How Non-Permanent Workers Learn and Develop

How Non-Permanent Workers Learn and Develop is an empirically based exploration of the challenges and opportunities non-permanent workers face in accessing quality work, learning, developing occupational identities and striving for sustainable working lives. Based on a study of 100 non-permanent workers in Singapore, it offers a model to guide thinking about workers' learning and development in terms of an 'integrated practice' of craft, entrepreneurial and personal learning-to-learn skills. The book considers how strategies for continuing education and training can better fit with the realities of non-permanent work.

Through its use of case studies, the book exams the significance of non-permanent work and its rise as a global phenomenon. It considers the reality of being a non-permanent worker and reactions to learning opportunities for these individuals. The book draws these aspects together to present a conceptual frame of 'integrated practices', challenging educational institutions and training providers to design and deliver learning and the enacted curriculum not as separate pieces of a puzzle, but as an integrated whole.

With conclusions that have wider salience for public policy responses to the rise of non-permanent work, this book will be of great interest to academics and researchers in the fields of adult education, educational policy and lifelong learning.

Helen Bound is Principal Research Fellow and Head of the Centre for Work and Learning at the Institute for Adult Learning, Singapore; Honorary Lecturer at the School of Education, University of Tasmania; and Honorary Principal Research Fellow with Griffith University.

Karen Evans is Emeritus Professor of Education at University College London and Honorary Professor with the Centre for Learning and Life Chances, University College London.

Sahara Sadik is Principal Researcher at the Institute for Adult Learning, Singapore.

Annie Karmel was Researcher at the Institute for Adult Learning, Singapore.

Routledge Research in Lifelong Learning and Adult Education

Books in this series:

Learning Trajectories, Violence and Empowerment amongst Adult Basic Skills Learners
Vicky Duckworth

Vocational Education of Female Entrepreneurs in China
A Multitheoretical and Multidimensional Analysis of Successful Businesswomen's Everyday Lives
Mary Ann Maslak

Life and Learning of Korean Artists and Craftsmen
Rhizoactivity
Dae Joong Kang

Enhancing the Wellbeing and Wisdom of Older Learners
A Co-research Paradigm
Tess Maginess

Global Networks, Local Actions
Rethinking Adult Education Policy in the 21st Century
Marcella Milana

UNESCO's Utopia of Lifelong Learning
An Intellectual History
Maren Elfert

Adult Education and the Formation of Citizens
A Critical Interrogation
Andreas Fejes, Magnus Dahlstedt and Maria Olson

How Non-Permanent Workers Learn and Develop
Challenges and Opportunities
Helen Bound, Karen Evans, Sahara Sadik and Annie Karmel

How Non-Permanent Workers Learn and Develop

Challenges and Opportunities

Helen Bound, Karen Evans,
Sahara Sadik and Annie Karmel

LONDON AND NEW YORK

First published 2019
by Routledge

2 Park Square, Milton Park, Abingdon, Oxfordshire OX14 4RN
52 Vanderbilt Avenue, New York, NY 10017

Routledge is an imprint of the Taylor & Francis Group, an informa business

First issued in paperback 2020

British Library Cataloguing-in-Publication Data
A catalogue record for this book is available from the British Library

Library of Congress Cataloging-in-Publication Data
Names: Bound, Helen, author. | Evans, Karen, 1949- author. | Sadik, Sahara, author. | Karmel, Annie, author.
Title: How non-permanent workers learn and develop : challenges and opportunities / Helen Bound, Karen Evans, Sahara Sadik and Annie Karmel.
Description: New York : Routledge, [2018] | Series: Routledge research in lifelong learning and adult education | "Chapter 1: What constitutes non-permanent work and why is it significant? Chapter 2: Being a non-permanent worker Chapter 3: Dispositions towards learning and becoming for non-permanent workers Chapter 4: Contexts in Non-Permanent Work Chapter 5: Integrated practice Chapter 6: Using the spaces of NPW for learning, curriculum design, and delivery type Chapter 7: Implications for Workforce Development : A Comparative Perspective Appendix A: The research project: Genesis and methodology."
Identifiers: LCCN 2018013723 | ISBN 9781138103115 (hardback)
Subjects: LCSH: Temporary employees—Singapore.
Classification: LCC HD5854.2.S55 B68 2018 | DDC 331.25/729095957—dc23
LC record available at https://lccn.loc.gov/2018013723

ISBN: 978-1-138-10311-5 (hbk)
ISBN: 978-0-367-48409-5 (pbk)

Typeset in Bembo
by Apex CoVantage, LLC

Contents

List of figures and tables vi
Preface vii
Acknowledgements x

1 What constitutes non-permanent work and why is it significant? 1

2 Being a non-permanent worker 29

3 Dispositions towards learning and becoming for non-permanent workers 49

4 Contexts in non-permanent work 69

5 Integrated practice 89

6 Using the spaces of NPW for learning, curriculum design and delivery type 109

7 Implications for workforce development: a comparative perspective 140

Appendix A: the research project: genesis and methodology 158
Index 172

Figures and tables

Figures

1.1 Total sample of non-permanent workers (n=97) 23
2.1 Two theoretical lenses 30
3.1 Spectra of dispositions 52
4.1 Occupational affordances in non-permanent work 74
5.1 Integrated practice 91
5.2 Non-permanent workers' capabilities 103

Tables

6.1 Traditional and integrated practices assumptions about teaching, learning and knowledge 117
6.2 Some pedagogical strategies for implementing the integrated practice model 120

Preface

In John Maynard Keynes's (1930) short essay on the 'economic possibilities for our grandchildren', he envisaged a future characterised by technological unemployment, eliminating the need for mass employment and leaving people to learn new ways of living a fulfilled life. Despite being written in the early decades of the twentieth century, Keynes's essay continues to have contemporary relevance not because we have arrived at the end of work: waged employment remains the dominant life-support system for individuals and families. Its relevance stems from the widely shared view that advances in digital technologies are leading to a 'second machine age', or 'fourth industrial revolution', finally making Keynes's predictions of technological unemployment a reality, requiring a fundamental rethink of the role of education, employment and the distribution of income and wealth.

I suspect that waged work is going to remain a significant part of most people's lives for some time to come, but there is little doubt that what people do for a living, the way they train for it, how they do it, where they do it and how much they get paid for it are being transformed. Technological innovation is enabling companies, especially in a context of economic globalisation, to develop global value chains that include the international distribution of highly skilled work at different market prices, alongside the development of digital platforms that enable the creation of an on-demand workforce.

Although the wider implication for the future of work will not be resolved anytime soon, the major focus of this book is on the non-standard or non-permanent workforce, which is now estimated to account for 20–30 per cent of the working age population in the United States and Europe. The challenge confronting all those who have written on this subject is how to analyse the various types of non-standard employment and the different working relationships they entail, including part-time work, fixed-term contracts, zero-hour contracts, freelance consultants and others in self-employment. The authors of this book take great care to identify different kinds of employment relations in their qualitative fieldwork but also recognise that these different arrangements are often associated with inequalities in individual market power. In much of the literature on non-standard work, there is a focus on either 'contingent' workers, who are sufficiently confident about the market value of their knowledge and skills to work on their own account, or 'precarious' workers, who are presented as having little market power, operating at the margins of the formal labour market. This book seeks to avoid this bifurcation by examining non-permanent workers in different market situations.

This is one of a number of strengths. I particularly like the way the authors attempt to bring 'to life' the experiences of people engaged in non-standard or non-permanent work. This extends the focus on labour protection, working conditions and low wages to address the question of how people learn, develop skills and maintain a sense of individual purpose and dignity. Typically, training provision after entry into the labour market has been left to employers to organise with their employees in stable employment, but how can this be organised when people are engaged in short-term employment or project work?

What are the implications for national models of skill formation premised on standard models of full-time, stable employment?

The fact that the study is set in the context of non-permanent work in a non-Western, advanced economy is another strength, although the findings have major significance for all developed and emerging economies. Research evidence is collected in Singapore, with additional comparative work on low-wage, non-permanent work in India, South Korea and United Kingdom. There is a surprising lack of studies on advanced Asian economies at a time when we are witnessing a transformation of the world economy driven by China and other Asian economies. The focus on Singapore is particularly fascinating given its 'developmental state'. Since independence in 1965, it has developed one of the most sophisticated skill formation systems in the world. It has found ways of encouraging employers to upgrade the quality of jobs at the same time as reforming the education and training system to meet the rising demand for skilled workers. However, this 'developmental worker' model, as Johnny Sung has called it, is no longer working to plan and new ways are being sought to create meaningful, well-paid jobs for the Singaporean workforce. How they approach this will have major lessons for other national economies, given that all confront similar challenges, including the growth in non-standard employment.

But the authors correctly highlight there is no 'one best way', for reasons that are clearly spelt out in this engaging and insightful book. Context matters, which rules out any magic formula for skills policy or labour market reform. The study of non-standard work is not only the study of different types of work organisation but different kinds of institutional context. Yet, one of the key ideas I take from this book is the need to extend the focus from an overriding concern with the definition of different kinds of non-standard or non-permanent jobs. While this is understandable given the need to ensure proper labour protection, holiday entitlement, enforcement of a nation's minimum wage etc. we should avoid pigeon-holing workers into specific labour categories, as the research evidence presented in this book shows how we need to develop skills policy as if people matter. In other words, we need to rethink what it means to be educated at a time when a front-loading model is no longer fit for purpose. How can people be empowered to engage in lifelong learning and meaningful careers when employment no longer offers the workplace foundations on which individual careers are staged? This book offers some important answers.

Phillip Brown
Distinguished Research Professor
School of Social Sciences
Cardiff University
Wales, UK.

Acknowledgements

This book originated from a Roundtable discussion of international scholars on the topic of workplace learning and the mediation of context held in Singapore in 2013. The Roundtable was funded by the Institute for Adult Learning, Singapore (IAL) and organised and conducted by IAL's research Centre for Work and Learning (CWL). From this discussion we developed a project – funded by IAL – spanning almost three years researching the learning and identity of non-permanent workers across three sectors that forms the basis of this book. We are grateful to IAL for the opportunity to undertake this research, which proved to be a fascinating journey as we built and refined our conceptualisation iteratively by studying first one sector, then another.

The constant evolution of non-permanent work and the varied journeys and identities of those of us who have engaged in and are currently engaged in this form of work, mean there are important messages to be heard. Our research not only contributes to giving voice to a growing number of workers who, for the most part, are without collective voice, but, also in this book, we stress the dignity of work and thus the importance of quality work. We stretch and challenge the current conceptualisation in the literature of contingent and precariat and, importantly, bring focus to the growth and development of non-permanent workers. It was the stories of our research participants that enabled the conceptualisation and challenges to current thinking that we present in this book. We thank those who generously gave their time to be interviewed.

The research team who worked on the project varied over the time of the project. With the exception of Sahara, the authors of this book were present from the first discussions. Sahara joined us one year into the project, adding research expertise, commitment and important insights. Associate Professor Peter Rushbrook (RMIT, Australia) was also part of the first discussions and remained with us to the completion of the first of five reports for the project, 'The entrepreneurial self: Becoming a freelancer in Singapore's Film and Television industry'. In the first year of the project, Dr. Edmund Waite (IOE, UK) contributed to review of the literature and conceptualisation of identity. Magdalene Lin, a much-valued researcher who was still with the team in the first year of this research, supported the data collection and analysis. Maha

Sivalingham also contributed to this part of the project. Thereafter, the research was conducted by the four of us writing this book, covering technical theatre, adult educators and what at that time we termed low wage non-permanent workers (we have since reconceptualised this terminology as a result of the research findings). We are deeply grateful for the contributions of those who joined us for first stage of this research. All five research reports are available on the IAL website.

We are deeply grateful to Emeritus Professor David Ashton (Leicester University, UK), who was our guest author for our final chapter. Our many conversations over email and Skype were invigorating and thoughtful. He raised important considerations which have added greater depth and insight to the book.

We are also grateful to our intern Gabrielle Suppiah, who was with us undertaking her internship from Ngee Ann Polytechnic in the last quarter of 2017. She generously gave her time and attention to detail in helping us with the references.

Without the support and funding of IAL, the research and this book would not have been possible. Since October 2017, IAL moved from being a Division of the Ministry of Manpower to a Division of SkillsFuture, under the Ministry of Education. We are deeply appreciative of the support structures and support of individuals within IAL who have in one way or another contributed to supporting the journey in undertaking the research and the writing of this book.

Chapter 1

What constitutes non-permanent work and why is it significant?

The rise of non-permanent work and non-traditional work patterns is a global phenomenon. As expectations of a job for life, dependable benefits, steady work rhythms and union protection are being eroded in the advanced industrial economies; work patterns based on informal and part-time work, short-term contracts, self-employment and freelance work are expanding. This growth is characterised by both risks and opportunities for those who are increasingly caught up in these work patterns. Some perspectives focus on the social and economic risks associated with polarisations between the highly paid who can invest in their own future security and those caught in the revolving doors of short-term contracts and low pay, with precarious working lives and few safety nets. Others focus on the opportunities created by new working patterns, pointing to flexible work as a convenient cultural choice, particularly among young adults, while imagining future prospects for the realignment of labour with new flexible modes of production as 'friction-free capitalism'. Social commentaries pragmatically analyse the policy options based on the empirical facts of the increasing incidence of precarious or contingent work. Whatever the perspective, most books on the subject approach this phenomenon from the standpoint of Western, advanced economies. This book is unique in exploring the realities of precarious and contingent work from the standpoint of an advanced Asian economy rooted in a version of the developmental state model that characterises much of the region.

Conceptually, the book moves beyond the characterisations of a new 'precariat' trapped in work patterns that are increasingly contingent or precarious. In modern forms of employment, both work and workers are continuously changing across and beyond traditional boundaries, enabling a new, empirically based exploration of the challenges workers have to negotiate in becoming knowledgeable practitioners, developing occupational identities and striving for sustainable working lives. It also enables a constructive exploration of what public policy, in an advancing, developmental state context, can and should do to support and protect workers in securing futures for themselves and their families. It considers how strategies for continuing education and training can move towards more inclusive and progressive approaches to supporting learning and development that have better fit with the realities of changing work patterns and the changing composition of the workforce. The conclusions have wider salience for public policy responses to this global phenomenon in both Asian economies and the advanced, industrial economies of the West.

What constitutes non-permanent work and why is it significant?

Non-permanent work is significant, if not dominant, in many parts of the world, including in industrialised countries. Recent estimates, for example, found that 20 to 30 per cent of the working-age population in the United States and the European Union engage in what they term 'independent work'. For the International Labour Organisation (ILO, 2015), non-permanent work is part of what it terms Non-Standard Employment, which includes part-time work, temporary work, fixed-term contracting and subcontracting, self-employment and homework. These forms of employment are far from new. It is the growth and patterns in the use of these forms of work that have new features, with potentially far-reaching consequences for economies, businesses and workers.

Most countries, in one way or another, are accommodating diversified working arrangements in the formal economy with the proliferation of different modes of flexible production. In low-income countries, paid employment is often poorly regulated and lacks basic worker protections, and self-employment remains the main form of work. In middle-income, developing countries, multiple types of labour markets co-exist, with differing degrees of connection to the globalised economy.

The growth of non-permanent work is surrounded by controversies about the interests that non-standard forms of employment serve, how the benefits gained from them are distributed and the protections that are available for those who participate. Non-permanent forms of work are argued to be 'beneficial to both employers and employees if they can accommodate the needs of enterprises for flexibility, while at the same time providing decent employment that also enables workers to balance work and personal responsibilities' (ILO, 2015). Conversely, their potential to fuel employment insecurity and allow exploitation in society are sources of considerable concern, particularly as the risks often fall disproportionately onto the most disadvantaged groups in society. The increasing prevalence of non-permanent work is leading to reviews of employment practices and regulatory frameworks as well as roles of unions in many countries in which non-permanent forms of work are increasingly being incorporated into more traditional employment frameworks (OECD, 2014; ILO, 2015).

Each country has a different mix of forms of temporary work which have always existed, combined with others that are new; this evolving mix reflects different modernisation trajectories/journeys and how different parts of the economy are connected to the globalised economy. There are myriad reasons for the use of non-permanent work arrangements in employment, which themselves vary considerably according to sector and occupational field. Temporary employment, whereby workers are engaged for a specific period, includes fixed-term, project or task-based contracts, as well as seasonal or casual work. Many organisations employ a mixture of permanent and directly employed temporary staff, often using agencies and, in some cases, sub-contractors. ILO investigations have shown that comparable cross-country data on the incidence and trends of temporary employment are lacking. Comparisons are often confounded by the use of different statistical definitions in national surveys. In many countries, some sectors are traditionally associated with non-permanent work; for example, work in agriculture and construction is often seasonal and entails complex contracting arrangements with many parties, and in the creative arts sector, work has traditionally been project-related. The spread of the use of non-permanent work has, however, expanded and broadened in industries where the labour market has been progressively casualised, including the transportation and hotel industries (Bamber et al., 2009; Weil, 2014).

For the purposes of this exploration of how non-permanent workers learn and develop, we defined non-permanent workers as those who were engaged in work for 12 months or less. This includes those who work 'on their own account' (freelancers) or who work on a series of short-term, fixed contracts (with or without written contracts), often project-based or task-based, in industries in which these forms of work are dominant. It also includes those who are engaged on an hourly or daily basis (casual workers) for anything from a once-off arrangement to working intermittently for the same employer for several years. But the employer is not obliged to offer them work, nor is the employee required to take up work when it is available and offered. Under these arrangements, the employment relationship is limited only to the period for which the employee actually works, allowing considerable variations in the recognition and exercise of wider responsibilities towards such workers. Ambiguous employment relationships are a feature of non-permanent work. Non-permanent work, or what the ILO (2015) calls 'non-standard', implies a departure from standard employment models favoured in advanced economies in which most workers are employed on permanent contracts whose terms, conditions and features are based on human resource policies that manage mutual expectations and obligations in ways that are designed to bolster the psychological contract between employer and the workforce.

Reasons for use of non-permanent work

Three major reasons why organisations use non-permanent workers include cost advantages, flexibility and technological change (ILO, 2015). The extent to which non-permanent work arrangements are used vary by industrial sector, the practices of competitors and the regulatory framework that governs the employment relationship in the country of operation. According to the Institute for Employment Research, the use of non-standard employment contracts is increasing in sectors such as hospitality and retail, where it is possible to break down less highly skilled jobs into discrete tasks, apparently without damage to service quality. Furthermore, some labour-intensive organisations have adopted non-standard contracts that transfer part of the risk to employees, citing as their reason the highly competitive nature of the markets in which they are operating (Purcell, Hogarth, & Simm, 1999). Such arrangements become open to abuse when ambiguous employer-worker contracts take on the characteristics of 'bogus self-employment' (or 'false' self-employment) in which workers who would have been employees in standard business models are forced into self-employment status in which they bear risks and costs that previously the employer would have carried (Böheim & Muehlberger, 2006). Surveys in the United Kingdom (UK) have estimated that a quarter of UK employers use 'zero hours contracts' (CIPD, 2013, 2015) and various forms of 'false self-employment' have been identified as a growing problem (Taylor, 2017).

The societal costs associated with such arrangements include negative consequences for the national 'tax take' as well as negative social consequences for populations of workers exposed to exploitative work practices that do little to develop their capabilities. The costs of individual 'skills' curtailment or atrophy, aggregated at the national level, have considerable implications for skills levels in the workforce. Calls for creative and highly skilled workforces are at odds with patterns of employment that could well be eroding capabilities through practices that fragment jobs, 'cut corners' and are detrimental to worker well-being potential. A twenty-first-century reworking of the debates about the consequences of Taylorism is underway (Green et al., 2016).

The 'gig economy' highlights changing work arrangements. When technology is harnessed by businesses in the search for innovative products and services to meet changing consumer demand, there is a tendency for greater public attention initially to be given to the product or service and only subsequently to the changes in working practices that are consequent upon its introduction. As Jacobs (2017) says, there is a lack of clarity about the workers who are actually involved and affected, when the term 'gig economy' seems to range from freelance consultancy to letting out rooms on Airbnb.[1] The use of on-demand, online work platforms for paid 'gigs' constitutes a relatively small proportion of this non-permanent work, but its growth is acknowledged to be part of a trend. The McKinsey report (2016) sees this in positive terms:.

> Digital platforms are transforming independent work, building on the ubiquity of mobile devices, the enormous pools of workers and customers they can reach, and the ability to harness rich real-time information to make more efficient matches.
>
> (In Brief p. 1)

'Gig workers' have fewer outlets for stresses and anxieties than employees (Amy Wrzesniewski in Jacobs, 2017). Workers who are managed through digital platforms can become relationally disconnected. They rarely meet or chat with co-workers and are often directed impersonally in their tasks as, for example, old-style 'radio-controller roles are replaced by 'faceless' technology. This lack of human connection can be alienating, as Jacobs's interviews with gig workers revealed. These insights reinforce the case for paying closer attention to the socio-psychological consequences of changing work practices and a better understanding of how people direct their energies and capacities in the social relations of workplace environments.

An opposing view to the valuing of the product or service through the use of 'gigs' enabled by technology is that the innovation lies in the technology and not in the casualisation that accompanies it. The Trades Union Congress (TUC) demonstrates how casual working arrangements have important continuities with past working practices of casualised labour. The extension and acceleration of casualisation by technology generate the new challenges to which unions have to respond (TUC, 2017).

Trade unions are actively searching for new responses to the growing numbers of people working on their own account, but developments have proceeded slowly within mainstream unions. As a consequence, employee representative bodies in this field have tended towards mutuals or cooperatives that both provide business support as well as representing and fighting for worker rights. For example, the Freelancers Union has been formed for the self-employed in the USA; the Netherlands and Spain have general unions for self-employed; legislation introduced in France in 2016 recognises business and employment co-operatives that support members not only with accounting, but also access to the sickness pay and benefits of employees in standard permanent forms of employment. Examples can also be found in Asia, as in India, where the Self-employed Women's Association is a co-operative that acts as a trade union in representing and protecting member rights while providing services such as micro-insurance. (ILO, 2014).

The rights of workers to 'decent work' and sustainable working lives are challenges for modern economies seeking to manage socially sustainable employment and workforce development strategies under conditions of global capitalism. These themes are intertwined in the exploration of non-permanent forms of employment.

Contingent or precarious: different facets of modern employment?

We observed at the outset of this research inquiry (Rushbrook, Karmel, & Bound, 2014) that the growth of non-permanent work is characterised by both risks and opportunities for those who are increasingly caught up in these work patterns.

Firms' costs and benefits of non-permanent working arrangements can yield benefits disproportionately for managerial, professional and clerical workers with specialist or scarce expertise. For most manual and lower-skilled workers, however, flexibility means insecurity and unpredictability, particularly where working patterns fluctuate according to consumer or employer demand, and workers cannot, in many cases, decline shifts without a penalty (Purcell, Hogarth, & Simm, 1999; TUC, 2017).

The term 'contingent' worker tends to be used for workers who have chosen to shape their own working life journey outside the paths of standardised careers (see, for example, Fournier, 2015). These workers are portrayed as exercising choices about how and when to use their expertise and are characterised as able to navigate the labour market, obtaining, keeping or declining work to their own advantage. They use social capital networks, have choices concerning work-life balance and have the resources to maintain current workplace skills and knowledge capabilities. These contingent workers are perceived as able to pursue meaningful, creative and self-fulfilling work, maintaining a 'comfortable' income and self-selected lifestyle. They are also sometimes portrayed in the literature as 'boundaryless' or 'protean' workers, in terms chosen to encapsulate trends in flexible capitalism (Allan, 2002; Arthur & Rousseau, 1996; Hall, 2002, 2004; McKeown, 2005, McKinsey Report, 2016).

Precarious workers, highlighted by the work of Guy Standing, are, by contrast, characterised as marginal and prone to exploitation, experiencing anxiety because of inconsistent income, reduced benefits and deskilling, as well as unclear prospects for career progression. The precarious workers, it is argued, experience rupture, exploitation and disadvantage in their relationship with their employer (Brophy, 2006; Ross, 2008; Kalleberg, 2009; Rushbrook, Karmel, & Bound, 2014; Standing, 2011).

The terms 'contingent' and 'precarious' represent two distinct perspectives. The contingent perspective tends to emphasise benefits of flexible working and is usually considered to be more closely aligned with employer perspectives, while the precarious camp emphasises individual and social risks and is considered to be aligned with union and worker perspectives.

There is a third perspective which emphasises the 'transitional' nature of some forms of non-permanent work. Non-permanent work, in this perspective, can offer useful ways of gaining work experience and provide entry points into the labour market for school-leavers and college graduates through arrangements such as internships. Non-permanent work is a feature of the many schemes for people who are long-term unemployed, with the aim of providing ways back to work (Gangl, 2003; McGinnity, 2005). While such schemes help to develop skills and networks, they can also contribute to 'churn' under conditions of high unemployment, where people move from scheme to scheme. Temporary employment agencies also hire and provide limited support to individuals who may have difficulty finding employment (Autor & Houseman, 2010).

Forms of work which can be characterised as precarious, contingent or have a combination of features are facets of evolving labour markets everywhere. While many of these employment forms are far from new, their increasing prevalence is becoming a feature of 'modern employment'. The key challenge is how societies can manage this phenomenon in ways that ensure 'decency of work' (ILO) or rights to what Taylor, adviser to the UK Government on this matter in 2017, terms 'good work' (RSA, 2015; Taylor, 2017). Progress towards the goal of decency of work can potentially be measured by the extent to which poor and exploitative working practices are minimised and the extent to which customs and practices associated with decency of work, or good work, become embedded beyond minimum legal requirements.

The challenge is to find better societal solutions to the evidenced problems of precarious and exploitative working practices. In 'Self-employed: rich, poor or something more?' (2016), Dellot argues:

> Many clearly struggle to make a living – a problem exacerbated by the absence of conventional safeguards, such as sick pay, maternity/paternity pay and employer pension contributions. But overstating the perils and pitfalls of self-employment risks tarnishing it as a form of work altogether, and distracts us from the real task of creating a proper tax, regulatory and welfare regime that runs with the grain of self-employed lifestyles . . . , our goal should not be to try and 'save' people from self-employment, but rather to *help more people take part* in the meaningful kind that at its best allows workers to flourish and find purpose.
>
> (p. 1)

Taylor, leading the UK government inquiry, summarises the challenge in a series of negatives: to find ways of managing 'non-standard' forms of employment in ways that do not incentivise behaviours that are not economically productive or unfair to workers while taking care not to reduce innovation and flexibility (Taylor, 2017).

The characterisations of decent work and good work in these debates beg many questions. Decent work, in the ILO definition, involves opportunities for work that is productive and delivers a fair income, security in the workplace and social protection for families, better prospects for personal development and *social integration*, freedom for people to express their concerns, organise and participate in the decisions that affect their lives and *equality of opportunity* and treatment for all women and men. The European Union has endorsed the concept, and the promotion of decent work as a way to achieve sustainable development is embedded in the new European Consensus on Development (European Commission, 2016).

In the United Kingdom's Modern Employment review, a notion of 'good work' has been proposed and made the subject of consultations and invited responses (Taylor, 2017). Reviewing the available evidence on the persistence of 'bad work' entails 'bad working conditions, poor legal safeguards and job insecurity'. Taylor, charged with advising government on the matter, asserts the need to focus on the 'quality of work, and not just quantity' and defines good work as 'fair and decent with realistic scope for development and fulfilment' for the whole workforce, at all levels and stages of their working lives (Taylor, 2017). This perspective is supported in the UK by the TUC, the Institute of Directors, Federation of Small Businesses, CIPD and Business in the Community.

Surprisingly, these characterisations of decent and good work pay scant regard to the human development aspect. Beyond lip-service to the notion that 'people are our most important resource' and to the importance of well-being and human flourishing, detailed attention is lacking to questions of how the development of non-permanent workers' capabilities can be supported over time and how the scaling up to the highly skilled workforces espoused by policies can realistically be achieved.

The context – why study Singapore?

This book is unique in exploring the realities of precarious and contingent work from the standpoint of an advanced Asian economy rooted in a version of the developmental state model that characterises much of the region. There are several ways in which the Singapore context can be informative globally in a study of how non-permanent workers learn and develop. First, Singapore brings together East and West, with multiple inheritances that have influenced its growth as an economy. According to Tan (2011), Singapore represents an 'ideology of pragmatism', as economic radicalism and moral conservatism combine within a totalising government framework.

The economy depends largely on the city-state's human resources and is characterised by marked increases in non-permanent work, estimated to have reached approximately one-fifth in 2015. Second, Singapore is one of the countries identified in *The Economist's* 'Special Report on Lifelong Learning' (2017) as substantially enacting lifelong learning policies, alongside the Nordic countries. Singapore is judged, in this context, to have introduced a proactive set of policies under the banner of SkillsFuture, involving the development of 'industry-transformation maps' drawn up for the city-state with substantial subsidies for adult learning.

As a city-state, Singapore has set out to import practices from around the world and mobilise them, but there has been an enduring disconnect with segments of the labour market engaged in the least secure forms of non-permanent work, reflected in low take-up of the national offers. Labour market context is of course important to understanding the situation of non-permanent workers. The caveat is that Singapore's size and political system putting limits on replicability is met by emphasising that any lessons that can be drawn have to be actively recontextualised to other settings. These lessons and their limits are explored in Chapter 7.

Third, Singapore embodies a social dialogue approach (expanded on below) to the challenges of non-permanent work. In societies where there is limited collective bargaining coverage of non-standard workers, social dialogue can provide a useful approach for addressing the needs of non-standard workers (ILO, 2015). Singapore exemplifies an approach to national tripartite cooperation and partnership to address the growth of contract and casual workers associated with the expansion in outsourcing.

East-West interfaces

Both European and Asian countries are very diverse, yet there are shared features that make insights into the interplay of values, interests and wider economic forces instructive for audiences that extend beyond national borders.

Asian populations are experiencing changes in understanding what jobs are, according to Han (2011), in ways that depart from norms and expectations that are traditional for Asian societies. Most Asian economies are now divided between that part of the economy that belongs to global knowledge capitalism – the much-debated knowledge economy – and the part of the economy that belongs to pre-modern or, at most, the modern industrial economy. The extent to which the pre-modern and modern local industrial or agricultural parts of the economy still dominate varies by country, and many people in Asia are exposed to the vulnerable work conditions of manufacturing industries with no connection to the global knowledge economy and the lifelong learning resources that are designed to support it. The extent to which this still remains true in the advanced Western economies has been highlighted in the anti-globalisation backlash experienced in America and parts of Western Europe, long-predicted by globalisation theorists (including the most enthusiastic proponents, such as Micklethwaite (2004). Despite the high degree of variation and the acceptance of non-linear trajectories/journeys of modernisation, it is evident that most Asian countries are undergoing transitions of some kind from industrial to post-industrial economies.

Singapore, as a city-state, was able to recover relatively quickly from the 1990s economic crises and has made faster progress towards its goal of becoming an advanced economy than many countries in the region. Identifying and quantifying the scale of non-permanent work in Singapore is problematic, given the change in labour markets and the limited statistical categories in use. In this respect, it illustrates the situation identified in ILO Global Dialogue Forums, which showed that quantification is globally challenging, given that the 'presence of one concept in national data and not of the other may in itself signal recognition of the importance of that specific form of employment in a given country. It does not, however, signal that other forms are absent' (ILO, 2015, p. 4).

In Singapore, based on the data collected by the Ministry of Manpower (MOM), the statistical categories that are the closest fit to non-permanent workers are term contract[2] (11.8 per cent) and own-account workers[3] (8.7 per cent). These two categories combined account for 20.5 per cent of Singapore's resident labour force. These figures exclude the foreign workforce, who also tends to be on non-permanent work arrangements, albeit tied to the issuance of various types of employment passes issued by MOM.

Interviews with key informants carried out between 2012 and 2015, as part of this research indicated that up to 70 per cent of those in the creative sector and adult educators in Singapore are non-permanent workers. In addition, our interviews indicate that in sectors such as logistics and food and beverage, a considerable number are non-permanent workers. Non-permanent work is thus a characteristic of the Singapore labour market that to date has received limited attention. This is a form of work that is here to stay, and if global trends are indicative, then Singapore can expect this segment of the workforce to grow, perhaps more so due to the hollowing out of the middle class (Brown, Lauder, & Ashton, 2011) and the likelihood of some of these middle-class workers moving into non-permanent work. In low-paid work, Singapore appears to be differentiated from many first-world economies where there is a high degree of precarity and lack of choice associated with this form of work. When there is a tight labour market, unlike experiences in the US and Australia, it appears that non-permanent workers in Singapore who are doing work that is traditionally low paid sometimes *choose* this form of work as they tend to *earn a better income and experience less rigid conditions than if they undertook permanent work*. The same could apply with some forms of agency work in the European Union.

An understanding of the interdependencies inherent in work and learning requires appreciation of the distinctive social processes involved (Sung, 2006). Wider socio-political considerations of, for example, the maintenance of social cohesion within Singaporean society are also part of the social-ecological dynamic, as cultural expectations and practices in sectors and workplaces are likely to be highly differentiated and segmented.

Failure to respond to the challenges of increasing non-permanent, fixed-term and casualised working arrangements are associated with wider societal risks, ranging from the widely recognised economic risks of a reducing tax take to the hidden risks of allowing skills and knowledge to atrophy in substantial elements of the working population; and, in social terms, risks to well-being, fairness and social cohesion. Where these risks have been identified, initial attempts to address them have focused on the regulatory gaps between non-standard and standard forms of employment. Singapore's approach in this area, a form of social dialogue, is also of wider international interest.

Social dialogue approach

In Europe, the growth of non-standard forms of employment has led to policy-makers and institutions, including the European Commission (European

Commission, 2006, 2013), advocating labour reforms to reduce the regulatory gap between workers in standard and non-standard forms of employment. In other parts of the world, there has been an opposite movement towards the liberalisation of such forms of work as a partial response to growth in unemployment. Some reforms in some Asian countries have attempted to introduce controls into the practices of agencies, or 'labour dispatch' firms, countering wage discrimination and ensuring financial viability, with some protections for the non-permanent workers themselves.

Non-permanent workers are rarely covered by collective bargaining arrangements, and, in such situations, social dialogue is argued to provide a useful approach for addressing the needs of non-standard workers (ILO, 2015). Singapore has engaged in national tripartite cooperation and partnership to address the growth of contract and casual workers associated with the expansion in outsourcing. In 2008, it issued the Tripartite Advisory on Responsible Outsourcing Practices to encourage end-user companies to demand that their service suppliers or contractors raise employment terms and benefits and take due account of the Central Provident Fund status of low-wage contract workers as required by the law (ILO). This social dialogue approach is also found in many other countries, as noted by ILO surveys, and has limitations which are indicated by our evidence and discussed in later chapters.

The learning and development of NPWs – what are the issues?

Support for the learning and development of non-permanent workers is often a side issue in public debates, if it is present at all. When the learning does come into view, debates tend to focus on the need for individuals to continually reskill and on how individuals can best be equipped to meet the challenges of moving between different types of job.

The Economist (2017), reviewing the lifelong learning challenges arising from increasing automation and consequences for changing labour markets, focuses on costs and restrictions on individuals who constantly move in the labour market and do not have access to internal pathways to learning and qualification that are afforded to permanent employees in large corporations. When opportunities for 'reskilling' are dependent upon having sufficient savings to afford costs and upon having sufficient control over your working hours and personal circumstances to participate effectively, it is unsurprising that for most lower-graded workers, the standard pathways to learning and qualification are closed off. The problem identified, what are possible solutions? *The Economist*'s 'Special Report on Lifelong Learning' (2017) highlights the example of a company that supplies agency workers for temporary work in many industries also acting as a conduit for the workers to earn qualifications by 'iterative learning and working' through a programme mounted in collaboration with a higher education provider. It is claimed that the agency's programme allows its 'army of temporary workers in America to earn a degree . . . at no financial costs to them' (p. 14) by interleaving episodes of work with periods of education, guided and facilitated, it is claimed, by the agency's 'good overview of the skills leading to well-paid jobs' (p. 14). This example highlights one dimension of the problem and a potential solution – the development by employers of agency workers of pathways to qualifications that mirror those that might be available to more privileged permanent workers in larger corporations, with company support. This is adapting the standard view of learning to circumstances of the individual workers.

Competence frameworks, as imported, thrive on perceived needs for standardisation in order to provide the certification that people need and demand within the socio-political context of Singapore; yet the benefits of standardisation may begin to be outweighed by the limitations these approaches impose on what can be done and created. The responses to the learning and development challenges associated with the rise of temporary work has to be substantially expanded beyond adaptation of standard models.

Lifelong learning strategies and disconnects

There are often major disjunctions between globalised policy assumptions about large-scale competence requirements and employees' (often larger and richer) capacities to develop their existing competencies and knowledge. Disjunction is exacerbated through adoption of narrowly defined skills agendas and vague assumptions about the needs of a post-industrial 'knowledge economy'. The adoption of minimum competence frameworks often fails to take account of individuals' capacities to use and build on their existing knowledge in all its forms and the support needed to 'put knowledge to work' in meeting the actual demands of the workplace. Furthermore, workplace learning can support participation in employee-driven, 'bottom-up' development as workers engage with others to vary, and eventually to change, work practices, as Scandinavian experiences have shown (Høyrup, 2010).

The disconnects between standard competence-based frameworks and the development needs of workers applies particularly in the case of non-permanent workers moving between tasks and assignments in fixed-term contracts for multiple employers. Even with a shift globally towards greater support and recognition for workplace learning (now embraced by Singapore in SkillsFuture), the questions of whether, how and how effectively support for workplace-based learning of non-permanent workers assigned to fixed term project-based or casualised task-based activities pose particular problems with few obvious solutions. Ways in which the learning and development of these workers might be enlarged or constrained depend crucially on the strategic interplay of workforce development policies and the wider organisational and societal terrains created for worker development. Fragmentation of work in neo-Taylorist forms or movement between low-grade exploitative assignments threaten to limit or erode skills, as they did historically when Taylorist work practices became dominant then widely jettisoned in favour of more participatory work practices. The risks of skills atrophy in growing sections of the working population are societal risks, when scaled up, and at odds with espoused aims for highly skilled and knowledgeable workforces.

Furthermore, how can learning and development support become attuned to the principle of learning for long-term transformation rather than compliant adaptation? This is a necessary consideration if policy aims of upgrading workers (Ministry of Trade and Industry (MTI), 2016), creating better jobs (Channel News Asia, 24 October, 2017) and embracing innovation (MTI, 2017) apparent in Singapore's national Industry Transformation Maps (ITMs) overseen by The Future Economy Council[4] are to become more than a slogan. And where non-permanent workers who seek development opportunities do so under the radar or beyond the scope of workforce development provision, it is important to understand the reasons for this. How can initiatives such as SkillsFuture actually serve non-permanent workers' needs and preferences for forms of learning and development that work for their lifestyles and everyday life and work realities?

As well as focusing on access for non-permanent workers to learning resources and platforms that are independent of the employers to whom they are contracted at any one time, it is therefore necessary to deepen the debate about support for the learning and development of non-permanent workers by attending to:

- the variety of situations;
- the quality of the work assignments they undertake and of the work environments in which they are carried out;
- learning dispositions of the workers themselves;
- the regulation of employment relationships in the particular national and industry contexts, including entitlements and obligations.

The interplay of these dimensions creates fundamentally different learning and development spaces around non-permanent work. To what extent do these spaces enable the expansion of human capacities and well-being, and how are the participants themselves situated in the wider sphere of social, cultural and economic changes?

How learning is connected to changes in the organisation of work

Much attention has been paid to ways in which competition has led to changes in the way work is organised and to ways in which these changes at work are experienced, as shown in the previous section. Continuous pursuit of performance improvement and reduction of unit costs have far-reaching consequences for employees' experiences of work. They are reflected in management strategies at the company level, in changes in regulatory frameworks that govern the worker-employee relationships and in priorities in education and training systems. They are also reflected in the access workers have to learning opportunities in the workplaces of everyday life. New forms of work, associated with fragmented, smaller, high-tech organisations combined with the burgeoning of short-term employment contracts in many economies, are making insecurity one of the dominant realities of the work of the future. Metaphors of the life course capture this in a shift from 'pathways' and 'trajectories' to 'navigations' of risks, opportunities and uncertainties (Evans & Furlong, 1994). A debate about whether this shift represents limited diversification of patterns of activity in societies still dominated by standard templates for working lives or signifies a long-term, fundamental disruption of existing models (Evans, Schoon, & Weale, 2013) is paralleled in the 'trajectory' of job markets. Patterns of employment are gradually diversifying. To what extent might this represent a de-standardisation process by which 'modern employment' will depart substantially from standard modes of the past? These are questions facing many societies. Singapore, where segmented labour markets attached to the global economy co-exist with local indigenous forms of employment, provides a telling case, not only in the context of Asia (Han, 2011), but also for many other countries experiencing these tensions and trends.

Workers' 'flexibility' – what does it mean?

Workers who have 'flexibility' in the labour markets of the present time are seen to be mobile or potentially mobile. A European-wide typology of job-changers (Hendrich & Heidegger, 2001) revealed considerable variation in experiences, positive and negative, and associated competences, according to how people are positioned in the labour market and in the social structure. These considerations are relevant to workers involved in non-permanent forms of employment, for whom 'job change' is an ever-present feature of working life. The types identified were broadly as follows:

Advancement-oriented, work-centred individuals: 'labour force entrepreneur'; frequent job moves geared to advancement; high awareness of key competences and 'know how'.

Precarious occupational biography in low-graded jobs: awareness of social competences for adaptation to new work situations; little confidence in ability to draw on other experiences or skills in new work situations or recognise their relevance, both males and females.

Return to the labour market after occupational breaks for personal/family reasons: predominantly stability-oriented females; awareness of competences gained outside work, but also knowledge that these are seen as equipping them for helping/caring occupations or low-graded jobs (seen as women's work?!).

In or aiming for self-employment: both males and females; high awareness of wide range of competences gained and exercised through experience used to pursue business opportunities in ways that do not rely on accreditation by others.

Highly skilled, professional career/job changers: usually entails moves to different roles, e.g. advisory or consulting with a focus on updating and regaining confidence and networks. Wider competencies gained outside work are valued.

The development of this typology purposefully included both highly skilled and lower-grade workers, many of whom manifest higher levels of skill in their day-to-day work than are attributed to them in their job gradings. The latter include the workers for whom flexibility and mobility are often enforced, as they attempt to move between home and work environments or experience the harshest effects of downsizing. While labour market entrepreneurs style themselves as knowledge workers and add to their portfolio through mobility, their relatively insecure labour market position is often offset by their ability to command high pay and package and sell their experience. Such benefits are unusual for lower-grade workers or those whose skills have often been gained in settings that are disregarded because they lie outside the economic sphere.

Workers on short-term contracts who have to navigate work opportunities engage with many different workplaces and work teams over time. Prior experiences shape if they perceive non-permanent work as an opportunity or a threat and how they view the risks associated with mobility in a changing labour market. The situations and learning dispositions of workers themselves depend on the socially positioned lives they lead. For example, highly flexible non-permanent work is often held to suit those people whose main activity and focus lie elsewhere. Two examples provided in Purcell's 1999 study came from a study of the further (post-school) education sector: students were staffing hotels for part-time or weekend shifts which fitted in with their study commitments, and staff and colleges of further education were 'providing piecework contracts that allowed people to happily pursue one or more careers, such as musicians supplementing their income with some teaching work'.

Many such examples can be found. What is more important, however, is a realistic appraisal of non-permanent work arrangements on the mainstream labour force and on employment opportunities for socially excluded groups. If employers can meet their staffing needs with part-time or casual employees, will they have any incentive to create more stable job opportunities which imply longer-term commitment to members of the workforce? Key considerations, for both employers and non-permanent workers, are the terms and conditions of employment specified in the contract or practised through internal human resource policies.

It is recognised that non-standard forms of employment can potentially contribute to improved employment outcomes and a better work–life balance, provided that the working conditions are 'decent' (Fagan et al., 2014). Particular challenges arise, however, when non-standard employment is an involuntary choice, or when significant barriers exist against transitioning to standard forms of employment (Purcell, Hogarth, & Simm, 1999)

Learning in the contexts of organisational work practices and cultures

How do organisational work practices and cultures influence non-permanent workers' opportunities for learning? We know that individuals bring prior abilities and experiences to the workplaces in which they participate and that their dispositions towards work and learning influence the use of workplace learning affordances. (Evans, Kersh, & Kontiainen, 2004; Billett (2006; Hodkinson et al., 2004). The extent to which workers on short-term contracts can personalise the working environments and influence the workplace cultures and practices which in turn influence learning is likely to be less than those in more permanent positions. However, Cavanagh (2010), in a study of legal auxiliaries, found that their learning was mostly shaped by their dispositions to take action (agency) and reflexivity in the face of work challenges. The interaction between context and dispositions would seem to be important in understanding how non-permanent workers learn and develop as they navigate different assignments.

Workplace environments are shown to be as important as training methods and supervisory practices in developing adults' skills and knowledge in the research of Felstead et al. (2009); Williams (2010); and Fuller and Unwin (2004). Less attention has been paid to the ways in which individuals involved in contract-based work navigate the learning affordances of different workplaces. This is likely to be as strongly influenced by biographical and out-of-work factors as it is by workplace environments. More generally, while workplace learning may have immediate or obvious relevance to job skills, the long-term impact of learning on adults' capabilities – and thus on productivity as well as on life satisfaction – will often depend on out-of-work activities as well as workplace participation (see Malloch et al., 2011). An understanding of both workplace participatory practices and individual agency is required particularly for an understanding of short-term and contract-based work.

The significance of agency and identity for non-permanent workers' learning

As Billett (2006) has observed, an individual's personal history provides a platform for their coming to know and make sense of what is encountered in workplaces. This sense-making process fundamentally shapes and reflects the person's intentionality and agency in the ways in which they engage with work roles, learning opportunities and the wider social environment. In Asian contexts, the wider social and political environment of 'community before self and nation before family' has profound implications for this process of sense-making (Tan, 2013).

Workplace learning is seen by Rainbird and Evans (2006) as constituted in sites in which both antagonistic and cooperative relationships are expressed. For workers on short-term contracts, navigating changing employment relationships and work spaces can be particularly hazardous. As Cavanagh's (2010) study of legal auxiliaries shows, accessing affordances for learning often becomes a highly individualised process. The female legal assistants identified themselves as pragmatic learners and demonstrated how they navigate subjectivities and find 'self' through agentic actions and reflexivity. These workers, and others like them, inhabit 'figured worlds' (Holland et al., 1998) and often rely on transgressive deployment of knowledge, skills and judgement in their work practices.

Reflexive changes in the environments and practices of work demand new ways of thinking that go beyond preoccupations with the direct managerial surveillance of workers and manipulation of work 'performances'.

Reflexivity and learning in 'liquid lives'

Destandardised and flexible working patterns call for greater reflexivity on the part of both institutions and individuals as well as a greater emphasis on learning (Edwards, 1998, p. 382). Reflection becomes a 'general pedagogic stance' (Edwards, 1998, p. 386) that is vital to the effective navigation of shifting work patterns and a fast-changing technological environment.

Learning in relation to flexible work is usually associated with 'informal learning', which is, in turn, increasingly associated with relationships forged through collaborative work (Marsick, Watkins, & O'Connor, 2011). Workers on short-term contracts are often assigned to working teams. Several types of workplace-based learning arise naturally as people work collaboratively on tasks: seeking out and observing those who are 'knowledgeable' about the task or activity; peer support; focused workplace discussions; practising without supervision, searching out new information, ideas and solutions; and mentoring and coaching (Taylor, Evans, & Mohamed, 2008). Learning that results from combinations of activities, such as observation and focused workplace discussions, depends on worker motivation, their orientation to practice, workplace relationships and the affordances of the wider environment. This interplay can offer rich learning engagements, for example, where 'doors are opened' to opportunities to expand and share knowledge and skills in supportive workgroups. Conversely, unintended negative influences on learning may occur, for example, where the interdependencies of the workplace are undermined by feelings of lack of trust (Billett, 2002, 2006). Workers who move between sites and settings can potentially experience the advantages of exposure to a challenging and varied range of environments. They also experience the disadvantages of marginalisation and limited access to in-house opportunities. Thus, Rainbird, Munro and Senker (2005) have shown that learning opportunities for cleaners and care workers are related, amongst other things, to the relatively low status of the predominantly female, working-class and often ethnic minority workers concerned. There are also significant differences, depending upon the different ways in which cleaning, social care in residential homes, domiciliary social care and carer support are organised, with contract-based cleaning staff often experiencing isolation and fewer opportunities for training than permanent staff cleaners.

If such workers experience greater risk, often resulting in occupational health and safety issues for them (Evans & Gibb, 2009), are less likely to access and participate in training and tend not to work alongside other workers from whom they can learn on the job, how do these workers continue learning? Owen and Bound (2001) found that Australian contractors working in alliances need to recognise their own and others' strengths and weaknesses. Furthermore, metacognitive strategies and cultural understanding were found to be critical in contractor alliance work. These authors suggest that technical proficiency for contractor alliance members can be maintained through a combination of formal vocational courses, working with others and learning from them, actively seeking information and talking with others. In a study of the learning of Australian seasonal agricultural workers (who are low-paid workers), Kilpatrick and Bound (2005) found that these workers relied very much on learning from each other; however, where follow-up was structured and consistent, workers reported that they learnt the job thoroughly and product quality was generally much better. Given constantly changing relationships with employers, co-workers and peers, how do these workers connect and interrelate given multiple employment locations and relationships?

At a theoretical level, Bauman (2005) shows how individuals are being increasingly positioned to lead a 'liquid life'. Expertise is increasingly deployed in relational and multifaceted ways, cutting across areas of specialisation. Workers develop multiple identities according to their positioning and contribution to different work teams they participate in. Fox (1997), moreover, argues that Lave and Wenger's COPs do not provide researchers with the intellectual resources to engage with the decentred nature of work and expertise or the distributed nature of much learning, a point re-iterated by Lahiff and Guile (2016), in relation to cultural and creative sector apprenticeships. The concept of figured worlds has assumed greater salience for understanding learning in and through work in the liquid life course. In occupations of all kinds, and at all levels, people come to *figure out* who they are through the worlds in which they participate and by the ways in which they relate to others both within and beyond these worlds.

In the liquid life, success can be seen as arising from the development of capabilities to make multiple transitions and to navigate these 'figured worlds'. This involves 'reflexivity', as Edwards (1997) argues, with reflective practice a key condition of flexibility. Edwards argues that reflective practice, which revolves around the bringing together of thought and action, 'reflecting whilst doing' is a key condition of flexibility:

> the significance of reflective practice becomes clearer when it is situated within the socioeconomic and cultural changes of reflexive modernization. It is not simply the nature of professional practice that necessitates reflection-in-action. It is also a part and an outcome of a particular organisation and division of labour within which flexibility is a key component.
>
> (p. 164)

For workers reliant on short-term contracts and 'freelancers' navigating work opportunities, reflexivity becomes all important, but, as Edwards takes care to note, the possibility for enterprise of the self is neither uniform nor equal. Felstead et al. (2009) show how new modes of self-governance enable workers to conceive of themselves as autonomous authors of their own lives. These new modes involve self-inspection, self-monitoring and self-regulation as 'internalised restraints', modes that can be characterised as workers taking responsibility for their working and learning and, equally, as colonisation of the self by forms of social control. 'Technologies of the self' (Foucault, 1998), referring to the self-governing processes that shape the development of people's capabilities and life directions, are apparent in the work and life negotiations of the liquid life course. Maintenance of internal points of reference and a continuous internal life appear important in navigating fluid work opportunities, but casualities of non-permanent work are likely to occur where workers lose a sense of continuity and direction and are unable to access support that could help them.

For many, a rethinking of 'what jobs are' and of identities that were tied to particular conceptions of work and community were experienced as existential crises during the economic crises associated with the 1990s 'crash' that affected most of the economies of Asia that required for many. 'More people do not only have to acquire specific skills – they also need new ways of perceiving the world' (Han, interview, 2011). Family support and the 'one company' lifetime commitments started to become less dependable, and commitments to collectivism over individualism become more complicated to realise in practice.

The ways in which people forge identities, individually and collectively, within and through their work practices have been captured by Kirpal (2011) and Allan et al. (2016), showing how IT professionals and nurses, for example, radiate different senses of themselves as workers as well as people with particular personal interests and commitments. These senses of self are thus many dimensional and represent the variety of ways in which people position themselves in relation to their employment, professional development and other purposeful activities that constitute work. All forms of work contribute to identities, which are realised through unpaid as well as paid work, whether in home, family or community.

Keeping knowledge in view: how non-permanent workers' recontextualise knowledge

The literature on learning and reflexivity in figured worlds often acknowledges, but struggles to keep in view, the different types of knowledge (personal, procedural, ethical, propositional) that are brought into play in these multi-faceted engagements with work and learning. The significance of prior knowledge and skills is widely acknowledged, as is the evidence that moving into and between new workplaces involves much more than the simple transfer of prior skills and knowledge. Lobato (2003) for example, has shown the importance of the actor's/learner's perspective; the influence of prior activity on current activity and the different ways in which actors may construe situations as being 'similar'; that what experts consider to be only a 'surface feature' of a work task or problem may be structurally important for a participant; that multiple processes involved include attunement to affordances and constraints in the work environment; and that 'transfer' is distributed across mental, material, social and cultural planes. Skills and knowledge have to be developed and changed as they are operationalised in the culture of new workplaces. Furthermore, it is not the skills and knowledge that develop, but the whole person, as s/he adjusts, with greater or lesser success, to working in a new environment, as Hager and Hodkinson (2011) have argued. That adjustment depends as much upon the receptive or expansive nature of the new workplace as upon the prior experiences that workers bring to it.

Put differently, the processes entailed involve a series of knowledge recontextualisations (see Evans, Guile, & Harris, 2009; Evans et al., 2010; Evans & Guile, 2012) that can be significantly helped or hindered by the actions and dispositions of employers and co-workers. Processes of knowledge recontextualisation lie at the heart of workplace learning, as knowledge is put to work in different environments. This concept moves thinking and practice beyond the dominant metaphor of 'transfer' of learning by concentrating on the ways in which different forms of knowledge are used and developed as people move between sites of learning and practice. All knowledge has a context in which it was originally generated. Contexts extend to the 'schools of thought', the traditions and norms of practice, the life experiences in which knowledge of different kinds is generated. For knowledge generated and practised in one context to be put to work in new contexts, it has to be recontextualised in ways that simultaneously engage with and change those practices, traditions and experiences. This approach to recontextualisation has drawn on van Oers's (1998) idea that concepts integral to practice change as practice varies from one workplace to another. These notions have been substantially expanded to embrace the ways in which workers themselves change as they recontextualise concepts and practices. This is integral to the ways in which people think and feel their way into occupational and professional identities or think and feel their way beyond them and is highly significant for workers who move between workplaces on short-term contracts. As contingent workers move between sites of practice, they think and feel their ways into occupational and social identities, necessitating different modes of knowledge re-contextualisation as well as a capacity to develop and maintain 'mobility capital', or the ability to transition from one job to another (Forrier, Sels, & Stynen, 2009). Knowledge re-contextualisation, including attitudes, values and beliefs, leads to longer-term and ongoing 'whole person' development in professional life, part of the process of 'becoming' highlighted by Hager and Hodkinson (2011) and Zukas (2012).

Where the contexts of work are constantly changing, part of what one learns is how to vary performance, how to fit in, how to re-contextualise forms of knowledge to make it useful and how to 'keep a narrative of identity going over a constantly changing terrain' (Gill, 2002, p. 123) For non-permanent workers, where figured worlds (Holland et al., 1998) are likely to be constantly in flux, these dimensions of performance, fitting in, knowledge re-contextualisation and multiple identities in shifting terrains merit further investigation, in the contexts of contrasting occupational contexts and cultures. A deeper understanding is needed of how workers' identity development is intertwined with changing work demands and societal shifts, not least because the ways in which people identify with their work is fundamental both to workplace practices and life journeys, and to exploration of the ways in which existing or new programmes of lifelong learning support might be made more effective.

Exploring non-permanent workers' learning and development in practice – the research

This book aims for an extended dialogue between ideas and evidence in exploring how non-permanent workers learn and develop. In understanding how non-permanent workers learn and develop, the authors have carried out empirical investigations in Singapore alongside wider explorations of the phenomena of non-permanent work globally.

Many studies of non-permanent workers have focused on particular groups; it is rare to find a study that looks systematically across different groups. Our inquiry has investigated contrasting groups of non-permanent workers in order to develop a unique, differentiated account of their experiences and the contexts of their work:

- creative sector: film and television, technical theatre workers;
- continuing education and training (CET) sector: adult educators, trainers, consultants;
- occupations commonly understood as being 'low-wage': despatch riders, removalists and food and beverage help.

Another original feature of our study stems from the debates that have categorised non-permanent workers as either precarious or contingent, a debate which itself tends to polarise into views of precarious workers at the mercy of the structures within which they work, contrasting with the abilities of contingent workers to exercise choices in the ways in which they navigate work opportunities. In our exploration, we have explored these and other facets of modern employment from the standpoint of workers who are differently positioned in the social landscapes of changing employment. Furthermore, our point of departure in exploring the learning and development of non-permanent workers recognises this learning as both existential and profoundly social. Questions of identity are central to the questions we address, as we work from socio-cultural (and socio-material) perspectives that mean we also seek to understand societal contexts and the actualities of each industry sector, their ways of working and the structures and practices that mediate the identity and learning of the non-permanent workers who participate in them. Consequently, from the individual respondents, we have gathered data capturing their experience, their story and the contexts in which they work. This provided data that we analysed through multiple theoretical lenses while always letting the 'data speak'. Our theoretical lenses include practice which does not separate out agency and structure but rather embeds each in the other, identity, socio-cultural (and socio-material) perspectives of learning, as well as some borrowing from cultural historical activity theory, namely the concept of mediation.

Given the strong theme of precarity and contingency, we posed questions of the data in relation to these concepts and found that in our sample, 'non-permanent workers are neither contingent nor precarious, rather they experience aspects of contingency *and* precariousness to varying degrees, thus these labels are not helpful as binary definitions, which hide the reality of the lived experience of these workers.

The qualitative study has entailed semi-structured interviews with 97 non-permanent workers, designed to explore and to understand the identity, learning and development of non-permanent workers in the three chosen sectors (see Figure 1.1).

Our qualitative analysis has been iterative; as each sector was completed, we built on the insights we had gained to inform the investigation in the next sector. The findings are a result of further building on this iterative analysis where we undertook a systematic approach across all of our studies, explained further below. The research questions we addressed in our study are:

- How does the experience of non-permanent work contribute to or constrain the learning of workers?
- How do non-permanent workers identify with their work, and how does this influence learning opportunities?
- How can the learning of non-permanent workers be supported and enhanced?

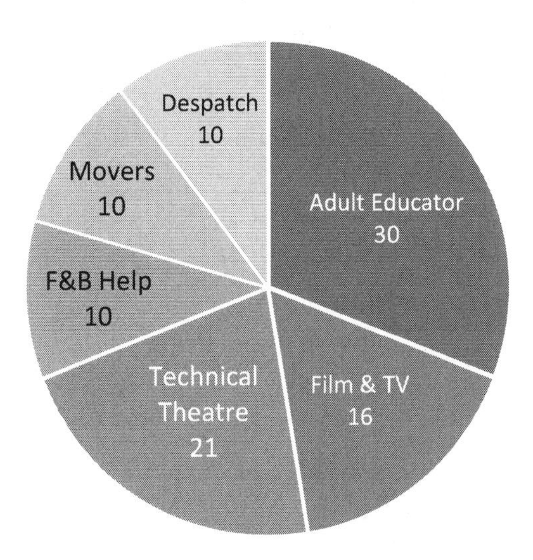

Figure 1.1 Total sample of non-permanent workers (n=97)

In addition to the 97 non-permanent workers interviewed, we held discussions and interviews with stakeholders such as employers, policy makers, career coaches and representatives from industry bodies such as professional organisations. Stakeholder perspectives were also gathered in 'reference group' sessions we conducted towards the end of each sector-specific investigation. In these discussions we gathered inputs, reactions and responses to our interpretations as stakeholders were invited to reflect upon the implications of our findings. Detailed information about our methodology and methods can be found in Appendix A.

In analysing, interpreting and reflecting upon our findings, we have aimed throughout to keep in view the wider societal factors that drive the employer-worker relationship and the differential ways in which work of various kinds is valued in different societies, reflecting wider power relations. As Sennett reminds us, these are, everywhere, oblivious to the personal goals of workers.

The interpretation of non-permanent or non-standard employment patterns in contemporary societies requires new ways of understanding the relationships between workers, workplaces and learning. The decoupling of individuals and their skill sets from ongoing or continuous relationships with any one employer or enterprise also means a decoupling of work identities from traditional roles and modes of learning. Our extended dialogue between ideas and evidence points the way towards more inclusive and progressive approaches to supporting learning and development that have better fit with the realities of changing work patterns and the changing composition of workforces.

Notes

1 Airbnb – online marketplace for leasing or renting short-term accommodation.
2 Term contract workers are defined as those on fixed-term contract of employment that will terminate on the expiry of a specific term unless it is renewed, as well as workers on casual or on-call employment (i.e. where persons are employed on an ad hoc basis, as and when the company requires additional manpower). The difference between a permanent and fixed-term contract worker is that there is no guarantee of contract renewal and thus of continued employment, unlike a 'permanent' worker. This definition of fixed-term contract by MOM can include a wide spectrum of contracts ranging from, for example, a number of years, months or weeks.
3 Own account workers are defined by MOM as persons who operate their own business without employing any paid workers. Own account workers were evenly distributed in PMET (e.g. working proprietors, real estate agents, insurance sales agents/brokers, private tutors) (54 per cent) and non-PMET (e.g. taxi drivers, hawkers/stall holders) (46 per cent) occupations.
4 The Future Economy Council has responsibility for 23 Industry Transformation Maps (ITMs) and has established five focus areas (called 'the Five Futures'), including jobs and skills. The rationale for developing industry maps to drive transformation in each of the 23 elected industries includes the need for 'cross-cutting solutions from multiple agencies and stakeholders', the need to 'upgrade', to 'move the productivity and innovation needle' and for organisations and unions and workers to take ownership of the transformation effort. Four pillars support each ITM's plan, including equipping people 'with deep skills to support the shift to greater value creation' (MIT, 2016).

References

Allan, H. T., Magnusson, C., Evans, K., Ball, E., Westwood, S., Curtis, K., & Johnson, M. (2016). Delegation and supervision of healthcare assistants' work in the daily management of uncertainty and the unexpected in clinical practice: Invisible learning among newly qualified nurses. *Nursing Inquiry, 23*(4), 377–385. Retrieved from https://doi.org/10.1111/nin.12155

Allan, P. (2002). The contingent workforce. *American Business Review, 20*(2), 103–110.

Arthur, M. B., & Rousseau, D. M. (1996). *The boundaryless career: A new employment principle for a new organizational era.* New York: Oxford University Press. Australian Bureau of Statistics (ABS), (2013). ABS 6359.0 Nov 2013.

Autor, D. H., & Houseman, S. N. (2010). Do temporary-help jobs improve labor market outcomes for low- skilled workers? *American Economic Journal: Applied Economics, 2*(3), 96–128.

Bamber, G., Gittell, J., Kochan, T., & Nordenflycht, A. Von. (2009). Up in the air: How airlines can improve performance by engaging their employees. *Journal of Periodontal & Implant Science*, 2–3. Retrieved from https://doi.org/10.7591/j.ctt7v6r5

Bauman, Z. (2005). *Liquid life.* Cambridge: Cambridge University Press.

Billett, S. (2002). Workplace pedagogic practices: Co – participation and learning. *British Journal of Educational Studies, 50*, 457–481. doi:10.1111/1467-8527.t01-2-00214

Billett, S. (2006). Relational interdependence between social and individual agency in work and working life. *Mind, Culture and Activity, 13*(1), 53–69.

Böheim, R., & Muehlberger, U. (2006). *Dependent self-employment: Workers on the border between employment and self-employment.* Retrieved from https://doi.org/10.1057/9780230288782

Brophy, E. (2006). System error: Labour precarity and collective organizing at Microsoft. *Canadian Journal of Communication, 31*(3), 619–638.

Brown, P., Lauder, H., & Ashton, D. (2011). *The global auction: The broken promises of education, jobs, and incomes*. Oxford: Oxford University Press.

Cavanagh, J. (2010). Women, subjectivities and learning to be adaptable. *Multicultural Education & Technology Journal, 4*(3).

Channel News Asia. (2017, October 24). *New industry transformation map launched to create new, better jobs in construction sector*. Retrieved from www.channelnewsasia.com. Accessed 2 January 2018.

CIPD. (2013). *Zero-hours contracts: Myth and reality*. London: CIPD.

CIPD. (2015). *The growth of EU labour: Assessing the impact on the UK labour market*. London: CIPD.

Dellot, B. (2016). *The self-employed: Rich, poor or something more*. Retrieved from www.thersa.org/discover/publications-and-articles/rsa-blogs/2016/10/the-self-employed-rich-poor-or-something-more

Edwards, R. (1997). *Changing places? Flexibility, lifelong learning and a learning society*. Abingdon: Routledge.

Edwards, R. (1998). Flexibility, reflexivity and reflection in the contemporary workplace. *International Journal of Lifelong Education, 17*(6), 377–388.European Commission. (2016). *The new European consensus on development "our world, our dignity, our future". Joint statement by the council and the representatives of the governments of the member states meeting within the council, the European parliament and the European commission*. Brussels: European Commission.

Evans, K., & Furlong, A. (1997). Metaphors of youth transitions: Niches, pathways, trajectories or navigations. In J. Bynner, L. Chisholm, & A. Furlong (Eds.), *Youth, citizenship and social change in a European context*. Aldershot: Ashgate. ISBN 9781859725412.

Evans, K., & Guile, D. (2012). Putting different forms of knowledge to work in practice. In J. Higgs, R. Barnett, S. Billett, M. Hutchings, & F. Trede (Eds.), *Practice-based education: Perspectives and strategies* (pp. 113–130). Rotterdam: Sense Publishers.

Evans, K., Guile, D., & Harris, J. (2009). *Putting knowledge to work: The Exemplars*. London: WLE Centre for Excellence, Institute of Education, University of London.

Evans, K., Guile, D., Harris, J., & Allan, H. (2010). Putting knowledge to work: A new approach. *Nurse Education Today, 30*(3), 245–251.

Evans, K., Hodkinson, P., Rainbird, L., & Unwin, L. (2006). *Improving workplace learning*. (Chapter 1). Abingdon: Routledge.

Evans, K., Kersh, N., & Kontiainen, S. (2004). Recognition of tacit skills: Sustaining learning outcomes in adult learning and work re-entry. *International Journal of Training and Development, 8*(1), 54–72.

Evans, K., Schoon, I., & Weale, M. (2013). Can lifelong learning reshape life chances? *British Journal of Educational Studies, 61*(1), 25–47. Retrieved from https://doi.org/10.1080/00071005.2012.756163

Fagan, C., Norman, H., Smith, M., & González Menéndez, M.C. (2014). In search of good quality part-time employment. Geneva: ILO.

Felstead, A., Fuller, A., Jewson, N., & Unwin, L. (2009). *Improving working as learning*. London: Routledge.

Forrier, A., Sels, L., & Stynen, D. (2009). Career mobility at the intersection between agent and structure: A conceptual model. *Journal of Occupational and Organizational Psychology, 82*, 739–759.

Foucault, M. (1998). *Technologies of the self* (Luther H. Martin, Huck Gutman, & Patrick H. Hutton, Eds., pp. 16–49). Amherst: University of Massachusets Press.

Fournier, J. (2015). *What is contingent worker?* New York: HCMWorks.

Fox, S. (1997). Situated learning theory versus traditional cognitive learning theory: Why management education should not ignore management learning. *Systems Practice, 10*(6), 727–747.

Fuller, A., & Unwin, L. (2004). Expansive learning environments: Integrating personal and organisational development. In H. Rainbird, A. Fuller, & A. Munro (Eds.), *Workplace learning in context*. London: Routledge.

Gangl, M. (2003). The only way is up: Employment protection and job mobility among recent entrants to European labour markets. *European Sociological Review, 19*(5), 429–449.

Gill, R. (2002). Cool, creative and egalitarian? Exploring gender in project-based new media work in Euro. *Information, Communication & Society, 5*(1), 70–89.

Green, F., Felstead, A., Gallie, D., & Henseke, G. (2016). Skills and work organisation in Britain: A quarter century of change. *Journal for Labour Market Research, 49*(2), 121–132. Retrieved from https://doi.org/10.1007/s12651-016-0197-x

Hager, P., & Hodkinson, P. (2011). Becoming as an appropriate metaphor for understanding professional learning. In *"Becoming" a professional, lifelong learning book series* (Vol. 16, pp. 33–56). The Netherlands: Springer.

Hall, D.T. (2002). *Careers in and out of organizations*. Thousand Oaks, CA: Sage Publications.

Hall, D.T. (2004). The protean career: A quarter-century journey. *Journal of Vocational Behaviour, 65*(1), 1–13. doi:10.1016/j.jvb.2003.10.006

Han, S-H. (2011, January). Asia needs lifelong learning. *ASEM Magazine*.

Hendrich, W., & Heidegger, G. (2001). *Tacit forms of key competences*. Flensburg: BIAT.

Hodkinson, P., & Hodkinson, H. (2004). The significance of individuals' dispositions in workplace learning: A case study of two teachers. *Journal of Education and Work, 17*(2), 167–182.

Hodkinson, P., Hodkinson, H., Evans, K., Kersh, N., Fuller, A., Unwin, L., & Senker, P. (2004). The significance of individual biography in workplace learning. *Studies in the Education of Adults, 36*(1), 6–24.

Holland, D., Lachicotte, W., Skinner, D., & Cain, C. (1998). *Identity and agency in cultural worlds*. Cambridge, MA: Harvard University Press.

Høyrup, S. (2010). Employee-driven innovation and workplace learning: Basic concepts, approaches and themes. *Transfer: European Review of Labour and Research, 16*(2), 143–154. Retrieved from https://doi.org/10.1177/1024258910364102

International Labour Organisation. (2014). Self employed women's association (SEWA). In *Learning from catalyst of rural transformation*. Retrieved from www.ilo.org/employment/units/rural-development/WCMS_234890/lang-en/index.htm. Accessed 3 January 2017.

International Labour Organisation. (2015, February 16–19). *Non-standard forms of employment*. Report for discussion at the Meeting of Experts on Non-Standard Forms of Employment. ILO, Geneva.

Jacobs, E. (2017). *The gig economy: Freedom from a boss, or just a con? The New Statesman*, March 20, 2017.

Kalleberg, A. (2000). Non-standard employment relations: Part-time, temporary and contract work. *Annual Review of Sociology, 26*, 341–365.

Kilpatrick, S., & Bound, H. (2005). *Skilling a seasonal workforce: A way forward for rural regions*. Adelaide: NCVER.

Kirpal, S. R. (2011). *Reflections on empirical findings: In labour-market flexibility and individual careers* (pp. 201–210). The Netherlands: Springer.

Lahiff, A., & Guile, D. (2016). It's not like a normal 9 to 5!' The learning journeys of media production apprentices in distributed working conditions. *Journal of Vocational Education & Training, 68*(3), 302–319.

Lobato, J. (2003). How design experiments can inform a rethinking of transfer and vice versa. *Educational Researcher, 32*(1), 17–20.

Malloch, M., Cairns, L., Evans, K., & O'Connor, B. (2011). *The Sage handbook of workplace learning*. London and New York: Sage Publications.

Marsick, V. J., Watkins, K. E., & O'Connor, B. N. (2010). Researching workplace learning in the United States. In L. Cairns, K. Evans, & B. O'Connor (Eds.), *The SAGE handbook of workplace learning*. London: Sage.

McGinnity, M. F. (2005). A bad start? Fixed-term contracts and the transition from education to work in West Germany. *European Sociological Review, 21*(4), 359–374.

McKeown, T. (2005). Non-standard employment: When even the elite are precarious. *The Journal of Industrial Relations, 47*(3), 276–293.

McKinsey Global Institute. (2016). *Independent work: Choice, necessity, and the gig economy*. Retrieved from www.mckinsey.com/global-themes/employment-and-growth/independent-work-choice-necessity-and-the-gig-economy

Micklethwaite. (2004). *A future perfect: The essentials of globalisation*. London: Random House.

MTI. (2016, September). *Integrated roadmaps to drive industry transformation: Broader sector-focused strategies to sustain growth and competitiveness of our economy and industries*. Media Facrt Sheet. Retrieved from www.mti.gov.sg/MTIInsights/SiteAssets/Pages/ITM/Images/Fact%20sheet%20on%20Industry%20Transformation%20Maps%20-%20revised%20as%20of%2031%20Mar%2017.pdf. Accessed 2 January 2018.

MTI. (2017, October 30). *Speech by Mr Ong Ye Kong Minister for Education (Higher education and skills)*. Launch of the financial services industry transformation map. Retrieved from www.mti.gov.sg/MTIInsights/SiteAssets/Pages/ITM/Images/Financial%20Services%20ITM%20Speech.pdf. Accessed 2 January 2018.

OECD. (2014). *OECD employment outlook*. Paris: OECD.

Owen, C., & Bound, H. (2001). *Contractor alliances and the new world of work*. Adelaide: National Centre for Vocational Education Research.

Purcell, K., Hogarth, T., & Simm, C. (1999). *Whose flexibility? The costs and benefits of non-standard working arrangements and contractual relations*. New York: Joseph Rowntree Foundation.

Purcell, K., & Purcell, J. (1998). In-sourcing, outsourcing, and the growth of contingent labour as evidence of flexible employment strategies. *European Journal of Work and Organizational Psychology*, 7(1).

Rainbird, H., Munro, A., & Senker, P. (2005). Running faster to stay in the same place? The intended and unintended consequences of government policy for workplace learning in Britain. In *International handbook of educational policy* (pp. 885–901). The Netherlands: Springer.

Ross, A. (2008). The new geography of work. *Theory Culture & Society, 25*(7), 31–49.

Royal Society of Arts. (2015). *Boosting the living standards of the self-employed*. London: RSA.

Rushbrook, P., Karmel, A., & Bound, H. (2014). Staying in a certain state of mind: Becoming and being a freelance adult educator in Singapore. *Australian Journal of Adult Learning, 54*(3), 413–433.

Standing, G. (2011). *The precariat: The new dangerous class*. London: Bloomsbury Publishing.

Sung, J. (2006) *Explaining the Economic Success of Singapore*. Cheltenham: Edward Elgar.

Tan, K.P. (2011). The ideology of pragmatism; neo-liberal globalization and political authoritarianism in Singapore. *Journal of Contemporary Asia, 42*(1), 67–92.

Tan, J. (2013). *Negotiating the occupational landscape: the career trajectories of ex-teachers and ex-engineers in Singapore*. Doctoral Thesis. London: UCL

Taylor, M. (2017, July). Good work: The Taylor review of modern working practices. *Employment*. Retrieved from https://assets.publishing.service.gov.uk/government/uploads/system/uploads/attachment_data/file/627671/good-work-taylor-review-modern-working-practices-rg.pdf. Accessed 3 May 2018.

Taylor, M., Evans, K., & Mohamed, A. (2008). *The value of formal and informal training for workers with low literacy: Exploring experiences in Canada and the United Kingdom*. Ottawa: Partnerships in Learning. Retrieved from http://www.nald.ca/library/research/interplay/value/value.pdf.

Trade Union Congress. (2017). *The gig is up*. Retrieved from www.tuc.org.uk/sites/default/files/the-gig-is-up.pdf. Accessed 3 January 2018.

Van Oers, B. (1998). The fallacy of decontextualization. *Mind, Culture & Activity*, *5*(2), 135–142. Retrieved from https://doi.org/10.1207/s15327884mca0502

Weil, D. (2014). *The Fissured workplace: Why work became so bad for so many and what can be done to improve it*. Cambridge, MA: Harvard University Press.

Williams, C. (2010). Understanding the essential elements of work-based learning and its relevance to everyday clinical practice. *Journal of Nursing Management*, *18*(6), 624–632.

Zukas, M. (2012). Regulating the professionals: Critical perspectives on learning in continuing professional development frameworks. In *Second international handbook of lifelong learning* (pp. 455–467). The Netherlands: Springer.

Chapter 2

Being a non-permanent worker

In our study, we explored how non-permanent workers' capabilities are employed in differing contexts. In doing so, we are in a position to take issue with questionable assumptions about needs and demands for competence development that focus wholly on the 'supply side' for the accumulation of human capital without addressing the contexts, spaces and their practices in which capabilities are used and developed. The contexts, spaces and practices of non-permanent work mediate the learning and development that take place, simultaneously facilitating and/or undermining the learning, development and work performance of non-permanent workers.

Analytical perspectives

There are two analytic perspectives and two theoretical lenses that have relevance for the investigation of how non-permanent workers learn and develop. The two analytic frameworks start with the social organisation of learning and the learning individual. The first theoretical lens focuses on the individual knowledge and skills that are part of human capital and on learning and development as human capital accumulation. The second theoretical lens sees human capabilities as shaped by context and social practices, with learning and development embedded in the uses of capabilities in practice and in context. These lenses focus attention, in different ways, in which the learning and development of non-permanent workers are connected with personal and work situations in adult life. In four separate quadrants, Figure 2.1 summarises the assumptions and beliefs in these different analytic perspectives from the perspective of an individual focus on learning and a social perspective on learning. An explanation of each quadrant follows.

Quadrant I: non-permanent workers' learning as human capital development that focuses on the learning individual

The concept of 'human capital' as coined by Becker (1993) emphasises the way in which an individual's skills and abilities can be applied again and again over time, to produce things – as can fixed capital. The research literature taking this approach has come to be dominated by studies of how higher levels of skill

	Learning and Development of NPWs as Human Capital Accumulation	Learning and Development as Social Practice
Focus on the learning individual	*Quadrant 1* Non-permanent workers perceived as requiring defined set of technical skills, the absence of which can impact negatively on an individual's economic and social opportunities.	*Quadrant 3* Emphasises the social context of using capabilities, often framed by relativist and hermeneutical perspectives.
Focus on social organisation of learning	*Quadrant 2* Emphasises shaping and organising education and adult learning 'provision' for socio-economic ends such as increased productivity, social mobility.	*Quadrant 4* Emphasises contexts, spaces, environments, socio-materiality and mediational means for learning; communities of practice; informal and 'everyday' learning; tools and historicity, appropriation and expertise.

Figure 2.1 Two theoretical lenses

Source: Adapted from Evans (2010)

(and higher levels of education) are associated with higher incomes and more favourable economic opportunities for the individuals who possess them.

In the context of non-permanent worker development, this perspective translates into policy arguments which assume that developing 'transferable' competences will bring greater likelihood of a sustainable working life, moving between short-term contracts and tasks. In this view, standardised 'employability skills' are cast as the defined set of required technical skills, the absence of which can impact negatively on an individual's economic and social opportunities. The recommendations of the Taylor (2017) study of non-permanent work in the United Kingdom, 'An Independent Review of Employment Practices in the Modern Economy', exemplify this human capital approach in arguing that 'it is time to take a standard approach to the concept of transferable skills and widen it across the economy as a whole' (p. 87).

Ideally, Quadrant 1 research inquiries would have to track individuals' journeys over time to demonstrate sustainability of working life, and they also have to address the complexity of the relationship between adult learning and adult experiences in ways indicated by Reder and Bynner (2009) and Comings

(2009). The links between acquisition of skills knowledge and experiences in adult life and later life journeys are evidently far from simple (Machin & Vignoles, 2005).

Quadrant 2: non-permanent workers' learning as human capital development that focuses on the social organisation learning

Although most of the literature on human capital examines the relationship between individual human capital and individual earnings and life-experiences, human capital development is recognised as having broader social dimensions in health, welfare, social participation and poverty reduction (McMahon & Oketch, 2013). It is argued that higher levels of human capital have spillover effects. In other words, a society with large numbers of educated and skilled people is believed to benefit as a whole in ways which go beyond the higher incomes and better life-chances of the skilled individuals themselves. The people who work alongside skilled people will also be more productive, and there will organisation-wide changes which would not occur without the presence of skilled individuals. Researchers such as Koepp (2002) and Riley (2012) have found some evidence for the phenomenon, but although policy-makers and public agencies argue that upgrading individuals' skills will have spillover effects at a societal level (e.g. DfES, 2003), the spillover effects of non-permanent workers' learning and development have yet to be addressed. Indeed, the effects of spiralling down skills and abilities in successive poor-quality work assignments may also have negative spillover effects, but these are as yet unresearched.

Quadrant 3: non-permanent workers' learning as social practice that focuses on the learning individual

In this perspective, learning journeys in adult life are defined in terms of biography and socially embedded learning. Chisholm, Evans and Biasin (2017) have argued that adult learning takes on a genuinely active, unpredictable quality when it takes the form of a critically reflexive engagement with personal and social life, drawing on resources in varied, autonomous and 'borderless' ways and feeding off critical life situations and turning points in the life course (Chisholm, 2008; Evans, 2009).

In this process, new forms of learning are superimposed on old forms, which retain much of their original power. Social institutions, old and new, continue to interlock to shape typical life courses, that is life courses which may still be typified according to social position. There is a need to understand better the reflexive ways in which people's lives are shaped, bounded or change direction as they interact with the social institutions which structure aspects of the social landscape in which they move. Furthermore, people's beliefs in their ability to change their situation by their own efforts, individually or collectively, are significant for the development of skills at work and beyond (Evans, 2002b). These beliefs change and develop over time and according to experiences in the labour market and beyond. The ways in which these beliefs are translated into action is achieved rather than possessed (Biesta & Tedder, 2007); capabilities are limited by bonds that can be loosened (Evans, 2002a, 2009). Notions of 'borderlessness' view learning as becoming more extensive (lifelong), more specialised (life-near), more differentiated (life-wide), more flexible, more individualised and more contingent (Chisholm, 2008, p. 142). Research that focuses on complexities and contingencies in the adult life course examines how learners' dispositions to learn relate to a wide range of differing environments as adults recontextualise their knowledge and use their learning in and through their domestic situations, community involvements and family environments.

Quadrant 4: non-permanent worker development as social practice, focusing on the social organisation of learning

Non-permanent workers' learning as a social practice emphasises the social context of knowledge and capabilities that are learnt and developed over time, as workplaces become important milieus for development of capabilities and immersion in work cultures as well as places for improving employment and income for the workers (Rismark & Sitter, 2003). The new spaces themselves are characterised by being both work and learning spaces where the boundary between the two is considerably blurred (Solomon, Boud, & Rooney, 2006, p. 6). Situated learning theory further enriches the concept of learning space, emphasising socialisation into a wider community of practice that involves membership, identity formation and expertise development through participation in the activities of the particular work practice (Lave & Wenger, 1991; Fuller & Unwin, 2004; Hughes, Jewson, & Unwin, 2007). In this view, the group is seen as important, rather than the individual, and people learn through shared practices of the community (Billett, 2004) who shows how individuals actively influence one another's learning and enculturation through a process of 'co-participation'. Non-permanent worker development thus becomes an expanded concept which locates learning in the lived experiences and social relations of work.

Exploring non-permanent workers' lived experiences at the limits of analytic and theoretical perspectives

Researching the learning and development of non-permanent workers takes each of these analytic and theoretical perspectives to the limits of their explanatory and exploratory power. For example, modelling the acquisition of qualifications and competences using a human capital lens eventually concludes, tentatively, that work returns are likely to be enhanced when there is a good match between the qualification and the requirements of the job in practice, but lacks a way of capturing and modelling the qualities of social practice that are involved. Furthermore, situated learning theories, which are well able to capture the significance of learning in the non-permanent workers' exposure to different workplace environments, often struggle to explain *what* is learned in practice and in the interplay between practice-based learning and prior skills and knowledge. The idea of 'borderlessness' in learning suggests new conceptual and practical connections between learning subjects (who), learning sites (where) and learning pathways (when and how).

The idea of 'borderlessness' moves away from looking at and understanding phenomena as separate from each other. Rather, in using a 'borderlessness' lens, researchers and practitioners focus on relational aspects and the dynamic in relations between different aspects and phenomena of activity. For example, understanding context as embedded in everyday actions (Bound & Rushbrook, 2015) and using concepts such as spaces of learning (Kersh, 2015; Evans & Kersh, 2016) potentially bring together ways of studying and understanding how everyday actions, decisions, judgements and relations are imbued with not only the spaces, environments and materiality of situated contexts, but what lies beyond the situated context. An important aspect of the embeddedness of context in everyday actions is that of mediation. Historically, the concept of mediation comes from the work of Vygotsky in the 1920s, who argued that human action is mediated by culturally meaningful tools and signs. Wertsch (1998) takes this concept and further develops it, suggesting that historical cultural and institutional patterns and precedents are embedded within tools, and these mediate our conceptualisation of skills and intelligence, and what is perceived as possible or not. When subjects master tools, these patterns are learnt, but not necessarily valued or internalised. However, when subjects appropriate (Wertsch, 1998) these tools (rather than master them), the patterns and beliefs inherent in (embedded in) the tools are valued. Despite historical, cultural and institutional patterns and precedent influencing subjects, these patterns and precedents are often invisible to subjects. Further, there are social relations between tools, subjects and desired goals not always visible to the subjects. Socio-material approaches (e.g. Fenwick, 2012) emphasise the mediation of tools in learning within situated contexts. The practice lens (e.g. Schatzki, 2012; Nicolini, 2011) also enables close-up examination of interactions, sayings, doings and relatings within situated contexts. Using these theoretical understandings enables a rich investigation and understanding of the complexities of work and learning.

However, as indicated in the discussion of Figure 2.1, the complexities of work and learning, particularly for non-permanent workers, go beyond these frameworks. We also need to take note of the theoretical perspectives referred to in quadrant 3, namely the life history of the individual within their social context and the ways in which this mediates learning and work; agency and identity in relation to work and learning. Learning and development of social practice using both an individual and social organisation perspective thus provide new conceptual and practical connections between learning subjects (who), learning sites (where) and learning pathways (when and how).

In the process of sharing with readers the lived experienced of the non-permanent workers we interviewed, we bring together explicitly and implicitly these theoretical frames for understanding the work, learning and identity of these workers. Given that the bulk of our data is interviews, the richness of ethnographic approaches used in applying practice and socio-material approaches is not part of our data. Nevertheless, the theoretical concepts driving these approaches offer some useful means for explaining the lived experience non-permanent workers shared with us in these stories. Importantly, the use of theoretical lenses discussed in this section strongly inform our theoretical frame of integrated practice expanded in Chapter 5. This chapter and Chapters 3 and 4 provide the basis for the integrated practice framework that is brought together in Chapter 5.

In the remainder of this chapter, we pick up the theoretically contingent, precarious debate discussed in Chapter 1 and introduce elements of our theoretical framework of integrated practice. In Chapter 1, we pointed out that the labels of precarious and contingent are not helpful in capturing the lived experience of non-permanent workers and in fact get in the way of understanding the day-to-day experience. Integral to this discussion, in this chapter we privilege the concept of identity as the strength of identification with the work is important in the journeys and learning and development of non-permanent workers. We consider how non-permanent workers think and feel their way into occupational identities. We commence the chapter by unpacking what we mean by 'identity'.

Identity and non-permanent workers

Identity brings into focus the individual *and* their social practice in various contexts (see Figure 2.1); indeed, as Eteläpleto (2015) argues, 'professional identities are negotiated at the intersection of the individual and the social' (p. 40). This relation between the individual and the social, the nature of the intersection between them, not only rejects a simplistic individual-social dichotomy, but provides a frame for understanding the development of identity and appreciating identity as a continuous process. Wenger (1998) highlights the importance of the relations between individual and context when he states that identity is

> the social, the cultural, the historical with a human face. Talking about identity in social terms is not denying individuality but viewing the very definition of individuality as something that is part of the practices of specific communities. It is therefore a mistaken dichotomy to wonder whether the unit of analysis should be the community or the person. The focus must be on the process of their mutual constitution.
>
> (Wenger, 1998, pp. 145–146)

What is meant by this 'mutual constitution' or the intersection of the social and individual? Wenger argues that we produce our identities through the practices we engage in (Wenger, 1998, p. 164) or do not engage in. We define ourselves through lived experience in multiple communities of shared practice, what we think and say about ourselves, through our history and our future plans, our learning journey; identity combines competence and experience and develops our 'ways of knowing'. It determines what matters to us, with whom we share information and who we decide to trust. It also recognises multiple memberships of practice communities and boundary crossing (Wenger, 1998). The limitations of this concept are that it underplays the role of individual agency and of power differentials and does not fully explain engagement in learning in practice, nor how beliefs about learning, knowledge and power shape that learning. This perspective is also limited in how it accounts for affordances and constraints from situated settings and the ways in which wider socio-economic contexts impact learning and identity. As Du Gay (1996) notes, 'any identity is basically relational to its conditions of existence, any change in the latter is bound to affect the former' (p. 184).

So in understanding and considering identity and its development, it is important to consider the context(s) of workplace learning; professional identity is a dual process of identity negotiation and the development of work practices that is specific to particular contexts, cultures and occupational fields (Eteläpleto, 2015). This conceptualisation of the processes of identity formation points to what it is we can focus on when investigating work identities: work identities would be investigated 'from the perspective of how they are constructed and negotiated within workplaces and work organisation in different cultural contexts' (Eteläpleto, 2015, p. 47). For example, in investigating how vocational teachers negotiate their professional identity in the context of a major curriculum reform, Vähäsantanen and Eteläpelto (2009) considered individual backgrounds, teachers' sense of their professional selves, prior working experiences and expectations of their professional future *and* the affordances from the practices and traditions of the context in which these teachers worked. In short, we understand identity as a negotiated process in light of how individuals negotiate material conditions of the context, work practices, discourses and their intersection with the discourses of individuals' ideals, values and goals, their work history and professional knowledge and interaction with community members. Identity, then, is about being and becoming to particular occupational practices. Holland et al. (1998) conceive of identity as 'self-authoring' within a contested social and cultural space, what they call a 'figured world', and as contributing to making the figured worlds (p. 272) linked to 'positionality' (p. 271) (referring to power, status and rank within 'figured worlds' that 'carry disposition, social identification and meaning' (p. 271)). When considered in this way, it can be said that Holland et al. unpack Eteläpleto's (2015) claim that identity is negotiated at the intersection of the individual and the social. The theoretical lenses identified in Figure 2.1, quadrants 3 and 4 are also evident in this interpretation. In the following section, we explore what it means for our interviewees to *be* a non-permanent worker.

Being a non-permanent worker

> 'It [being a freelancer] means you are free'! (Gail, producer, film and television)
> 'As a freelancer, you are only as good as your last job'. (Kevin, director, film and television)
> '[T]he biggest one [challenge] would be getting payment sometimes'. (Kerry, keygrip, film and television)
> 'I would say every one of us always have this little voice that tells us you're not good enough and all those things'. (Daisy, adult educator, CET sector)
> 'I don't want to freelance anymore because it's very unstable'. (Ashely, lighting designer, technical theatre)

These short quotes are illustrative not only of what it requires to be a freelancer, or non-permanent worker, but of motivations for being a non-permanent workers and of its challenges. Our research found there are those who appear to thrive on non-permanent work arrangements, as well as those who struggle. Despite the discourse particularly amongst those who called themselves freelancers, that this way of working allowed them to exercise their professional judgement, to grow and develop and gain a deep sense of satisfaction, to exercise choice and experience freedom, in reality it appears that uncertainty of payment, long working hours and highly fluid boundaries between work and home qualify the freedom, choice and control of non-permanent work, as we will illustrate below.

Thriving or struggling or somewhere in between is, of course, dependent on many factors, including, for example, the ability and access to opportunities to turn passion into a continuous flow of work and income, lifestyle and life stage choices, access to networks and ability to work these networks, access to mentors, role models, opportunities for challenging work, competencies, positioning and a range of other factors explored in detail in the following chapters. Such factors mediated the journey of the non-permanent workers we interviewed, their entrepreneurial and craft capabilities and identities. Entrepreneurial and craft identities were also mediated by the opportunities for learning afforded not only by the structure of the work, but of the industry sector (e.g. ways of working together, spaces and forms of interaction) as well as individual learning-to-learn capabilities and dispositions.

Varied 'career' journeys

The career path or what we are calling the journey of non-permanent workers is fluid, moving horizontally, vertically and at angles in between at different points in time. Such journeys are mediated by the context the non-permanent worker works in and their dispositions.

Awareness of what it takes to persevere and find satisfaction and recognition as a non-permanent worker was quite varied. For example, Kevin, a freelance director, revealed that his willingness to be exploited in the early stages of his career led to an especially burdensome work schedule, low income and issues of late payment:

> But when I was directing, I was very poor when I started. And the payment come late. Because there's no regulatory body in Singapore to say, to help us. There's no union. So basically I, to get into the industry, I had to undercut myself. Undercut, I know this production company is sort of like, raping me up. But I let them rape me. Once again, no choice, because you got to get in you see.
>
> (Kevin, director, film and television)

Kevin's story tells us not only of his commitment and desire to become a successful director (he is now well known in Singapore and considered highly successful), but is revealing of the film and television sector, its structures and ways of working. It is a cut-throat, competitive industry that does not lend itself well to supporting and mentoring new entrants. Despite this, many individuals in the sector do actively commit, as individuals, to providing such support. Kevin's story of struggle, long hours, poor and uncertain income and being exploited was echoed by others who became successful in other industry sectors and occupations.

To protect their choices to continue along this uncertain and difficult journey of what is essentially risky work, the large majority of 'professionals' who positioned themselves as freelancers spoke about their passion, also evident in Kevin's story as well as their commitment to others.

Bagus, an adult educator in the healthcare industry, shared with us that despite uncertain income, his priority was service to others.

> I can get good money this month, I may get little money next month but that doesn't concern so much but as long I can cover with the requirements of my living . . . but service to people is my main priority.
>
> (Bagus, adult educator, CET sector)

Like a number of others, particularly those in occupations such as removalists, couriers and food and beverage assistants, Bagis was undertaking a variety of different kinds of work. At the time of the interview, Bagus was busy developing a programme on clinical massage and physical rehabilitation. His secondary activity was freelancing as a cardiopulmonary trainer and auditor. In addition, he also spent time providing holistic massage/rehabilitation services to the elderly, doing part-time/seasonal catering of Nonya food (his own small enterprise) and was also a sales representative for a health product brand, something he had been doing for over 20 years. Due to the diversity of these activities, Bagus emphasised quality and care, rather than a particular subject matter or type of educator, as his core.

> I'm very particular, I'm very focused . . . I must give the best that means I'm willing to help a person. . . . and the same when I do all preparation of the catering or the food. . . . As a therapist you must be very professional. . . . you are a professional trainer, you are a professional assessor, you are a professional auditor and that is where you build up the confidence.
>
> (Bagus, adult educator, CET sector)

For Bagus, his identity was bound up with quality of service and care; service and care are key threads that run through all his different kinds of work. Kevin, on the other hand, identifies as a freelance director. His identity is bound up with his craft and whatever it takes to achieve his required 'sense of aesthetics' to achieve 'beauty'. He says it is

> all hard hours. Because my aim is to direct drama . . . But basically I try to do it with a taste that is above and beyond what you see every day. That's how I blow the competition out of the water. By putting in 110 basically.
>
> (Kevin, freelance director, film and television)

He has reached a position in the industry that allows him in many situations to exercise decisions that reflect his style and the crew he prefers to work with. 'My influence is substantial because I'm in the position of influence'.

Kevin's strong sense of craft identity and Bagus's identity as a caring professional contrast sharply with the identity of those in occupations that are quickly learnt. Thirty-eight-year-old Lai Ming, for example, started work at the age of 14 in a range of casual food and beverage jobs immediately after completing his primary eight education. After National Service (compulsory in Singapore for all males), he worked as a despatch rider in a permanent position for four years before opting to work on a commission basis. He made the switch because 'it pays better'. 'You work more, [you] earn more'. The pay for permanent work, on the other hand, never increases, he says. Freelancing also offers greater flexibility or 'freedom', as he calls it. Once he completes his work, he can head home, and this is difficult to do for permanent work. He laments the lack of CPF contributions and medical benefits in his current work. He puts in some contributions into his Medisave account, but is unable to save more. For these reasons, he is thinking of securing a permanent job as a delivery man driving a 'big lorry', but only if the pay is right.

Lai Ming's identity is as an entrepreneur who can earn more and access greater flexibility by doing this kind of work. Kamal, who was 51 at the time of interviewing, similarly identifies as a freelancer who can earn more and can access flexible working times. His need to earn more was related to his stage of life; namely, the need to support his children, who were entering into higher education. He amassed 20 years of experience in the hotel industry, but was laid off as part of his company's cost-cutting measures. His attempt at finding a similar job as a bell captain met with little success. Employers wanted him to begin all over again as a bell boy, drawing a monthly pay of $1 400–$1 500. This was unacceptable to him, as his children were entering higher education. He took on two despatch jobs, a main position to deliver letters on a commission basis, and a part-time position in a fast-food outlet. This currently nets him $3 500 a month in total, much higher than the $2 000 pay that he drew as a bell captain. Understanding that he is identified by government as 'self-employed', he makes sure that he has insurance coverage and makes self-contributions to CPF. It has been ten years since he moved to the despatch position. From time to time, he would try to apply for permanent jobs (e.g. as a tower crane operator) when he gets tired of the hours and income uncertainty in his current position. However, the generally higher income and greater flexibility as a non-permanent worker remain compelling.

Like many of the non-permanent workers in work that is task-based and with low discretion amongst our interviewees, Lei Ming and Kamal identified as entrepreneurs rather than with a craft. As such, they were prepared to try for other kinds of permanent work in other industries, such as Kamal's efforts to work as a crane driver. Decisions to stay as a non-permanent worker are largely based on the amount of pay that they can earn.

For these non-permanent workers, their entry into the industry is often motivated by personal circumstances, such as low initial qualifications, retrenchment or caring responsibilities. Freelance or casual work gives them access to higher income, fits their lifestyle better or functions as an interim measure. It is not fundamental to craft development, as they would prefer a permanent job if their needs or wants are met. This motivation for entry stands in sharp contrast to the 'way of being' for most freelancers in professional sectors who value the non-permanent work arrangement as a means to access diverse jobs and experiences that are vital to honing their craft.

Who you need to be as a non-permanent worker

Clearly, who you need to 'be' as a non-permanent worker differs not only across individuals but across occupations and industry sectors. What it means to 'be' is at the core of identity. Being a non-permanent worker involves both the public face individuals present in different settings, a process of matching the requirements of the practices in the setting. These are aspects of what Holland et al. (1998) would call self-authoring and positionality. This nexus between the individual and the social can be one of tension, calling for considerable resilience on the part of the non-permanent worker. For Bagus, it was being caring and focusing on service; for Kevin, it was about striving to be the best director with his own distinct style. It is these aspects of identity that remain 'core' or being anchored, important given the requirement for 'malleability' – an interesting term given that it refers to materials that have the property of being able to be hammered into shape without breaking or cracking. In the literature, this is called shapeshifting. Shapeshifting is the 'behind-the-scenes' work non-permanent workers need to do while appearing fit to adapt to each client's needs and be able to offer knowledge only in contexts where it is valued (Fenwick, 2008). At a theoretical level, Bauman (2005) shows how individuals are being increasingly positioned to lead a 'liquid life' where workers develop multiple identities according to their positioning and contribution to different work teams. In the liquid life, success can arise from the development of capabilities to make multiple transitions and to navigate the diverse worlds they operate in. In this sense, one needs to *be* a shapeshifter and skilled time manager while *presenting* a coherent brand for the particular client at hand. Retaining some type of visible identity marker to avoid a sense of fragmentation can be very difficult in this situation, but is important for psychological and pragmatic reasons (Edwards & Usher, 1996).

Howard, a freelance video editor and trainer, described this flexible state of mind as being 'cultivated over time'. He described himself as a naturally 'stubborn' person who has been forced to cultivate a flexible disposition through the necessity of working in a variety of different work environments:

> It's definitely a state of mind that is cultivated over time. You won't be so malleable at the very beginning of your freelancing career. But as time goes by, the more you work in different environments, the more you come to an understanding that you have to change to fit yourself into different environments. There's no point complaining that we don't have this, we don't have that. Every company you go to is very different and no company will change for a freelancer. So you change for them and not the other way around. So it was something that took me a long, long, long while, to cultivate myself to be malleable. But it's a very precious experience definitely.
>
> (Howard, video editor and trainer, film and television)

He describes the advantages of being 'malleable' as a freelancer, as 'it makes you see the world in a more realistic sense. And you are more fair to yourself and fair to others as well'.

Gavin, a sound technician also from the film and television sector, gives a slightly different perspective on what being malleable means in day-to-day practice. It is a quality required to gain a continuous flow of work and to be considered as 'good'. He states you have to '*swallow a lot of pain. The more pain you swallow, the more popular you'll get*'. Stamina and endurance are combined with a degree of performativity in the form of a willingness to stifle grievances that arise out of onerous working conditions. As Gavin further explained:

> And always remember . . . never put on a long face on the job. Even if you've been scolded or you've had a fourteen-hour day, you still have to put a smiling face because you're a non-salaried worker. Because if you're a salaried worker, you could scold your boss. You could use whatever words you want. But as a non-salaried worker, do not forget that your pay could be withheld.
>
> (Gavin, sound technician, film and television)

Recognising and paying deference to chains of command on sets is important for building a reputation that will help maintain regular work. This is part of the day-to-day exercise of judgement and self-management that are integral to the freelancer's role in the creative sector. The presentation of the 'smiling face' is part of a social process which Coté (2006) describes as image projection that occurs in contextually specific ways. These are part of the day-to-day practices of being 'malleable' or a shapeshifter.

To be seen as 'good' on set is important, as it often translates into getting a flow of work. But for those new to freelancing, this is problematic. It is not just how one presents on set but other entrepreneurial capabilities that are important, particularly networking. Ron's story illustrates the importance of being seen as 'good' by those in the sector who will engage you. Ron had very advanced skills when he entered the industry at the age of 21, made possible because of a rare opportunity to hone his skills on a lighting board at church. Yet he had difficulty securing jobs in the initial years. After he joined a diploma programme the job offers come in as a result of an opportunity to work alongside professionals from the industry at school:

> I had very advanced skills . . . but nobody would give me a chance because they don't know [who] I am, and they don't know what I can do. It wasn't until the last year [before I] graduate that I started to get a bit more work . . . [The practitioner-lecturers] don't look at your study results. They want to know . . . when a prop is missing, how this person reacts? The light is flickering, what does this person do? . . . If you are good, [the practitioner-lecturers] will just pull you out and say, I want you to work on my show. Once you get a foot in and someone well-established says this guy can work, people will say good, come and work on my show and it is very much that way.
>
> (Ron, lighting designer, technical theatre)

Ashley was not so successful in making the needed connections. He was undertaking a Technical Theatre Training Programme hosted at one of Singapore's major concert and theatre complexes. As will be discussed in Chapter 6, this programme was excellent for developing technical capabilities but did not enable exposure to other parts of the industry and professionals outside the site. Consequently, Ashely found it difficult to gain work. He says,

> I started out with passion, but slowly the passion became money and money became a job . . . my passion kind of died. . . . I definitely feel I didn't know the difficulty . . . of being a freelancer.

He opted for a permanent job in the shipping industry after two years of trying, despite being seen as a promising practitioner.

The combination of having a resilient core or anchor, of networking and other entrepreneurial capabilities and how these connected with and related to affordances of the context the non-permanent worker was working in, was particularly evident for adult educators in the continuing education and training sector. This is a highly competitive and segmented market; there are many opportunities for freelance trainers to doubt themselves and the viability of their occupation. The more established freelance trainers we interviewed and those who operated partially in the private market seemed to be more resilient to setbacks. The less established private trainers, however, grappled with self-doubt. Those in the private market with less experience demonstrated a period of trying to figure out who they were. Daisy, who had been a freelancer for two years and taught life-skills, was still trying to find out which 'particular market' (Daisy, adult educator, CET sector) she could do well in and reported needing to try out different sectors.

There is a balancing process that non-permanent workers need to constantly juggle. On the one hand, they need to find a bread and butter (rice bowl) source of income; yet to survive, they need to branch out. It is important to have engagements with multiple organisations. For example, those who relied on one or two organisations for their source of work were the least stable. Seeing opportunities and deliberately positioning for future work is important for ongoing work; it moves beyond being good at the work the non-permanent worker does. Kevin, for example, had established a working relationship with one production house, so he '*lobbied'. He* knew that at the end of the year, the production house had a drama that he was interested in. He let the production house know this and says that in the meantime, he did whatever they asked of him, even if he 'hated' it. At the end of the year, he got to direct three episodes.

Kevin's vision is to eventually open his own company, but in the meantime, he chooses to work as a freelancer, as it provides a range of experience not available in the few permanent positions in this sector. He says, 'once you become a director, you have to prove that you are good. If you are not good, you slide into 'lighted bulb'. The hundreds of directors who came out and fade away'. Kevin's story is one of strong passion for the work he does and of resilience. He comments, 'if you have the balls, you can become a director very fast'. However, to achieve this, he has experienced exploitation, undertaken work he does not like and put up with poor conditions. It is also interesting to note that Kevin, like many others not just in film and television, but in other sectors, consider that the way to get challenging, rewarding work in their sector was to freelance, to be a non-permanent worker. This issue is addressed in Chapter 4.

Being 'malleable', a shapeshifter, yet having a strong craft identity are aspects of being a non-permanent worker that look different for those in task-based work that has limited discretionary power. These workers, generally described as casual, tend to demonstrate loyalty to one or a few employers at any one time in order to secure a steady stream of work. They distinguish themselves from permanent workers through subtle resistance and identifying as different. In the furniture moving sector, for instance, industry casual workers have official polo T-shirts provided by the company and don them just like their permanent counterparts. The difference, one supervisor tells us, is insidious. The casual worker tends to bend the rules such as tucking out his T-shirt or donning long hair. Permanent employees, however, have to abide by strict dress code of tucked-in polo T-shirts and neatly groomed hair. That the workers value demonstrating their worth to one or a few employers but openly flaunt company's rules and regulations suggest that they have the upper hand in the context of the tight employment market, in which the demand for such workers is high and the supply is short. Employers opine that it is not easy to get them, as they 'choose and pick their work and pay'. The demand situation is exacerbated when others or players in the same industry recruit from the same pool of casual workers.

Indeed, while freelancers in professional sectors stay in their industry to hone their craft, the casual workers are open to moving across industries to another casual job. Tisha, 32, is employed by a manpower agency to work as a food and beverage casual worker across a range of hotels. From time to time, she will take up other casual work assignments, such as stock-taking for supermarkets. Nazri is a freelance mover during the weekdays and a food and beverage casual during the weekends. Adequate income, and, for a number, but not all, of these casual workers, a sense of flexibility are important. It is these aspects of work they seek to actively manage, rather than development of craft or craft identity. The reason? Their work is often task-based and quickly learnt, offering limited challenges for learning and development.

Another aspect of what it means to be a non-permanent worker, particularly for professional occupations, is the need to be a constant learner and thus to have good learning-to-learn capabilities. For example, adult educators working across the Workforce Skills Qualification (WSQ) and private market note that much of their learning occurred through reflection; this assisted them in constantly realigning and refining products and drawing value out of past experiences. In addition, a reflexive component is evident when they learn from contacts about how the various markets in the sector function. Limited reflection and reflexivity can also limit possibilities. Borhan, for example, was keen to start a business running his own *kebab* stall but saw no need to pick up additional skills, despite struggling with numeracy skills. Nazri, working in the furniture removal industry, sought to deliver high-quality customer service but lacked information on the range of job opportunities in the furniture removalist industry. His networks were family and friends, providing him with limited or no access to resources outside the circle of people he moved within (Kilpatrick & Bound, 2005), thus mediating his potential for development without access to learning resources that often come with access to wider networks. Reflection and reflexivity become a 'general pedagogic stance' (Edwards, 1998, p. 386) that is vital to the effective navigation of constantly changing work. Reflexivity and knowing the industry and how it works are important in being able to be comfortable in working across different settings, requirements and expectations and being able to manage all that is required. Learning, adapting and applying or what Evans (2009) calls recontextualising knowledge from different work settings and other sources to new settings is a constant part of being a non-permanent worker. Development opportunities for such capabilities are denied to these non-permanent workers given the task-based nature of their work.

Many of our interviewees spoke of the importance of finding mentors. Nasser highlighted his reliance on a mentor to develop the intuitive and aesthetic aspects of his work:

> And he's the only guy who can explain to me from A-Z and even more if I just ask him a simple question. He don't just tell you how to read, he tell you the nuance of it. He tells you all the little things that is not in the books, through his experience and through his knowledge.
>
> (Nasser, key grip, film and television)

To sum up this section, *being* a non-permanent worker is not a singular experience or identity. Rather, there are multiple ways of being, mediated not only by the individual's life experience, biography and circumstances, but by the opportunities afforded these workers. The opportunities afforded non-permanent workers, their individual circumstances and biographies, industry, institutional and policy contexts they work within are in constant interplay. Tensions and contradictions surface, such as those experienced by non-permanent workers in task-based work who can earn more and have greater flexibility as non-permanent workers than being in permanent work that is low paid. The tension managed by these workers is the lack of security, the lack of contributions to the CPF compared to more sustainable income over time and greater flexibility. Other tensions include learning to be a shapeshifter and yet to maintain a core self-narrative, a clear sense of identity. Having good technical and craft capabilities, yet not having the necessary entrepreneurial capabilities; wanting to expand the scope of work, but not having that more developed understanding of the industry or specific entrepreneurial capabilities such as strong, diverse networks are other examples. *Being* a non-permanent worker in work that offers challenges and learning and development opportunities requires craft, entrepreneurial skills and learning-to-learn capabilities. *Being* a non-permanent worker requires managing the dynamic interplay between many elements. The stories told in this section illustrate the theoretical lens of learning and development as social practice that focuses on both the learning individual and the social organisation of learning, introduced at the beginning of this chapter.

Conclusion

This chapter has introduced two analytic perspectives and two theoretical lenses that are used in exploring different facets of adult learning. The two analytic frameworks start with the social organisation of learning and the learning individual. The first theoretical lens focuses on sets of individual skills that are part of human capital and on development as human capital accumulation. The second theoretical lens sees pluralities of learning mediated in and through context and reflected in social practices. The experiences of non-permanent workers have to be understood as part of a wider, social, highly dynamic context, keeping in view interdependencies within and beyond the workplace institutional and policy environments. This includes the recognition that workers are both part of the work system and have lives outside it; they are engaged in multiple overlapping structures and communities of social practice that can themselves be analysed in terms of interdependencies. While learning is seen as integral to practice, attention has be paid to the environment as a whole and the ways in which workers seek to bring their life situations under control, both within and beyond work. What it is to be a non-permanent worker is critical in understanding possibilities and barriers to their learning and development. For those engaged in complex work with discretionary power, their identity is primarily with their craft and secondly as an entrepreneur. For non-permanent workers undertaking solely task-based work, their entrepreneurial identity reflects issues around the quality of their work.

As previously argued, the family of approaches that starts with the 'learning individual' as the unit of analysis and argues that people do not act *in* structures and environments – they act through them. Learning and development processes are best understood when individual worker/learner perspectives are built into the dominant social–organisational view of learning at work. Wider social structures and social institutions can be fundamental in influencing the learning that is possible and held to be desirable and worthy of support. This includes the legal frameworks that govern workers' entitlements, industrial relations and the role of trades unions as well as the social structuring of business systems, the 'rules of the game' in different societies (Whitley, 2000, p. 88). The nature of the learning environments in organisations can expand or restrict learning (see Fuller & Unwin, 2004). For most employers, workers' learning is not a priority and a lower-order decision, and for non-permanent workers, hiring and firing may be a more immediate response to skills challenges than any investment in their learning and development. For the individual worker, their past experiences, dispositions and present situation will affect the extent to which they take advantage of the opportunities afforded by their immediate work environment. These factors change over time. That professionals and other highly qualified workers are more likely to have access to continuing training and professional development than less-qualified workers has been consistently demonstrated in national monitoring reports, such as those of the National Institute of Adult Continuing Education in the UK (Aldridge & Tuckett, 2002) and in Asia; they are more likely to experience work environments that are rich in opportunities for learning than workers in lower-level jobs. The challenge is to create the conditions in which all workers can take advantage of all of these kinds of opportunities. One mechanism may be through entitlements to learning, established in law, or through tax breaks or through the intermediary organisations, NGOs and mutuals, trainers and co-workers. The ways in which non-permanent workers can themselves, individually or collectively, influence their employment and life chances have to be understood as part of a wider dynamic, keeping in view the institutional and policy environments and the interdependencies set up within and beyond the workplace and recognising that workers are both part of the work system and have lives outside it; they are engaged in multiple overlapping structures and 'communities of social practice' that can themselves be analysed in terms of the conditions for integrated practice.

References

Aldridge, F., & Tuckett, A. (2002). *Two steps forward, one step back: The NIACE survey on adult participation in learning*. Leicester: NIACE.

Bauman, Z. (2005). *Liquid life*. Polity, Cambridge.

Becker, G. S. (1993). Human capital: A theoretical and empirical analysis, with special reference to education. In *Evaluation* (Vol. 24).

Biesta, G., & Tedder, M. (2007). Agency and learning in the lifecourse: Towards an ecological perspective. *Studies in the Education of Adults, 39*(2), 132–149. Retrieved from https://doi.org/10.1080/02660830.2007.11661545

Billett, S. (2004). Co-participation at work: Learning through work and throughout working lives. *Studies in the Education of Adults, 36*(2), 190–205. Retrieved from https://doi.org/10.1080/02660830.2004.11661496

Bound, H., & Rushbrook, P. (2015). *Towards a new understanding of workplace learning: The context of Singapore*. Singapore: Institute for Adult Learning.

Chisholm, L. (2008). Re-contextualising learning in second modernity. In *Research in post-compulsory education* (Vol. 13, pp. 139–147). Retrieved from https://doi.org/10.1080/13596740802141253

Comings, J. P. (2009). *Student persistence in adult literacy and numeracy programmes* (S. Reder & J. Bynner, Eds.) (Tracking A). New York: Routledge.

DfES. (2003). *21st century skills: Realizing our potential*. Retrieved December 1, 2017, from www.dfes.gov.uk/skillsstrategy

Du Gay, P. (1996). *Consumption and identity at work*. London: Sage Publications.

Edwards, R., & Usher, R. (1996). What stories do I tell now? New times and new narratives for the adult educator. *International Journal of Lifelong Education, 15*(3), 216–229. Retrieved from https://doi.org/10.1080/0260137960150307

Edwards, R. (1998). Flexibility, reflexivity and reflection in the contemporary workplace. *International Journal of Lifelong Education, 17*(6), 377–388.

Eteläpleto, A. (2015). The role of work identity and agency in workplace learning. In *Towards a new understanding of workplace learning: The context of Singapore* (pp. 36–53). Singapore: Institute for Adult Learning.

Evans, K. (2002a). Taking control of their lives? Agency in young adult transitions in England and the New Germany. *Journal of Youth Studies, 5*(3), 245–269. Retrieved from https://doi.org/10.1080/1367626022000005965

Evans, K. (2002b). The challenges of "making learning visible": Problems and issues in recognizing tacit skills and key competences. In *Working to learn, transforming learning in the workplace* (pp. 79–94). London: Kogan Page.

Evans, K. (2009). *Learning, work and social responsibility: Challenges for lifelong learning in a global age*. Dordrecht: Springer.

Evans, K. (2010). *Rethinking work-based learning*. Paper presented at the American Educational Research Association Conference, Denver.

Evans, K., & Biasin, C. (2017). *Exploring agency, learning and identity in women's life trajectories in United Kingdom and Italy* (Exploración de la agencia, el aprendizaje y la identidad en las trayectorias de vida de las mujeres en el Reino Unido e Italia. Revista Española de Educación Comparada) (pp. 15-32). http://dx.doi.org/10.5944/reec.29.2017.17212.

Evans, K., & Kersh, N. (2016). Understanding working places as learning spaces: Perspectives, insights and some methodological challenges. In A. Ostendorf and C.H. Permpoonwiwat (Eds), *Workplace as learning spaces—conceptual and empirical insights*. Innsbruck: Innsbruck University Press.

Fenwick, T. (2008). Women's learning in contract work: Practicing contradictions in boundaryless conditions. *Vocations and Learning, 1*(1), 11–26. Retrieved from https://doi.org/10.1007/s12186-007-9003-9

Fenwick, T. (2012). Matterings of knowing and doing: Socio-material approaches to understanding practice. In P. Hager, A. Lee, & A. Reich (Eds.), *Practice, learning and change* (pp. 67–84). Dordrecht: Springer.

Fuller, A., & Unwin, L. (2004). Expansive learning environments: Integrating organizational and personal development. In H. Rainbird, A. Fuller, & A. Munro (Eds.), *Workplace learning in context*. London: Routledge. Retrieved from https://doi.org/10.4324/9780203571644

Holland, D., Lachicotte Jr. W., Skinner, D & Cain, C. (1998). *Identity and agency in cultural worlds*. London: Harvard University Press.

Hughes, J., Jewson, N., & Unwin, L. (2007). *Communities of practice* (J. Hughes, N. Jewson, & L. Unwin, Eds.). London: Routledge.

Kersh, N. (2015). Rethinking the learning space at work and beyond: The achievement of agency across the boundaries of work-related spaces and environments. *International Review of Education, 61*(6), 835–851. Retrieved from https://doi.org/10.1007/s11159-015-9529-2

Kilpatrick, S. & Bound, H. (2005). *Skilling a seasonal workforce: A way forward for rural regions*. Adelaide: NCVER

Koepp, R. (2002). *Clusters of creativity*. Chichester: John Wiley.

Lave, J., & Wenger, E. (1991). *Situated learning: Legitimate peripheral participation*. Cambridge: Cambridge University Press.

Machin, S., & Vignoles, A. (2005). *What is the good of education?* Princeton: Princeton University Press.

McMahon, W. W., & Oketch, M. (2013). Education's effects on individual life chances and on development: An overview. *British Journal of Educational Studies, 61*(1), 79–107. Retrieved from https://doi.org/10.1080/00071005.2012.756170

Nicolini, D. (2011). Practice as the site of knowing: Insights from the field of telemedicine. *Organization Science, 22*(3), 602–620. Retrieved from https://doi.org/10.1287/orsc.1100.0556

Reder, S., & Bynner, J. (2009). *Tracking literacy and numeracy skills: Findings from longitudinal research*. New York: Routledge.

Riley, R., & O'Mahony, M. (2012). *Human capital spillovers: The importance of training*. Submitted as part of deliverable 2.4 of INDICSER (244 709): "Paper on links between productivity, innovation and ICT. European Commission, Research Directorate General".

Rismark, M., & Sitter, S. (2003). Workplaces as learning environments: Interaction between newcomer and work community. *Scandinavian Journal of Educational Research, 47*(5), 495–510. Retrieved from https://doi.org/10.1080/0031383032000122426

Schatzki, T. R. (2012). A primer on practices: Theory and research. In J. Higgs, R. Barnett, S. Billett, M. Hutchings, & F. Trede (Eds.), *Practice-based education: Perspectives and strategies* (pp. 13–26). Rotterdam: Sense Publishers. Retrieved from https://doi.org/10.1007/978-94-6209-128-3

Solomon, N., Boud, D., & Rooney, D. (2006). The in-between: Exposing everyday learning at work. *International Journal of Lifelong Education, 25*(1), 3–13. Retrieved from https://doi.org/10.1080/02601370500309436

Taylor, M. (2017, July). Good work: The Taylor review of modern working practices. *Employment*. Retreived from https://doi.org/10.1080/0140511012008938

Vähäsantanen, K., & Eteläpelto, A. (2009). Vocational teachers in the face of a major educational reform: Individual ways of negotiating professional identities. *Journal of Education and Work, 22*(1), 15–33. Retrieved from https://doi.org/10.1080/13639080802709620

Wenger, E. (1998). *Communities of practice: Learning, meaning and identity*. Cambridge: Cambridge University Press. Retrieved from https://doi.org/10.1023/A

Wertsch, J. (1998). *Mind as action*. New York: Oxford University Press.

Whitley, R. (2000). *Divergent capitalisms: The social structuring and change of business systems*. Oxford: Oxford University Press. Retrieved from www.jstor.org.gate3.inist.fr/stable/pdfplus/3445605.pdf?acceptTC=true

Chapter 3

Dispositions towards learning and becoming for non-permanent workers

Dispositions can be thought of as how people perceive and react to situations and opportunities. They orientate how a person makes meaning, participates and acts in any given situation. Non-permanent workers bring with them their own dispositions that are rooted in their lives outside work as well as within it. Dispositions towards learning evolve and inter-relate with social processes, pressures and structures (Bourdieu & Wacquant, 1992), including the contexts found within and between non-permanent work, as discussed in the next chapter. They are informed by a blend of the mind, body, individual, society, agency and structure, reminding us of the complexities as people co-construct their learning (Hodkinson et al., 2004). The discussion earlier discussion of knowledge recontextualisation in Chapter 1 acknowledges the relationship between these differing environments and an adult's disposition to learn in new work spaces. While this chapter focuses on individual dispositions, it does not argue that dispositions or the individual are the same as agency and the only dimension to consider when trying to understand how non-permanent workers learn and develop. The entwinement of worker/learner and workplace is complex, warning against oversimplifying the former as agency and the latter as structure when thinking about supporting the learning of workers (Hodkinson et al., 2004). As Hodkinson et al. (2004) argue, the interplay between individual and work means that work-related learning experiences cannot be thought of as uniformly guaranteed and should rather be encouraged in a way that recognises the variance without overemphasising the sole responsibility of the individual nor that of the workplace. Billett (2001) reminds us that different workplaces will offer different learning opportunities, which will differ for different workers depending on how work is organised, on positions and on job descriptions. This variance is related to the co-construction of work and learning cultures entwined with individual's dispositions. The individualised nature of much non-permanent work makes thinking of learning opportunities in a way that is inclusive of both individual dispositions and sites of and between work particularly challenging.

Dispositions towards learning can vary extensively. Adjectives such as cynical, enthusiastic, committed, focused, individualistic, communal, sympathetic, proactive, resistant, reserved and distrustful can be found in stories that describe the learning dispositions of people in work (Hodkinson et al., 2004). Dispositions to take action and be reflexive in action through mediating the creation and recognition of work-related learning affordances become a key feature of learning for non-permanent workers (Cavanagh, 2010; Billett, 2006). The development of reflexivity is particularly important for the notion of navigating the 'liquid life' prevalent in non-permanent work, where work patterns have become borderless, unpredictable and flexible (Bauman, 2005). As Elzen et al. (2017) point out in their discussion of reflexivity, its development is not the same as trying to teach people to reflect on reflection and may not be equal for all individuals, as it is likely to develop in unexpected ways and be dependent on many conditions that enable one to interact and affect contexts to change assumptions, practices and institutional arrangements and, by extension, to become 'reflexivity winners' to help navigate the 'figured worlds' of non-permanent work (Kelly, 2013, p. 67). Evans, Kersh & Kontiainen (2004) found that dispositions of autonomy and openness to learning made a difference in whether people took on-the-job learning opportunities and pursued personal learning outside the workplace. Participants' dispositions towards learning influenced whether they sought out learning opportunities to address areas personally identified as needing to be strengthened or avoided learning experiences that may expose areas of vulnerability or inadequacy. Much of this meaning-making, participation and action was coloured, not only by the individual's personal biography, but also their 'fit' and the culture of their workplace. Workers react and contribute to work structures and learning opportunities and become a part of the workplace culture, which feeds back into their dispositions towards learning.

Different senses of self and purpose as workers and as people with particular interests and commitments influence the variety of ways that people position themselves in relation to making meaning, participating and acting in employment, as well as learning and development (Allen, 2016). People in non-permanent work often emphasise the importance of personal interests and/or commitments to family in relation to their employment, making the role of disposition towards learning (as influenced by these features) particularly influential for their level of engagement in professional development. As access to learning affordances can become a highly individualised process (Cavanagh, 2010), particularly for non-permanent workers, the varying ways in which individuals make meaning of, participate and act in relation to such affordances have ramifications for their occupational trajectories (Bloomer & Hodkinson, 2000, p. 589). Dispositions towards learning and becoming mediate how individuals use and build on their existing knowledge and 'put knowledge to work' to navigate non-permanent work in different ways, how they feel about security and how they perceive events and interactions as opportunities or threats (Chapter One). As one's disposition towards learning is influenced by biography, personal history, prior and current work experiences, out-of-work activities and the wider social and political environment (Billett, 2006), which can change overtime, so too can dispositions towards learning and development.

Through discussing dispositions towards learning and becoming, we explore aspects of individual's meaning-making, participation and action (Bloomer & Hodkinson, 2000, p. 589) as they engage in various forms of non-permanent work. Our data illuminates the ways in which individuals' dispositions towards learning and becoming a non-permanent worker, consisting of associated meanings and justifications, various forms of engagement and participation and through decisions and actions, mediate individuals' trajectories and feelings of non-permanent work as 'good work'. Our data supports the notion that individuals' dispositions are not fixed like the notion of attributes, but are co-created along with wider personal, social and economic contexts, which change over time. It is important to emphasise fluidity and movement in dispositions, as it is rare for circumstances around family, finances, colleagues, hiring practices, work roles and other structural or societal facets to remain fixed. This means individuals may enter non-permanent work for particular reasons, but their disposition towards learning and development may not continually align with these initial motivators, which may change, reflecting the entwinement of an individual's circumstances and the context of their work and their further development (or not). Likewise, they may experience trajectories of struggle, stagnation and growth at different points in time relating to their learning and becoming. Although our study was not designed to be longitudinal, the stories of our participants' lives, as they engaged in non-permanent work, often expressed a temporal element as experience was gained and meanings, participation and actions related to their occupational learning and becoming were made and re-made.

To explore our participants' dispositions, two intersecting spectra are used along which varying stories can be discussed, as shown in Figure 3.1. The spectrum along the x-axis refers to a 'purposeful' disposition on one end and, on the other, an 'opportunistic' disposition to learning and becoming, whereby 'purposeful' refers to specific intent, and 'opportunistic' indicates a disposition of 'happen-stance'. The y-axis refers to the concepts of 'broad focus' and 'contained focus', with the individual's disposition towards their learning being open to opportunities related to their occupation and navigating non-permanent work more broadly, as compared to focusing on a particular job in a more contained manner. Our participants' stories illustrate the thick entwinement of varying personal circumstances and work contexts for their dispositions towards learning in non-permanent work.

A 'purposeful' disposition towards learning refers to a specific intent to pursue learning to strengthen capabilities for navigating and meaningfully participating in non-permanent work specifically. This openness and interest in learning for non-permanent work are often related to the nature of the industry, where moving based on project work is a norm and/or presents the greatest career prospects. Alternatively, this can be related to non-work

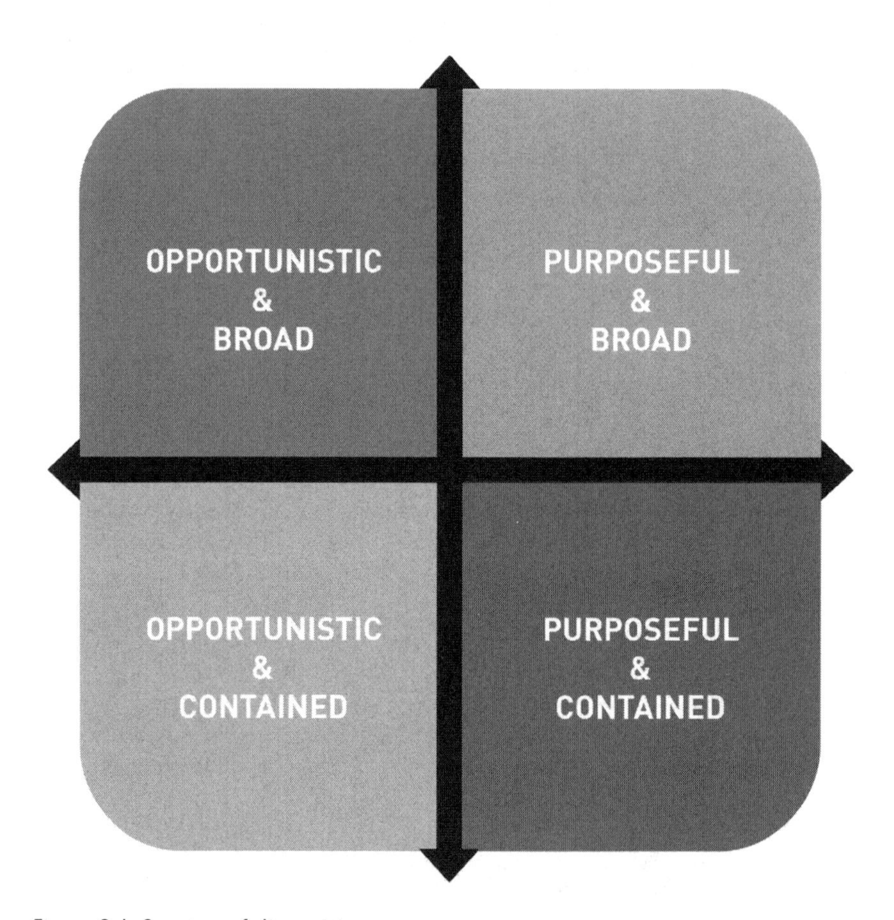

Figure 3.1 Spectra of dispositions

circumstances that make a non-permanent work arrangement more appealing, as committing to a permanent and full-time job may not be possible due to caring responsibilities (for example, children or ageing parents), or as a choice related to remaining engaged in work during retirement. The key feature of *intent* at this end of the spectrum appears to have significant implications for individuals' learning and becoming by orientating meaning-making, participation and action.

An 'opportunistic' disposition includes features of a willingness to try, often relating to entering non-permanent work due to a limited range of alternative forms of employment other than non-permanent work. Opportunists have not specifically sought out non-permanent work, but rather have found work that happened to be packaged in a non-permanent work arrangement. People with characteristics of an 'opportunistic' disposition may feel as though they have found themselves, or landed up, in non-permanent work arrangements as more permanent work arrangements had not worked out or had been unattainable due to issues of fit, work culture and/or personal circumstances. This has implications for individuals' meaning-making, participation and actions in relation to their learning, being and becoming as a non-permanent worker. A sense of 'floating' or 'drifting' appears to be stronger than that of having specific career goals or intentions that may provide focus for learning and development. For some people, this equates to a lower sense of personal identification with their work or its associated 'craft', which may or may not grow over time, mediated by experiences and changes in learning disposition that encourage movement towards or away from developing a more purposeful intent.

Along the spectrum of non-permanent workers with opportunistic to purposeful dispositions, we can also observe movement between those who focus on navigating non-permanent work more broadly as compared to those who focus on a single assignment or client. Peoples' focus may differ for a number of reasons, having implications for their disposition towards learning. Those with a broad focus tend to emphasise the economic viability of their work arrangement and are often interested in acting in an entrepreneurial manner to both maximise their financial gain as well as their professional engagement in their craft. Optimising non-permanent work, in this sense, requires building up a client base, continuously networking, growing a good reputation, providing products or services that meet client needs and being competitive. Here, dispositions towards learning may be orientating meaning-making, participation and action related to opportunities that enhance the ability to navigate the 'liquid life' of non-permanent work. In work that depends on project cycles and short-term engagements, this space can be very individualistic, with the sole worker being the consistent thread throughout their work engagements, but it also heavily relies on communal learning through networking to build up portfolios and work opportunities. Those with a more contained focus may be less interested in running themselves like a business, but be more interested in engaging in a specific type of work isolated from both extra organisational or entrepreneurial roles. This may be because of a strong passion for only the craft with a limited view of entrepreneurialism, a lack of interest in pursuing this type of work long term or due to time limitations. Some people with this focus start to appear as pseudo permanent workers, as they rely on a single client. Their dispositions towards learning may become more siloed, with an openness or distrust towards co-creating learning opportunities for their craft, but learning for navigating the movement between projects slipping off the radar. The interrelations between workers' dispositions and the expansiveness of their worksites may see learning for work and navigating work become perceived as valuable and important, or pointless, with little recognition. We put forward that the four resulting quadrants provide useful spaces for exploring the varying meanings, participation and actions of our participants' dispositions towards learning and being and becoming non-permanent workers.

Purposeful and broad

Our purposeful and broad space includes people who have not necessarily 'mastered' non-permanent work, but who pursue it with intent and a degree of an understanding of what such a work arrangement in their field may consist of. The purposeful and broad disposition was found amongst interviewees from the creative and CET sectors rather than those undertaking peripheral work. The different occupational settings of people in the creative sector and adult educators in the CET sector also inform variance in what constituted their purposeful narratives. For the creatives, the passion for their craft was an acute driving force behind the decision to pursue non-permanent work. The nature of the industry, based on project cycles, a degree of geographical mobility and access to challenging work as the best avenue to participate in good work with opportunities to learn signalled to many of the creative workers we interviewed that non-permanent work was the better avenue for deepening their craft. As most of the purposeful narratives came from people with five or more years in the line of work, a common feature of the creative narratives was that entrepreneurialism was acknowledged and developed later in order to attain work that could help deepen the craft. This signals a shift over time from a slightly more contained 'craft' focus towards a broadening of the entrepreneurial focus necessary for further developing their craft. Adult educators with purposeful and broad dispositions often entered non-permanent work through planning a gradual exit from permanent work. They talk about strategically building their networks and client base to bolster their craft identification before considering that freelancing would be a viable option. Timing is a key element for this group compared to the creatives, as adult educators depend on their prior work experience to form the basis of their reputation for providing and developing their products and services. The emphasis from both creatives and adult educators is intent and a strong feeling of purpose behind a choice to start non-permanent work, alongside a calculated decision that they will be able to make it economically viable.

This sets us up with an optimistic picture aligned to the 'contingent' worker image who is able to seamlessly navigate, through agile and precise movements, the bountiful terrain of non-permanent work. Although none of our narratives were quite as strong as that, of our 33 purposeful narratives, 24 expressed that they were growing to some degree through their work. Both occupational groups talked about the importance of building and maintaining strong functional networks, moving across projects and clients for growth (locally and internationally), shapeshifting to appear to align to client expectations, strategically positioning themselves in the market, recontextualising knowledge, being reflexive and building credibility through specialisation as integral features of their growth. These facets of their learning and development had been informed through drawing on past experiences, being attuned to what was working or not working for themselves and others and trying their best to surround themselves with, or interpret their surroundings as, learning opportunities. This type of disposition seemed to position them well to make constructive meanings of their work involvement through strategic participation and actions by being open to creating, seeking and using learning opportunities. Karthik, an adult educator in leadership, expresses this in terms of aligning work choices to help you learn and reach your 'highest goal'.

> creativity comes only when you go beyond your passion because passion is not sustainable. You need to be grounded in your deepest goal, the highest goal and most of the time we compromise ourselves with lower goals. . . . My real work is based on my highest goal and what I do and what I contribute . . . [everything else] are means to get me there.
>
> (Karthik, adult educator, CET sector)

Karthik expressed a highly reflexive practice that enabled him to feel he gained something for his practice through daily interactions, decisions and actions related to his work. Although not everything he did was directly related to his highest goal, he approached his work very intentionally and tried to increasingly tailor the jobs he applied for and accepted to ensure his experience and networks were aligning with his highest goal, rather than diverging his energy elsewhere. His purposeful and broad disposition towards learning and becoming a non-permanent adult educator enabled him to feel a sense of growth from his participation in certain practices for getting and maintaining work, such as making connections with like-minded people. His actions related to getting and engaging in the work, including his effort to be well informed about potential clients and maintaining relevance with latest practices and his ability to make meaning from his participation and actions in relation to them aligning to his higher professional goals.

Norashid and Shar are similar to Karthik in so far as having an interest in their craft and an understanding that entrepreneurial facets can bolster this. Notions of an explicit higher goal and plan are not strongly articulated. Rather, their voices can help illustrate how their varying dispositions towards learning and becoming non-permanent lighting or sound technicians appear to mediate their growth or stagnation, despite being both purposeful and broad to some extent. Norashid appears to participate in his work and with his colleagues more openly to actively learn, make his work meaningful and have a sense of growth through the concept of a 'journey' and 'taking a bit from there and from here'. Shar, on the other hand, appears to belittle the meaning of his work, and, although he feels he is knowledgeable, he also feels his learning has stopped with little room for growth.

> I think in this industry [you need to be] hard working and not shy to ask and be funny, make everyone laugh . . . Whoever is near to me I will just ask I don't care whether full-time or casual I will just ask . . . like for us we

> just see what they (more experienced people) are doing and take a bit from there and from here and that is where you get your own style . . . you got to try and try and try, you try and do this and then we learn new stuff. For me, the journey is fun.
>
> (Norashid, lighting technician, technical theatre)

> I just mix on sound . . . As stuff got bigger, you just learn a bit more, like how that particular equipment works, that's all. But the same . . . if I'm working with smaller equipment . . . I tend to get laid-back. I think now I'm still waiting for bigger and bigger shows. Yes, I think more concert scale. . . . I think mainly my personality that it cannot be too mundane. . . . The company I work for basically I'm the only sound man who knows most of the things. . . . If I don't know, no one knows. So what I do, sometimes I don't know whether it's right or wrong, and then I wait until someone does. If you want to learn the basics, YouTube is the easiest to learn basics. But then when you get advanced, it kind of like stops.
>
> (Shar, sound technician, technical theatre)

This comparison allows us to see the spectrum of a purposeful and broad disposition, placing Norashid further out and Shar closer to the centre of the x- and y-axes. The more purposeful and broad the disposition, the greater the openness to learning for craft and learning for navigating non-permanent work. Norashid appears to have an implicit interest in creating, seeing and making use of opportunities to develop his craft. His articulation of operating in the non-permanent space is not as explicit as Karthik's, but, by working hard, he is also conscious of building his reputation and networks for further work, both of which help him grow. Shar, on the other hand, seems more passive in his approach to furthering his trajectory. Like Norashid, he also talks about learning through equipment manuals; he clearly feels confident in having a degree of expertise and moves across different projects with different requirements, although largely under the umbrella of one company. He does not talk about reaching out to other people, but justifies his competitive edge by being the 'only sound man' and choosing to 'wait' for bigger assignments to come to him. With this, Shar expresses a sense of stagnation, as it does not appear to be easy to see, create or make use of affordances to grow, but rather, his participation and actions have become passive, justified by being the one 'who knows most things'.

Purposeful and contained

Having a more contained as well as purposeful disposition saw an intentional interest in a craft co-exist with a lower ability or interest in operating this craft in an entrepreneurial fashion. Here, individuals did not run themselves as a business and were less likely to entertain or pursue multiple clients. Rather, they made meaning of their work by focusing on doing a job that happened to be non-permanent well, while choosing not to participate in activities such as networking, building a broader client base and personal branding, either due to a lack of time and interest or a lack of knowing how to operate in such spaces. Those who could justify their contained participation, as it aligned well with non-work commitments, were often able to maintain a satisfactory sense of personal growth compared to the alternative of being out of the workforce. These circumstances were less common in the creative industries and more apparent in adult education and amidst our kitchen assistants who were taking care of young children or elderly parents or who were semi-retired. Here, the extra entrepreneurial roles earlier mentioned were replaced by a focus on learning to manage time, plan and schedule to juggle work and non-work duties, rather than managing multiple clients and trying to grow themselves as a business. This was largely operationalised through taking on a single client or project at a time and building a relationship that included an element of understanding the time limitations posed by the individual's non-work responsibilities or interests. The need for flexibility, and, particularly for those with domestic caring duties, the pressure to perform dual roles also required the individual to negotiate demands and contradictions between these two spheres of their lives. In this sense, this group of non-permanent workers needed to learn how to manage their dual roles or interests in order for them to co-exist. This was not always straightforward, as core notions, like flexibility, proved themselves to be rather different than initially presented, thus resulting in a more contained focus to aspects they were open to learning about.

> Free-lancing training you can't [cancel]. The minute you're training, you have to be there probably eight . . . you don't disappear at five. . . . By the time you are done . . . you get home seven plus. So if the child is sick, you cannot say sorry I call in sick. Because that is not responsible. . . . The stakes are high. You get learners who are very upset. And you lose your pay. Freelancer, they go by the hour, they go by the day, so it matters a lot. And there is no way to make up. You lose a client means you lose it. You lose a run means you lose it.
>
> (Tabitha, adult educator, CET sector)

Tabitha's sentiment also illustrates that low responsibility is not necessarily a feature of non-permanent work, where you have clients who are depending on your performance. While a purposeful element here can help an individual justify the nature of their engagement as satisfactory, the contained element can reign their disposition towards learning in such that for many in this quadrant, a sense of stagnation or skills atrophy was prevalent. This was commonly due to an underestimation of the challenges in attaining more desirable projects. A number of our participants felt they were able to attain work to provide a base-level income; however, such assignments soon became repetitive in terms of the skills and knowledge put to use. Often, these work arrangements depended on a single relationship with a client who was able to offer short-term, repeat contracts either for particular productions (film, television or theatre) or particular courses. The time dedicated to these jobs and the fear of losing what could become a relatively stable form of income contributed to a more closed disposition towards learning within non-expansive work arrangements, which trapped individual growth. This pattern of 'pseudo permanent' work offered the perfect environment for stagnation, with implicitly regular work seducing individuals away from intentionally learning to diversify or challenge their work experiences, build broader more strategic networks and find stretch opportunities to grow and deepen their craft as initially intended. The regularity and dominance of a single client can create a particularly vulnerable situation should that client no longer wish to engage a particular individual. This can happen if the hiring person is replaced, if the economy shifts, if the client goes bust or changes their programming or if someone more popular enters the scene. After a period working with a single provider, Lata found many of her freelancing colleagues were no longer getting jobs and that her feeling of security was not very sensible in her line of work. This realisation precluded shifting to work with a different provider, where she soon found she was 'settling' yet again.

> (I had this mind set), I am very well established here, so by hook or by crook, I will be staying here – to the extent that you think that it is a permanent job to you there even though it is freelance training . . . then realised I shouldn't put my eggs in one basket . . . But just to say, I am facing the same thing now at this point . . . but very difficult to balance it because sometimes, how to put it, it is not that I don't want them (other clients) but . . . it goes against my principles because I have already given my dates . . . and to tell them now (that I want to take other work would be) very difficult so.
>
> (Lata, adult educator, CET sector)

It is not easy for many people to know how to and be able to avoid 'putting all your eggs in one basket', even if they desire to do otherwise. Not only are these non-permanent work arrangements a complete contrast to more practised permanent employment relationships, but they are also riddled with the complexities of providing a quality service for a client while managing an internal and projecting an external image to secure, but also expand, one's reputation with current and potential clients. In non-permanent work arrangements, such as training in a classroom, isolation from other potential clients is a feature of the work, making it particularly challenging to organically engage with new jobs. This can create a discouraging site for learning how to better navigate non-permanent work and also provides little support for learning related to performing the work at hand. For the creative sector, where teams are more common and fluid, such isolation is less acute, but interactions with potential new clients on the job may still be hard to come by. Some individuals adjust their sentiments to feel content with more regular but less challenging jobs, while for others, this can become a source of great dissatisfaction.

Ashley, whose story was introduced in Chapter 2 was a theatre lighting technician/designer working at a single venue and some work at a school drama centre. His story helps illustrate the struggle that can result from a more contained disposition despite being initially purposeful. Shortly after his foray into non-permanent work, he found he was unable to make it financially viable, let alone provide a space for growing his craft.

> I definitely feel I didn't know the difficulty of the job itself, of being a freelancer . . . when I first started out in the theatre, it definitely was passion but slowly the passion became money and money became a job . . . calls were getting fewer . . . I didn't try (getting jobs at other venues) . . . . you feel that hey, the money is not coming in as much as before any more. So I need to look somewhere else already.
>
> (Ashley, lighting technician/designer, technical theatre)

Ashley began to struggle with his pursuit of working as a lighting technician/designer despite having a long-standing passion for the role developed through high school productions. Of particular note was his difficulty to network and fit in with his peers, which also made it increasingly difficult to find work.

> I feel that people are quite selfish. If they kind of share a bit, they might feel threatened that more people are sharing the same piece of pie . . . After work, I tend to just go back home. I don't really have a friend. I know some of them hang out and drink but I don't drink so it's a bit difficult and a lot of them smoke. So I don't smoke so it's a bit, it feels weird when I tag along with them to smoke because they all go on smoke breaks.
>
> (Ashley, lighting technician/designer, technical theatre)

Ashley recognised that he was unable to comfortably participate in such spaces, which translated into a meaning-making process of feeling like an outcast, curbing his openness to learn for this type of work arrangement and resulting in an action to farewell his pursuit as a freelance lighting technician/designer. He found work in a different field, pursuing theatre on the weekends for fun. It is not surprising that we found few narratives of purposeful entrants who struggled, as the early attrition rate is likely to minimise this pool of people who are able to find alternate forms of employment, and as their initial interest was a purposeful choice rather than a lack of one.

Ashley's story, along with those of stagnation, illustrate that 'passion' and intentional pursuit of a craft are not sufficient for the learning and development of non-permanent workers towards growth. Some people in this quadrant are able to maintain that their work is meaningful due to non-work responsibilities curtailing more extensive participation. Their disposition towards learning may be contained in such a way that enables growth for particular work assignments, or stagnation that can be personally justified. Yet for others, a sense of unease, resentment or frustration can settle in as their purposefulness becomes stunted by the contained aspect of their learning disposition towards the entrepreneurial facets of non-permanent work. This frustrating space illustrates the complex inter-relations of learning dispositions with learning affordances in non-permanent work contexts.

Opportunistic and contained

While our participants with purposeful learning dispositions felt a sense of intent in their orientation towards learning for navigating non-permanent work or for pursuing a craft, our opportunistic dispositions feature a sense of drifting, 'falling' or bouncing in relation to opportunities that appear to present themselves in non-permanent work. Those with a contained disposition towards their learning and work arrangement appeared to be stagnating or struggling to make non-permanent work 'good work'. This group of people told stories of having difficulty navigating and maintaining a position in the permanent workforce, with family or friends often introducing them to non-permanent work. This space is largely dominated by those in peripheral occupations whose situations were often complicated by wanting low responsibilities, having low educational qualifications and needing to figure out how to work without jeopardising government subsidies. Work equated to income more strongly than notions of learning and development towards becoming better at a craft or better at navigating non-permanent work. Decisions about which work to pursue were based on earning enough to meet daily requirements and trying not to jeopardise this, with less interest in pursuing work that would require learning significantly new skills. Jefri has managed this by mainly working for one boss who meets his daily needs and also allows for flexibility.

> One of them is the daily payment; $100 is enough for me. If I worked with the company, I have to have the capital. I have the freedom working as freelance. People cannot control us. If I am happy, I will work for him. If I get bigger offer, I will choose that place. The work is the same; the only different is the salary is higher. For example, other person wants to pay me $130 per day; you just follow me, take care of the workers. I have to consider that. It is because I have been following my current boss quite some time, so I feel hesitate to jump over another ship. I did receive such offers and company once.
>
> (Jefri, furniture mover, removalist sector)

Jefri's participation in non-permanent work suits his needs, and his action of staying with one boss helps offer familiarity and stability. At the same time, however, he can see a larger, broader picture at play, involving competition and other bosses that may pay more, but decides that jumping over imposes more risks than he is willing to take. Learning for occupational growth is not a feature of his meaning-making, participation or actions; rather, this is overshadowed by daily practicalities.

Although opportunistic contained dispositions appear to limit an openness to learning to be and become a non-permanent worker for growth, some people in this group hope their non-permanent work is a stop gap and have an eye towards finding permanent work with greater stability and reward.

> I try to go but some companies need two years of experience of car knowledge but I only graduate my automotive . . . they said you need to go for higher NITEC but your one is normal NITEC . . . I said never mind, not my luck. Then I just go for the movers. Got try [permanent work] before, but I feel like very lazy. . . . I want to take course, for tower crane course. That is my dream. Until now, I never get the course.
>
> (Luqman, dispatch driver)

> He actually tried to apply through CDC [Community Development Council] for the crane operator course but they say they already submit but there is no reply from them to say that he is selected for the course and things like that. . . . Because we no longer under them, we don't know how to go about it. To actually just enrol on our own, can but it costs a lot. It is $3000 for the course itself.
>
> (Luqman's spouse)

Luqman's story indicates that obstacles for upward mobility, such as low qualifications and difficulties in obtaining higher qualifications due to cost, support or motivation, often stand in the way. Such dejection has implications for how Luqman makes meaning of his non-permanent work as a dispatch driver, seeing his participation as necessary but not where he wants to be and his actions to change thwarted by obstacles he cannot see around.

Further complicating a number of the stories found in the opportunistic, contained quadrant is a distrust of authorities and a concern that a higher, more stable income will mean higher living costs, thus disincentivising actions to seek and create opportunities to develop craft or entrepreneurial identification for growth. De Wei (age 58), for example, had been working in daily-rated positions in the shipping industry for most of his working life. He was first an electrician and then did plumbing and fitting because 'the pay was higher'. He honed his skills by learning from others and also has a series of licenses. He claims that the entry of foreign workers into the shipping industry in the 1990s affected the job opportunities for Singaporeans in terms of availability of jobs, pay and job scope. He left the industry and has since been working in a range of casual positions, such as F&B helper, flyer distributor and removalist. He is unhappy, as the 'pay is low and the bosses' demands are high'. He claims that he can get a permanent job for $2 000, but it might lead to him losing his rental flat, which is more valuable to him. He also prefers to be paid daily, because it is easier to manage his finances that way. For these reasons, casual jobs continue to appeal to him. He states:

> You make more you have to pay more. . . . That's why, because of the rental make me no confidence to work in permanent job . . . I doesn't want CPF (Central Provident Fund Contributions). Because once I take my CPF, this job the pay is high. My rent will bounce up, but it won't come down again. So this is what the difficulty I have, you understand or not?
>
> (De Wei, works across sectors and roles)

This group of non-permanent workers illustrate that socio-economic circumstances can play a large role in an individual's disposition towards learning and developing in non-permanent work.

Opportunistic and broad

Opportunistic and broad dispositions seem to offer a space for more varied experiences than those in the opportunistic and contained space. There are stories that resonate with those shared in the earlier section but differ in that the work engaged in expands across many different types of jobs. There are also stories of people who have found themselves in non-permanent work, recognise the skills needed to navigate the terrain but are facing a very steep, and sometime dejecting, learning curve. And there are also Cinderella stories of people finding meaningful work and opportunities to grow through being open to participating in, and learning from, non-permanent work.

Barry's story is similar to that of Jefri's, from the opportunistic contained quadrant, in that he prioritises his daily needs. He differs, however, in that he talks of being happy to take on any work, rather than working with a single boss, and his participation is dependent on his mood. Non-permanent work is seen as flexible and comes with low responsibility and daily pay.

> Then after, the shipping industry is worse already, that means drop already, because all the foreigners come. So after it drop already, I run out. I just go around all sorts of casual . . . sometimes I mood good, I one week work four days, if I mood no good, three days. Okay like what I say four days my pocket money all spend finish, four days.
>
> (Barry, works across sectors and roles)

The nature of the jobs that Barry takes on intentionally requires little need to learn new skills, but rather need another body to do one job or another. He has learnt how to attain these jobs, in terms of where he needs to be or who to call when the bosses are looking for people for that day, but low competition and low desire to maximise his income beyond daily needs put little pressure on building further entrepreneurial capability or craft identification.

This contrasts with other opportunistic and broad stories that also expand non-permanent work participation beyond a single employer or type of job within an industry, but do so as an interim financial measure while looking for permanent employment. These stories suggest that, although there may be intent towards having a more coherent occupation, such 'interim' expansion can further complicate identification with an occupation and having a direction for one's learning. This was apparent in Benny's story, where he talked about hopping between different types of work as a temporary, but satisfactory, solution until he could find a full-time job again.

> I find that this freelance income is quite good to subsidise me for the moment when I'm still like trying to get a full-time job back . . . because from the beginning from visual merchandise I moved on to marketing role . . . I moved on because their business model they changed their business model . . . I also very keen to learn first aid . . . so I'm also a freelancer in that training part. . . . I don't know I'm kind of lost actually. So it depends on who I am speaking to, let's say I am in the training centre I say I'm a trainer in various training centres. So if I am in theatre.
>
> (Benny, theatre technician, technical theatre)

The patchwork nature of the jobs he is taking illustrates a broadness but does not offer obvious direction to help Benny feel less lost or able to stitch together his experiences into something more coherent to identify with. His work engagements do not easily build upon one another or translate easily into building credibility for his next job should it involve another jump. In this way, it is difficult for him to knit his identity or connect the people he engages with in his work into a useful network towards a more focused occupational identification or his desire to find more permanent employment. Tisha's story shares some similarities in that she sees her work as a stop gap while looking for another job, even though it has already been four years. She does not jump between hugely different types of work, but moves around hotels and roles related to banquets and events rather than focusing on a single hotel, which she suggests could offer something more stable but with long hours she would prefer to avoid.

> I've been in this line, banquet, for three to four years because I am mostly part looking for a job. . . . My previous experience was all in admin. . . . My boss asked me to just stop working because I'm pregnant . . . then I planned to continue working and I got hard time looking for job because of my

> qualifications . . . if possible I want admin because I can spend time with my kids after. . . . Because for banquet it's. . . . long hours and I keep on jumping hotels. Unless if I focus on one hotel maybe they will groom me . . . because not every day they have events right, so I just jump around . . . at least every day I have money with me.
>
> (Tisha, kitchen assistant, food and beverage)

Tisha's and Benny's stories illustrate how an opportunistic disposition, when associated with being an interim solution, does not equate to embracing learning for non-permanent work arrangements, or necessarily towards building experience that could make permanent employment more attainable. Openness to learning may be broad but undirected and unlikely to lead to deeper learning and identification along with a feeling of either being lost or uncommitted to jobs that are not seen as containing 'good work'.

Another common story amidst opportunistic and broad individuals involved those who were not hopping around disconnected types of work, but had recently found themselves attempting to build themselves up in a non-permanent work arrangement, as permanent employment had not turned out well. Here a feeling of being lost and overwhelmed about how to actually make freelancing sustainable was strong.

> Because you are not aware . . . and I think to be an entrepreneur is really not very easy. I notice that among the trainers who are successful, they are already in what they want to do. . . . So I'm starting . . . So I developed that [package] on my own, basically. . . . it was only this year that I decided that I needed to do something concrete in terms of my job and . . . because I looked for a job and I couldn't find. So I thought that . . . Friends may recommend, but when you talk to them you have to convince the managers.
>
> (Keegan, adult educator, CET sector)

An opportunistic broad disposition towards learning and development was particularly complicated for our participants who felt they could not see any achievable pathways into 'good work'. What they had initially thought was a possible solution to the problems they had faced in permanent employment became a new source of stress, heightened by earlier meaning-making processes that had disregarded their other employment options. While people with purposeful dispositions had normally planned their foray into non-permanent work, those with opportunistic dispositions were far less prepared for navigating the facets of this work such as finding clients, developing their own products and services or convincing potential clients of their credibility. They were also poorly equipped in terms of resources and networks for figuring out how to improve their chances, although they could see it was necessary and had an interest in becoming more entrepreneurial. Keegan's experience of an unexpectedly difficult learning curve related to the entrepreneurial nature of his work, coupled with his struggle to find permanent work, nevertheless contains a sense of trying to figure out how to build 'something concrete' in the adult education field. He is just unsure how to go about it, as it appears those who have succeeded just have it.

Although being opportunistic and broad do not guarantee growth, they do seem to better enable individuals who were open-minded towards unexpected experiences. By being open to new experiences, some participants found positive learning environments for re-making their meanings of their work. Non-permanent work offered gateways for some people to see what different types of work looked like, potentially leading to participation and the creation of further opportunities to try. Zac, introduced in Chapter 2, tells us:

> I joined this industry is basically when one of my friends . . . they said that do you want to work and I said okay what type of work are you doing? . . . when moving stuff and the term is called loaders . . . I was impressed with the other boys that are doing the work like they can run cable, they can make the lights move, they can make sound coming out from speakers . . . Basically I was just jealous. . . . So for me, it is getting the knowledge because tertiary wise I do not have anything. I want to learn new things, I want to explore what I can do, what is my capabilities by just learning the ropes of this entertainment so five years of doing lighting, another five years of doing sound and it is like really learn the in-depth things about sound and about lights. It is not just carrying lights, put there, run the cable, no, it is like learning the stuff, what is going on inside the light. So that is the passion I have for what I am doing now. So five years of sound, five years of lighting, then I get hooked on doing rigging till today.
>
> (Zac, rigger, technical theatre)

Here, Zac shares with us how his opportunistic and broad disposition towards learning to be a non-permanent worker in the creative sectors played an important role in expanding his opportunities, knowledge and identification. Although he started simply to have a job, he found an opportunity to make meaning of the job and use it to develop further pursuits. This also happened over a sustained period of time in which he saw depth and found interest in the work that he was initially involved in as a team member but in different roles. One key difference between his work and that of Keegan is that he joined a team that inspired him and helped him learn, while as an adult educator, Keegan operates solo with little easy access to more experienced peers who want him to do his job well. In this way, opportunistic and broad dispositions seemed to enable some individuals to grow through their work, but also highlight the importance of context, including peers, economic situations and occupational goals, for mediating changes in dispositions towards learning and becoming a non-permanent worker.

Conclusion

Dispositions towards learning and becoming a non-permanent worker orientate the various ways that individuals make meaning, participate and act in relation to learning affordances. Dispositions are entwined with personal biographies, out-of-work circumstances and activities, work culture and the co-creation of work related learning affordances. They do not exist in isolation; they can change over time or even be different in different contexts. Our data puts forward two spectra, purposeful to opportunistic and broad to contained, that we hope help illustrate the variance of dispositions towards learning, which mediates individual's trajectories of growth, stagnation and struggle.

A purposeful and broad disposition appears to set people up well for growth in non-permanent work. This is the space where awareness, preparation, economic and craft goals, occupational identification and intent seem to align to support learning and becoming in non-permanent work. We also see that there is variance in this group, as some people become more passive in their participation and actions to navigate non-permanent work for growth and thus experience stagnation. People may feel they have hit a glass ceiling, or that they should no longer need to hunt for better jobs.

A purposeful and contained disposition can also encourage sentiments of growth in non-permanent work, yet these sentiments appear to be more limited to specific jobs rather than growing the more entrepreneurial abilities associated with higher economic return and ironically greater stability in a non-permanent work arrangement. Here we find people with non-work responsibilities, such as caring for children, that limit the time to engage in paid work but do not necessarily limit an individual's intent to meaningfully participate in non-permanent work despite little interest in entrepreneurial expansion. We also find people who recognise the need to diversify their client base, but become pseudo permanent employees with a single client due to difficulties in developing more entrepreneurial skills, particularly functional networks, often resulting in feelings of stagnation or financial struggle.

For those on the opportunistic end of the spectrum, the intention to enter non-permanent work was not driven by intrinsic pursuits but rather feelings of necessity or as a 'best option for now'. When coupled with a contained disposition, we see stories that prioritise daily needs over occupational growth, obstacles for upward mobility related to educational qualifications and also an element of, or desire for, predictability in terms of maintaining a relationship with a single employer and participating in jobs that have a small learning curve.

Opportunistic and broad dispositions also share some stories of similar priorities such as daily financial needs over occupational growth, but they are operationalised through taking on any job rather than working with a single boss. Here we also find stories that associate participation in non-permanent work as an interim measure while looking for permanent employment, although this situation can continue more long term than initially intended. This type of meaning-making seems to minimise connections between jobs to build on each other for learning and development and encourages feelings of being lost. For those who enter non-permanent work as a solution to problems with permanent employment, we find underdeveloped entrepreneurial and craft identification make it very difficult to learn how to gain 'good work'. With financial pressure, this can lead to participating in work that does not help build a coherent occupational identification, but rather a sense of feeling unable to do so. There were a number of stories, however, of opportunistic broad dispositions becoming more purposeful over time as participation in different jobs, but within a single industry, offered exposure to learning opportunities previously unknown. Participating with intent to learn from these opportunities, developing an interest and intentionally engaging helped create a sense of meaningful work and growth over time. The meaning of engaging in non-permanent work shifted from 'I just need a job' to 'I want to be good at this occupation'.

There is no recipe for learning and becoming a non-permanent worker with a particular trajectory in mind. A feeling of growth, stagnation or struggle can be highly subjective, and moving between these trajectories is often a part of an individual's meaning-making related to their participation and actions in non-permanent work arrangements. Dispositions towards learning and development being more purposeful or opportunistic, and broader or more contained can mediate the co-creation of learning affordances to be expansive or restrictive. Such co-creation is set amidst wider contexts of both out of work and in work circumstances. We hope that by discussing movement and variance between people with purposeful to more opportunistic and broad to contained dispositions, we can help illuminate the stories of people as they embrace and reject, strive and disengage and negotiate and navigate their learning and becoming in non-permanent work.

Dispositions do not exist in isolation, and their fluidity points to the importance of the other facets when considering the learning and development of non-permanent workers. The relationships between the contexts of non-permanent work and an individual's dispositions provide many of the reference points from which experiences of learning and development are made and re-made, and are thus a timely component to discuss in the next chapter.

References

Allen, D. (2016). The resourceful facilitator: Teacher leaders constructing identities as facilitators of teacher peer groups. *Teachers and Teaching*, *22*(1).

Bauman, Z. (2005). *Liquid life*. Cambridge: Cambridge University Press.

Billett, S. (2001). Learning through working life: Interdependencies at work. *Studies in Continuing Education*, *23*(1), 19–35.

Billett, S. (2006). Relational interdependence between social and individual agency in work and working life. *Mind, Culture, and Activity*, *13*(1), 53–69.

Bloomer, M., & Hodkinson, P. (2000). Learning careers: Continuity and change in young people's dispositions to learning. *British Educational Research Journal, 26*(5), 583–597.

Bourdieu, P., & Wacquant, L. J. D. (1992). *An invitation to reflexive sociology*. Cambridge: Polity Press.

Cavanagh, J. (2010). Women, subjectivities and learning to be adaptable. *Multicultural Education & Technology Journal, 4*(3).

Elzen, B., Augustyn, A., Barbier, M., & van Mierlo, B. (2017). *Agroecological transitions: Changes and breakthroughs in the making*. Netherlands: Wageningen University & Research. doi:http://dx.doi.org/10.18174/407609

Evans, K., Kersh, N., & Kontiainen, S. (2004). Recognition of tacit skills: Learning outcomes in adult learning and work re-entry. *International Journal of Training and Development, 8*(1), 54–72.

Hodkinson, P., Hodkinson, H., Evans, K., Kersh, N., Fuller, A., Unwin, L., & Senker, P. (2004). The significance of individual biography in workplace learning. *Studies in the Education of Adults, 36*(1), 6–24. doi:10.1080/02660830.2004.11661484

Kelly, P. (2013). *The self as enterprise: Foucault and the spirit of 21st century capitalism*. Surrey: Gower Publishing.

Chapter 4

Contexts in non-permanent work

Contexts create affordances (Billett, 2001) for non-permanent workers in their journey of learning to be and to become. Contexts are not simply situated contexts; nor are they external to activity, practices and individual action (Bound & Rushbrook, 2015). Contexts are integral to the productive activity, entwined variously in everyday practices and meaning-making that are mediated by the socio-cultural, socio-economic and socio-political norms, discourses and practices of an occupation, of an industry sector, of a nation and more.

Identifying contexts in non-permanent work is challenging because boundaries are far more fluid than in permanent work. Due to their contractual arrangement, non-permanent workers traverse multiple work environments, social contexts and geographical boundaries on a regular basis, and engage in multiple communities and practices. In Singapore's creative industries, a non-permanent worker may be engaged in two jobs simultaneously – as an hourly-rated sound crew and as a sound engineer remunerated on a project basis – with different sets of contractual arrangements and work practices. An adult educator may develop a curriculum for service workers in Singapore one day, but fly off the next day to deliver a training programme to Myanmar public servants that requires operating in a far different socio-political context. An experienced lighting designer may take up work as a technical director that gives him the unusual opportunity to observe an expert lighting designer at work, which otherwise would not have been possible given that production houses in Singapore typically engage only one lighting designer per production.

Non-permanent workers thus inhabit multiple 'figured worlds' (Holland et al., 1998) that are always contested and entailing significant meaning-making. They frequently engage in 'boundary-crossing' as they take up multiple job roles with different remuneration structures and power relations, crisscrossing different industries. This way of being for non-permanent workers challenges existing paradigms of how learning in, at and through work takes place.

For instance, sites of work for the non-permanent worker challenge conventional understandings of workplaces. For non-permanent removalists in Singapore, the site where they carry out the packing and transporting of goods is indeed a worksite, but so are the local coffee shops around the island where work gets distributed every morning with employers indicating the available work for the day and signing up workers on the spot. New entrants are inducted into the norms of working in these industries through these coffee shops, which have evolved into entire support communities. In some sites, the workers are joined by their wives and young children after work hours. In other sites, gambling communities emerge by the coffee shops' narrow alleys just as the sun sets, where the men spend their daily wages in card games.

In the creative industries, a night out is not just for relaxing, but also for discussing job opportunities as well as work challenges, techniques and products that the workers encounter at different sites. Over supper, a new video product and its functionalities are discussed. A brainstorming session may informally emerge as friends discuss ongoing challenges at their various workplaces, such as alternative visual art projection techniques for a dinosaur exhibition. Pieces of serviette in a café become artefacts for learning as a senior draws out a technical problem and challenges the less experienced co-worker to come up with an appropriate solution.

Technology has enabled new ways of imagining work communities. A freelance sound technician makes it a point to watch YouTube videos of London concerts to observe how sound professionals conceal performers' microphones without compromising performance. Companies launching video editing software also create online communities where freelance workers can receive technical support as well as invitations to industry events.

In navigating this wide terrain of non-permanent work, significant meaning-making is required of non-permanent workers as they learn to be and become a practitioner. Some may find it difficult to 'see' possibilities on their own due to their dispositions or the inappropriate support they receive. Ashley, an aspiring lighting designer, enrolled himself into a year-long training programme jointly sponsored by a theatre venue and the Singapore government. The programme equipped him with a set of robust technical skills, including access to a full-time mentor. However, the programme did not cater to the development of entrepreneurial capabilities. Ashley himself never really understood the importance of cultivating a wide broader of clients, relying only on the theatre venue as his source of jobs. As he did not drink, he avoided evenings out with his colleagues, not aware that these were sites where jobs were negotiated and distributed informally. In other words, he could not make meaning of such activities that would have supported how he could be and become a practitioner. He became disillusioned with freelance work and applied to become a full-time shipping clerk instead despite the deep passion he had for his work.

Ashley's experience also highlights the socio-political context that mediates the delivery of workforce development programmes. The developmental state of Singapore has traditionally privileged permanent work, with a range of policies designed to incentivise workers to work with a single employer. Until recently, training was funded mainly through employers as shown by Ashley's case, where a theatre venue hosted the training programme. Such an approach was aimed at maximising the use of skills at the workplace but was fatal for Ashley because the theatre venue prioritised the development of technical skills, with no provision for developing the entrepreneurial capabilities that were important for a viable freelance career. Yati, another aspiring lighting designer, had similar criticisms of her diploma programme run by a government-funded polytechnic, where the curriculum limited students to working with a single venue. The consequence is that beginning freelancers often struggle to adapt to the diverse conditions in the multiple environments they work in, thereby compromising their performance and leading to a premature end to their freelance careers in some cases. In other words, her diploma programme provided the technical skills but never sought to start her off on her journey of being and becoming a practitioner.

Beyond the nation-state, the global context offers yet another setting that structures the opportunities and constraints for the learning and development of the non-permanent worker. In Singapore's creative industries, globalisation is a double-edged sword. At one level, globalisation facilitates access to international work that allows the non-permanent worker opportunities to be inducted into higher-level craft practices not possible in the local arts scene that have traditionally relied on imported shows. At another level, the increasing integration of the local industry into the global industry simultaneously facilitates the entry of foreign professionals with capabilities and rates that are more attractive to local employers. In the adult education industry, Singapore's adult educators face stiff competition from their foreign counterparts to deliver high-end training solutions in the local market but also enjoy good demand from the developing countries around the region.

Understanding contexts in non-permanent work thus helps us appreciate the complexity of being and becoming a practitioner. It gives us an important handle to understand why a particular group of workers may thrive while others drift. Contexts are also levers for the design of intervention to better support non-permanent workers in their learning in, at and through work.

Understanding contexts in non-permanent work through occupational affordances

The ubiquity of contexts in non-permanent work entailing significant meaning-making by non-permanent workers in their journey of being and becoming raises important questions in terms of how contexts can be meaningfully conceptualised in non-permanent work.

Contexts in workplace learning literature have traditionally been about the workplace, the organisation and its learning environment. The 'expansive-restrictive continuum' by Fuller and Unwin (2004) describes the extent to which a workplace creates opportunities for or barriers to learning. Skule (2004) similarly identifies learning conditions based on job-related factors. Ellström (2011) distinguishes between adaptive learning that focuses on efficient performance and developmental learning that focuses on innovativeness and discusses how an organisation may strike a balance between both types of learning. There have been recent efforts to expand the theorising of the context of workplace learning. For instance, Evans et al. (2006) integrate macro-level analysis with the characteristics of the learning environment. Felstead et al. (2009) highlight the relationship between the employee's position in the productive system and the ways in which their knowledge is 'developed, privileged and managed' (p. 198).

Still, theories of workplace learning are set in the context of a single workplace or industry whereas the context of workplace learning in non-permanent work is much broader with fluid boundaries. Non-permanent workers juggle a range of jobs, a range of workplaces and a range of learning environments. A wide client base is the hallmark of the wise non-permanent worker as a hedge against income risks through diversification of job sources. Non-permanent workers may knowingly opt for jobs that offer restrictive learning opportunities because these jobs bring in the income while also pursuing more expansive jobs that allow them to exercise their creative prowess. In other words, they may potentially be able to capture the full benefits of expansive environments while minimising the effects of restrictive ones. For example, in the adult education sector, jobs within Singapore's national credentialing system are seen as 'bread and butter', while the private adult education industry is seen as providing greater space for experimentation and self-actualisation. This is likewise happening in the creative industries, where directing corporate videos offer less prestige but often comes with a higher budget and therefore scope for experimentation, compared to local TV drama and films that always run on a tight budget, even though these work opportunities offer higher visibility to aspiring directors.

There is thus a need to understand the sets of non-permanent jobs in the market which tend to straddle industries and the various pathways to get them. This attention to the work journey is typically absent in many analyses of workplace learning privileging learning in stable, site-specific communities. An almost implicit assumption is that the availability of learning affordances and agency in accessing them should put the learner in a good position to progress in his career, since developmental pathways and trajectories are typically provided for by the employer. The world of the non-permanent worker, however, is marked more by elements of navigation, risks and uncertainties with unclear and yet-to-be discovered pathways and trajectories. They juggle the separate but overlapping processes of getting the work and the doing of work. Elsewhere, the work journey of non-permanent workers has been described as a 'vortex pathway', in that the type of work they engage in now shapes the learning and work opportunities they have in the future (Sadik, 2015).

Fundamentally, the pathways in non-permanent work are never linear and are not always clear. As Carl, a sound designer, explained, he had to reinvent himself a number of times, sometimes deliberately and at times due to circumstances.

Having joined the industry as a sound technician, he decided to make a niche for himself as a sound designer, turning down lucrative technical jobs in a bid to re-position himself as a designer in the market. Once he successfully made the transition, he started taking on sound technician jobs again if he found them attractive. He also taught in a degree programme on the sidelines. He then felt compelled to begin a business that would allow him to pitch for bigger contracts. At the point of our interview with him, he was juggling two businesses but still considered sound designing as his primary trade.

What strings the narratives of our respondents together is a particular identification with an occupation or with a craft. This was a critical frame in helping them make sense of the contexts they are in. They may or may not have purposefully pursued that particular occupation, but once in it, they could associate themselves with the practice. Carl was clear that the core of his work was sound designing. Borhan, a food and beverage help in a kebab makeshift stall, called himself 'run the show' because he did everything related to running the stall but imagined himself as a kebab-maker, which he called 'an art' to be mastered. Nazri, a freelance removalist during the weekdays and a part-time waiter over the weekend, spoke of these two jobs as separate because the occupational practices are different. Kevin, a freelance film director, likewise spoke of his practice as distinct from the work of his fellow soundmen and cameramen who had their own 'invisible union', despite recognition that they were all working in the same film and TV industry. How non-permanent workers imagine their craft or occupation is never identical, but mediated by their own disposition and the contexts they are in.

We could begin locating contexts in the 'occupation' of the non-permanent worker that cuts across work organisations and industry sectors. There may or may not be a common, widely accepted language or frame to describe these occupations. In technical theatre, a more or less common language exists to describe the lighting professionals that are required by the wide range of employers in the industry from arts production houses, to theatre venues, staging and equipment companies, as well as hotels. In adult education, the term 'adult educator' was introduced by the government agency overseeing continuing education and training. The term is typically used by those delivering services under the national credentialing system, but has little traction with practitioners in adjunct positions with polytechnics and universities, as well as those engaged as career coaches and business consultants. This lack of even a common language is part of understanding work contexts in the adult education sector, highlighting the high level of fragmentation in the industries that are associated with the sector.

We looked into our data to understand the particular factors in a work context that facilitate or inhibit the journey of being and becoming a practitioner. Identifying factors that were frequently mentioned by interviewees was one key approach. For instance, many of our interviewees shared experiences of co-workers who were instrumental in giving them vital tips and advice that

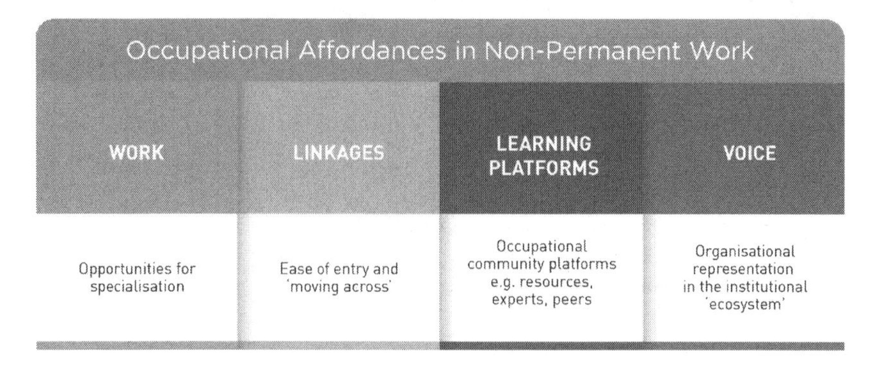

Figure 4.1 Occupational affordances in non-permanent work

then shaped their approach at work. In addition to frequency, we examined, compared and contrasted narratives of thriving non-permanent workers versus those exhibiting signs of drifting across occupations and industries. 'Occupational affordances' emerged as a meaningful way to describe contexts in non-permanent work, specifically the properties within an environment that furnishes the means for actions, independent of the actor's ability to perceive it or the actual action (Gibson, 1979).

Four key dimensions emerged as important in understanding occupational affordances in non-permanent work. These were:

- work, referring to the integration of non-permanent work roles into the production process, particularly the availability of specialised roles on a non-permanent basis;
- linkages, referring to how easy it is for workers to get work either at point of entry, across industries or across national borders;
- learning as part of an occupational community, linked to accessibility to peers, experts, and tools and artefacts; and
- voice, referring to the formal and informal organised representation of non-permanent workers within the industry institutional ecosystem, as well as the nation-state.

Figure 4.1 summarises the set of occupational affordances that could potentially support or constrain the learning and development of non-permanent workers.

Work: specialist integration into the production process

How non-permanent job roles are integrated into the production process has emerged as the most important occupational affordance to enable a robust journey of being and becoming a practitioner. The availability of specialist positions on a non-permanent basis in the job market is an important structural aspect guiding the work trajectory of the non-permanent worker. In the absence of career progression structures typically available in permanent work, the specialist roles that the market demands and rewards provide a signpost for the non-permanent worker to seek out work and evolve his or her capabilities in deeper ways.

In the removalist industry, there are plenty of entry-level jobs as packers and carriers. There are also a few team lead jobs as an assistant supervisor or a supervisor. However, there are no specialist job positions available on a non-permanent basis. Specialist roles such as a Sales, Customer Service and Quality Control are permanent positions. However, workers avoid taking up permanent entry-level jobs in the industry, as these jobs are perceived as paying too little and having rigid working conditions. The daily rates as a non-permanent worker were perceived to be much higher and closer to socially acceptable levels of income.

Omar, who worked primarily as freelance removalist but also doubled up as a part-time cleaner, spoke about his dream job to become 'the quotation guy' who goes to sites, assesses the items to be packed and draws up a quotation for customers. However, he could progress to such a position only if he was first employed as an entry-level removalist on a permanent position. The low take-home pay was a huge deterrence for him. As he shared, 'They offer me S$1 200 to work permanent with them. After CPF [Central Provident Fund] deduction, it is too low'. By eschewing permanent work, Omar was also kept out from higher-skilled work such as removalist jobs for data centres, which are entrusted only to permanent staff.

Omar's co-worker, Jefri, had been a freelance removalist for 30 years, and took up jobs as an Assistant Supervisor or Supervisor, commanding daily wages of S$100 per day. In the coffee shop we interviewed him in, he was seen as the expert and commanded respect from his younger peers. He once took up a permanent job briefly as a removalist, but it did not work out because he did not think he was paid fairly and has since avoided permanent jobs in the industry. Jefri and another co-worker tried to set up their own business, taking up sub-contractor jobs. However, the partnership did not work out, and he went back to working as a freelancer. He enjoyed working as a removalist particularly because of the physical exercise he got and the opportunity to work with diverse clients, but was worried about his retirement. Two years ago, he tried to apply for a permanent position as a cleaning supervisor, which was his last permanent job before he joined the removalist industry 30 years ago, but that did not work out.

The technical theatre industry offers a striking contrast to the removalist industry. Both entry-level and specialist jobs in the technical theatre industry are available on a non-permanent basis. The best in this industry is observed to be a freelancer. The example of Zac, a rigging expert in Singapore, demonstrated how he entered technical theatre opportunistically, tagging along with a friend to take on a casual job as a loader in a range of sites that included hotels, convention centres and stage companies. He so enjoyed the work that he started to specialise – first in lighting, then in sound before he finally came across rigging. Rigging so challenged him that he took it upon himself to pick up mathematical concepts. In his words,

> I did my own research, I went to all the websites and I read all the books about calculations, Pythagoras theorem . . . Because in rigging . . . you need to know your calculations. You need to know your angle, the angle of bridle, you need to know your points, the weight, the tension, this is all maths. And as a person without any education level, it is very hard to learn maths especially A Maths just to accommodate my job. So I learnt from scratch, I asked my sister, I asked my friends to help me with all of this.
>
> (Zac, rigger, technical theatre)

Zac soon became one of the top head flymen in Singapore. When a new theatre venue was set up in Singapore, he was talent spotted to join the venue. At the point of interview, he was a full-time technician at the theatre venue and also a part-time lecturer at a post-secondary education institution. As his contractual arrangements allowed him to also provide freelance services, he was involved in freelance projects from time to time, including being the Technical Manager at one of Singapore's top annual youth shows.

The contrasting work journeys of Jefri and Zac, both of whom had minimal formal qualifications and began through entry-level jobs, highlight the importance that industries providing specialist integration into the production process on a non-permanent basis if non-permanent work was to enable meaningful work journeys. It is the type of integration into the production process – whether purely peripheral or with specialisation opportunities – that provides either meaningful or limiting opportunities for development of the non-permanent worker. This finding takes the analysis beyond wage, skills and formal education. Common assumptions of precarity in low-wage and low-skill, non-permanent jobs do not hold up in Singapore. Non-permanent work in traditionally low-wage occupations such as food and beverage, despatch rider and removalists are in fact seen as paying better and offering less rigid conditions than in permanent work. These workers take up such work on a non-permanent basis despite the availability of those jobs on a permanent basis. Employers shared with us how they spent time to persuade these workers to join as permanent staff, with little success. What this means for non-permanent workers in these industries is that regardless of how motivated they are to perform their best at work, the lack of specialist roles on a non-permanent basis puts the brake on their development very early in their work trajectory.

Where specialist work is available in the industry on a non-permanent basis, entry-level, low-wage work may in fact be stepping stones to develop deeper expertise if adequate support is provided, as the case of technical theatre demonstrates. On the other hand, non-permanent work, even in higher-skilled sectors, may lead to precarity if there is no opportunity for specialisation on a non-permanent basis or if the links to permanent work are problematic. Elsewhere in Singapore, administrative, research and infocomm technology positions are increasingly available on a non-permanent basis in Singapore. If industries do not create meaningful specialist positions on a non-permanent basis, there are limits to the work trajectory of these workers unless there is capacity for them to join permanent work.

Specialist versus peripheral integration into the production process also offers a handle to help us better understand the impact of non-permanent work that the platform economy is throwing up through companies like Uber and TaskRabbit. These companies offer peripheral integration into the industry as drivers or helpers, as the pathways to further specialisation are absent. In contrast, the gig work that other platform companies such as Gigster and Toptal potentially offer expansive development opportunities, because the infocomm and finance industry are increasing their demand for specialists on a non-permanent basis.

Linkages: ease at entry and 'moving across'

The availability of specialist roles on a non-permanent basis does not, in and of itself, promise developmental opportunities for the non-permanent worker in their journey of being and becoming. When we spoke to employers in the creative industries, there was an acute sense of manpower shortage, especially at specialist levels. On the other hand, when we spoke to the freelance workers, a sense of stagnation linked to limited developmental opportunities was pervasive. As Rina, a sound crew member, said, she knew 'only a few people who are very successful but the rest of us are just there'.

The same situation prevails in the adult education sector. A veteran in the adult education industry informed us that certification programmes are churning out large numbers of qualified adult educators, but only a small proportion are in fact practising, and even fewer are practising at the specialist level.

Our data suggests there is a chronic lack of linkages in all the industries we studied that is limiting how workers can develop their work journeys. Linkages are critical to support the process of learning to be and become for non-permanent workers. Linkages enable non-permanent workers to get work and access to communities that are both meaningful to their craft development, and their standing in the market. Linkages may be personal, for instance, knowing the person who is offering the job or having someone vouch for you. Linkages could also be more formal for example through education and training programmes or a set of industry-recognised credentials that facilitates movement across jobs. Linkages could also be embedded in the production process through internship or apprenticeship arrangements. In the industries we studied, there was an over-reliance on personal networks for the distribution of work, and thus the access to opportunities to develop capabilities.

When we asked Yati, a beginning lighting designer, how she got jobs in the industry, she said emphatically, 'Contacts. Contacts. Contacts. Then skills'. Carl, a leading sound designer who runs two businesses, confirmed this recruitment practice. He refused to recruit based on resumes or interviews. He said:

> You give me CV [sic], I don't read, no point . . . because . . . it's so skill-based . . . Make sure that you worked with me before so I know.
>
> (Carl, sound designer, technical theatre)

His main mode of recruiting younger co-workers was by teaching in an arts degree programme. When he stopped teaching about six years ago, the pipeline stopped as well:

> I feel like I'm [a] HR director, I . . . struggle everyday. I still [have] one show [with] no operator because everybody is booked up. It's a big struggle, really . . . I stopped teaching . . . for about six years and I'm suffering the consequences.
>
> (Carl, sound designer, technical theatre)

The biography of Ron, now considered a top lighting designer in Asia, attests to the restrictive recruitment practices in the industry that is highly reliant on personal networks. By the age of 21, Ron already had very advanced capabilities through self-practice on his church's lightning board. Nobody would give him a chance because in his words, 'they don't know [who] I am, and . . . what I can do'. It was only after he enrolled himself into an arts degree programme and became exposed to practitioners who were guest lecturing that he started getting jobs. There is certainly space to evolve more sophisticated recruitment platforms that give opportunities to a wider pool of workers.

Linkages also include opportunities to access diverse jobs across industries. As we observe earlier, a wide client base allows non-permanent workers not only to hedge their income risks, but also their learning risks. One set of jobs may pay well, but offers limited developmental opportunities such as working as a lighting designer on rock-and-roll shows. Another set of jobs pays less well but stretches the capabilities of the worker because the demands are more sophisticated such as working in the theatre. Yet another set of jobs neither pays well nor offers developmental opportunities, but is readily available to offer a steady stream of income for the non-permanent worker, such as working as a stage crew. The ease with which workers can access a range of jobs will allow them to take advantage of expansive jobs and minimise the risks associated with restrictive jobs.

In the creative industries, linkages across the industries are fairly well developed. Film directors pursue work in the television genres as well as seek out work with corporate clients, among others. Sound technicians likewise work across theatre venues, arts production houses as well as staging companies. This suggests that occupational norms and practices across the various sub-sectors of the creative industries are fairly comparable, making traversing across sectors less problematic. This is less the case in the adult education sector, which is highly fragmented with different norms and practices associated with the different industries. For instance, trainers with the national credentialing system achieve higher credibility through repeated performance, without a need to articulate a particular specialisation. This practice stands in sharp contrast to practices in the private training market, where delivering niche products tends to be more highly rewarded by the market. Experience in the national credentialing system thus have little traction in the private training market, with some of our interviewees deliberately omitting the former in their resume because it signals a lack of innovation that the private training market demands.

Linkages are also global in nature. Our interviewees often articulated their work aspirations in global terms. This global orientation reflects Singapore's particular integration into the global economy that exposes its workforce directly to global markets through the ease with which both foreign companies and foreign workers can operate in the city-state.

The availability of foreign jobs locally did not automatically mean that locals had access to them. In the creative industries, the industry development model spearheaded by government agencies privileges the attraction of globally competitive companies through incentives as well as investment in excellent infrastructure such as world-class theatres and business mega-plexes. Successful shows from Broadway and elsewhere are brought in and compete with low-budget, local productions. The paradox is that those working in the local market have little need to build deeper sets of capabilities; this also means that they are kept out from the more sophisticated work created by these foreign companies. Gail, a former full-time producer who started a company that matches freelancers to jobs, found it difficult to get foreign companies to recruit local practitioners. One major foreign studio required a cameraman who knew how to edit but local shows running on tight budgets would not have those requirements. The experience of Hannah, a veteran video editor, who managed to get a job in the foreign work-market, reveals the narrow ways in which local jobs are organised. It is worth quoting her at length here:

> In [the] broadcast environment in Singapore, we always have tight deadlines. And whenever you are brought into editing room, the clock starts counting . . . So there isn't much discussion on the edit table. Most of the time is 'I have the script; this is what you can do'. They even have all the time codes, the in/out points of interview . . . But when I have a chance to work with [foreign broadcasting companies], the directors work very differently . . . The director will sit in and discuss with you how you feel, what

> his vision is . . . One of them made me sit through 12 hours of rushes . . . At the back of my mind, I thought 'This is a bit silly isn't it. You can save money but you didn't want to.' Interestingly, when watching through the footage with an ease of mind, it actually expedites your editing in the later part . . . because you know the footage so well . . . By watching through and getting the footage into your psyche, . . . you understand [the] footage . . . So it helps a lot when we decide to change the direction in the story later on. You can actually give a lot more to your director, because you know the footage so well.
>
> (Hannah, video editor, film and TV)

Issues of access to higher-quality jobs in foreign companies are complicated, because it links recruitment practices with occupational practices that look different in different markets. This does not mean singularly developing workers to a high level of expertise, as they may not be able to thrive in other markets. For instance, very early in his career, Kevin, a film director, learnt that a good aesthetics sense alone was not sufficient to survive in the local industry if he could not shoot fast and economical enough. Likewise, Singapore adult educators need to recontextualise their knowledge and experiences when performing jobs in less-developed countries in the region. What is needed is meaningful linkages across the different types of markets that support workers in this process of recontextualisation.

In summary, linkages facilitate 'boundary crossing' and give non-permanent workers space and flexibility to pursue their craft and make the most out of the different opportunities available in different industries and markets. The presence of linkages does not necessarily mean that the workers can 'see' the affordances and act on them. In fact, getting workers to 'see' the affordances is particularly problematic, given that the majority of the workers we interviewed enter non-permanent work opportunistically, without intentionally seeking out that particular craft or occupation, which poses a challenge in their journey of being and becoming. Rather, the presence of linkages, in and of themselves, takes away much of the pressure from those who can 'see', and those who has been coached to be able to 'see' these affordances, and empower them to drive their careers in ways that are meaningful to them.

Learning as part of an occupational community

We found it significant that the non-permanent workers tend to articulate in an exuberant manner, the learning experiences they had in the context of some form of informal mentoring or observation of more experienced peers at work assignments. We could understand this enthusiasm better in the context of the professional isolation faced by non-permanent workers where they are hired for a certain service and deemed as the 'expert', at least for that job. The affordances for learning from more experienced peers are thus difficult to access, which is a significant constraint for them in their journey of being and becoming.

In the UK's freelance-dominated TV industry, experienced workers are said to be not available for novices to consult or observe because of freelance arrangements, thus 'creating a community with a missing middle' (Grugulis & Stoyanava, 2011, p. 342). This is no different from the local creative industries. Kevin, a freelance director, shared his difficulty working on his first TV drama:

> When I directed my first drama, I know nothing at all. And you have to command people because you are the director. That's tough . . . I studied the structure of the television programs. I walked around with a tape recorder. I have no concept of lighting or anything, I just shot it the best way I know how.
>
> (Kevin, director, film and television)

Shar, a sound technician, similarly highlighted how lonely the freelance arrangement was:

> The company I work for, basically I'm the only sound man who knows most of the things. . . . If I don't know, no one knows . . . Sometimes I don't know whether it's right or wrong, and then I wait until someone [who] does.
>
> (Shar, sound technician, technical theatre)

It is usually serendipitous when someone comes along to guide. Yati was feeling jaded about her work until she was introduced to Ken, an experienced lighting designer. Ken gave Yati jobs that his schedule did not allow him to take up and mentored her to perform those jobs. Yati thus became an informal assistant to him. What was particularly useful for Yati was the learning conversations they had. She related their conversations:

> After every project, he will sit down with me and ask me did you learn anything . . . and he will do a recap with me. He [asked] me 'You know why I [left] you alone in the morning?' . . . Because we start work at 9 and he always comes in after lunch. I said not really. [He says] 'Because from there if you are alone then you have to make the decision yourself. I cannot be there all the time to make decisions for you.' In a sense, he knows that I will face trouble . . . in the morning because that is the point where we are going to start work . . . So that is where he tests and trains [me] at the same time . . . At the end of the project, he will always ask me 'Did you learn a lot? And then he told me, 'Your art is there, but your technique is not yet there' . . . There is not a lot of people who can tell me that. There is not a lot of people in the world that will actually help me up the ladder.
>
> (Yati, lighting designer, technical theatre)

The partnering of experienced and beginning practitioners is a powerful developmental model for supporting the learning to be and to become of non-permanent workers, but such opportunities are too few and far between. As Carl, a sound designer explained, local jobs paid badly so designers could not afford to hire assistants. Not only do beginning practitioners lose out, but the designers lose as well as they lack the bandwidth to do a good job. Carl avoided this stalemate by taking a cut from his fee to engage assistants. This puts him in a position where he could readily call upon a team to take up multiple jobs that were well-run under his name, but this practice was rare.

Those in the creative industries could cope to a certain extent with the lack of access to experienced peers because artefacts are visible and could be deconstructed. An effect in a movie could be deconstructed in terms of the equipment that was used and how the shot was taken. A preferred cinematography style could be conveyed by referring to previous famous movies. This is not the same in the adult education industry, which, at its core, involves highly private sessions between the educator and their clients, and with materials such as curriculum and course outlines not readily available in the public domain.

Lata, a freelance adult educator, observed that there was very little sharing among practitioners, and attributed it to the perceived need to guard 'trade secrets'. Given the low-trust environment in the adult education sector, it is not surprising that many of the thriving adult educators in our dataset were those who built experience and contacts while still under permanent employment arrangements. Permanent work, which comes with fixed income and organisational-mediated opportunities, provides a safe environment to try out the world of freelance training before taking the plunge. Karthik, a corporate trainer, made strategic shifts from the engineering department to the human resources department when he was in permanent work. To support that transition, he took up a master's programme in human resources and started networking with like-minded peers who opened opportunities for him to try out the world of freelance training in the weekends.

When Karthik made the switch to becoming a freelancer seven years later, there was already a network of what he calls 'partner and allies' who helped open doors and opportunities for him. However, the process continues to be very lonely and atomising, with limited opportunities to get feedback from peers and clients alike. Once, he tried to solicit feedback from a client for a programme he had been running for 2.5 years. The client's response was superficial, with just a one-liner that he was doing fine, since the company did not have any complaints. He discontinued with the assignments and is now careful to select more discerning clients. However, most entrants to the industry do not have networks like Karthik did to be in a position to turn down jobs. Practising their craft is a lonely affair.

Continuing education and training programmes are one important way to reduce the atomising effects of non-permanent work. Unfortunately, such programmes do not put much focus on the full range of occupational practices to be a freelance adult educator, focusing mainly on pedagogical aspects. Zeng Gong, a veteran corporate trainer, was highly critical of the way a popular credentialing programme for beginning adult educators was conducted, because of the focus on technical skills whereas entrepreneurial capabilities are equally needed to survive in the industry. Lata, as one of the trainers delivering the credentialing programme, made the same criticism:

> For freelance trainers, how do they start off? . . . Because when I am doing training, I am seeing a lot of potential learners who can become trainers but they have a challenge of going into somewhere to become a trainer . . . I don't know where to put them.
>
> (Lata, adult educator, CET sector)

In the creative industries, a handful of institutions do better at linking up students with practitioners, but in most institutions the same focus on purely technical skills persists. This set of affairs is the outcome of a particular discourse in the Singapore developmental state that is built around supporting permanent work, which means that business needs are prioritised that do not necessarily support the practice of workers. One course coordinator in technical theatre we spoke to saw no problem with attaching students to a single organisation for a six-month internship, whereas the reality of working in the industry would require students to seek jobs from a range of organisations. In fact, it was a source of pride that she could get big companies to host her students. A flagship programme in technical theatre for beginning freelancers has a significant work attachment component but only with one employer. Ashley, an aspiring lighting designer, did well to complete the course but failed to make the transition to become a practitioner because he was not able to get a steady stream of jobs. As part of the programme, he was assigned a full-time mentor whose focus was on technical skills. There was no space in the curriculum for entrepreneurial capabilities, nor conversations with experienced freelancers.

In many ways, the issues of poor linkages overlap significantly with the limited opportunities to learn from co-workers and experts. An important area for further examination is how the production process itself can evolve to support learning as an occupational community. The examples of Yati's informal mentoring by Ken and Carl's pool of assistants suggest that there are significant prospects for embedding some of these mentoring opportunities directly into the production process in ways that are meaningful to both beginning and experienced practitioners. In the adult education industry, Zeng Gong similarly had a number of what he called 'associates' who supported him to run some of the programmes he organised. Like Carl, he too was looking for people to take over some of his sessions because he could not cope with the demand. These are not the typical apprenticeship arrangements, because assistants can and do take up other work. The value of such loose apprenticeship programmes is to create spaces for observing and dialogue with a fellow practitioner, thus building a strong foundation for beginning workers in their journey of being and becoming.

How else do non-permanent workers learn as part of an occupational community? Social sites such as nights out are important platforms in bringing workers together during which conversations around specific work challenges inevitably surface. These platforms enable considerable problem-solving, but there are significant limits because such social settings are based on homophilous networks. Technology is another key platform supporting the occupational practice of non-permanent workers such as YouTube videos, chatrooms and discussion boards. For adult educators, books and conferences are also key sources for learning. Ultimately, however, it is minimising the loneliness and homophily that come from practising in an atomising contractual arrangement that requires support. The journey of being and becoming is necessarily a social one.

Voices

The discussion thus far suggests that there are important roles for various stakeholders in each of the industries we studied. In technical theatre, industry development efforts through the import of world-class shows is developing a disproportionate number of technical jobs with insufficient opportunities for engagement in the creative process. In the film and television sector, efforts to attract foreign companies through incentive schemes are not twinned with strategies to strengthen linkages with local practitioners. Polytechnics, universities and the adult education sectors also have an important part to play in appreciating the specific occupational practices associated with being a non-permanent worker to deliver more effective programmes. There are in fact existing industry platforms to discuss many of these issues which are typically led by government agencies as part of Singapore's unique developmental state model. The key feature of the developmental state in Singapore is a particular form of coordinated market planning undergirded by a strong partnership between the state and businesses and supported by a tight integration between the national education system and the labour market. What is significant is that the non-permanent worker's voice is absent or under-represented in all of these discussions.

In part, this is due to the atomising effects of non-permanent work arrangements that make self-organisation difficult. Carl candidly admitted:

> Unless . . . some governmental organisation wants to get us to organise, we will never do it. It's because we can't. The irony is the more vibrant we become, the less likely we will organise ourselves because everybody is booked for a job.
>
> (Carl, sound designer, technical theatre)

However, it is quite clear that part of the problem is the dominant model of industry engagement in Singapore that remains focused on supporting permanent work and prioritises business needs over those of workers. It is not surprising that at the point of our study, the committee overseeing skills and training for the technical theatre sector was represented by only one freelance professional, with the remaining 12 members made up by companies and government agencies. This is despite non-permanent workers in the creative sector making up some 70 per cent of the workforce

In addition, wider social cues, norms and discourses have yet to adequately evolve to support non-permanent work. A key tool by the developmental state to instil broad-based labour discipline and incentivise workers' participation in the state's economic activities is through the delivery of broad social security payments (Doner, Richie, & Slater, 2005). In Singapore, this is done through the Central Provident Fund (CPF), where forced compulsory savings is mandated through employers (Sung, 2006). Through the CPF, workers' access to basic needs such as housing and medical are greatly enhanced. Non-permanent work tends not to include CPF contributions, and thus has important consequences in the exercise of citizenry. Non-permanent workers have to adopt long-range financial planning for themselves if they are to sustain a professionally satisfying career, and this is not immediately apparent to many. As Ron, a freelance lighting designer, laments:

> [You] don't have [contributions to the CPF]. You don't have medical insurance, you cannot take sick leave and get paid, whatever you get paid, that is it. I have to buy my own insurance, I have to plan my own retirement, I have to plan for my own travels, insurance, everything is done on your own . . . A lot of people will not have that kind of knowledge or diligence to make sure that you plan for your future.
>
> (Ron, lighting designer, technical theatre)

Much of this advice is currently dispensed through experienced workers, or by figuring things out by oneself like Ron did. Jed, for instance, shared that he advised young freelancers to always file their income tax returns as there would be proof of income in the future if they had to get a bank loan to purchase a house. Given the poor linkages between experienced and beginning practitioners in the industries we studied, relying on personal contacts for the delivery of such critical information is insufficient.

Beyond financial planning, there needs to be deeper conversations on the risks and opportunities associated with non-permanent work, particularly through career guidance. This is especially if more workers are going into non-permanent work opportunistically. They would need significant guidance on evolving their work journeys. In the last few years, significant investments have been made to enhance career guidance services at school and for the workforce, but guidance on working as a non-permanent worker remains limited. At present, there is limited awareness of the way of being of non-permanent work, as the paradigm of permanent work continues to dominate.

A potential handmaiden that can give voice to non-permanent workers is professional or occupational groupings (Sadik, 2017). Such groupings are important support structures for non-permanent workers that can also act as an intermediary between non-permanent workers, industry and the government. To date, there has been little success in creating viable professional groupings of non-permanent workers in Singapore. Some reasons put forth are staffing and funding issues, although more research is needed to understand the difficulty of self-organising in a developmental state that manages worker organisations tightly.

Conclusion

Ellström (2011) highlights that 'learning in work is a matter of design. That is, it is a matter of organizing the workplace, not only for the production of certain goods or services, but also for supporting learning' (p. 107). In the case of non-permanent work, 'organising the workplace' is far more complicated because it requires changing practices in a number of industries, job markets, educational and training institutions as well as modifying government policies and schemes.

In this chapter, we put forth the conceptual frame of 'occupational affordances' for understanding contexts in non-permanent work. The four key dimensions are specialist versus peripheral work, linkages to ease movement across jobs and industries, learning as an occupational community and voice in the industry and nation-state. These occupational affordances do not absolve the individual of his or her agentic involvement in seeking out and acting on the affordances. The conceptual frame also offers signposts for areas of intervention to better support non-permanent workers in their learning in, at and through work.

Our identification of the distinction between specialist and peripheral non-permanent work creates a platform for deeper discussion on the impact of non-permanent work to the capabilities of workers in a country. Specialist roles that the market demands and rewards provide a signpost for the non-permanent worker to seek out work and evolve his or her skills in deeper ways. When these roles are absent, workers remain stuck at entry-level jobs with limited skill-sets almost in perpetuity. There is the risk that new technologies deployed in a neo-liberal economic environment is likely to create more of such peripheral non-permanent jobs. However, technological innovation does not take place in a vaccuum. There therefore needs to be deeper conversations not just on the number of non-permanent workers generated in an economy, but also on the type of non-permanent work being created.

Our identification of linkages and platforms to learn as an occupational community puts the focus on how workers learn and develop in a social setting, but raises issues of how the atomising nature of non-permanent work disrupts traditional ways of learning to be and become. Efforts to support the learning and development of non-permanent workers in Singapore have long given focus on classroom training, which is sorely found wanting when we examine how these workers learn and develop. Where there are funds available for these workers to develop such as through overseas work attachments, workers do not capitalise on them because it is hard to identify such opportunities. The atomising effects of non-permanent work are not inevitable. More importantly, it is not desirable as it leads to situations of workers lacking capabilities at specialist levels, while only a few succeed. Overcoming this stalemate requires workforce and industry development agencies to evolve suitable supporting arrangements such as embedding mentoring in the production process through fund support and more.

Our identification of the importance of the voice of the non-permanent worker is critical in the context of a developmental state that is traditionally about supporting big businesses and creating and supporting workers in permanent jobs. There is genuine attempt to better support non-permanent workers in their learning and development, but efforts continue to be framed by the range of tools available to the developmental state. For instance, apprenticeship programmes in technical theatre are conducted with big businesses rather than experienced freelancers who can offer more to the beginning practitioners. These are missed opportunities that could be avoided by developing a deeper understanding of the ways of being of non-permanent workers and exploring new models and partners in workforce development.

In all, learning and developing non-permanent workers in, at and through work requires a deft understanding of the contexts they are in, which stretches existing theories of workplace learning. Boundaries are far more fluid in non-permanent work, and subject to extensive meaning-making by the worker that requires support. Non-permanent work should not be seen as exceptional, given that we can expect more of the workforce to experience frequent job and career changes. The concept of 'occupational affordances' is an initial effort to evolve discourse to better support the learning and development of non-permanent workers and other workers in an era of higher job impermanence.

References

Billett, S. (2001). Learning through working life, interdependencies at work. *Studies in Continuing Education, 23*(1), 19–35.

Bound, H., & Rushbrook, P. (2015). Problematising workplace learning. In H. Bound & P. Rushbrook (Eds.), *Towards an expanded understanding of workplace learning*. Singapore: Institute for Adult Learning.

Doner, R., Ritchie, B., & Slater, D. (2005). Systemic vulnerability and the origins of developmental state. *International Organization, 59*(2), 327–361.

Ellström, P. E. (2011). Informal learning at work: Conditions, processes and logics. In M. Malloch, L. Cairns, K. Evans, & B. O'Connor (Eds.), *Sage handbook of workplace learning*. London: Sage Publications.

Evans, K., Hodkinson, P., Rainbird, H., & Unwin, L. (2006). *Improving workplace learning*. London: Routledge.

Felstead, A., Fuller, A., Jewson, N., & Unwin, L. (2009). *Improving work as learning*. Abingdon: Routledge.

Fuller, A., & Unwin, L. (2004). Expansive learning environments: Integrating personal and organizational development. In H. Rainbir, A. Fuller, & A. Munro (Eds.), *Workplace learning in context*. London: Routledge.

Gibson, J. (1979). *The ecological approach to visual perception*. Boston: Houghton Mifflin Harcourt.

Grugulis, I., & Stoyanava. D. (2011). The missing middle: communities of practice in a freelance labour market. *Work, Employment and Society, 25*(2), 342–351.

Holland, D., Lachicotte, W. Jr., Skinner, D., & Cain, C. (1998). *Identity and agency in cultural worlds*. Cambridge, MA: Harvard University Press.

Sadik, S. (2015). Vortex pathways: Understanding the dynamism of non-permanent work. In H. Bound & P. Rushbrook (Eds.), *Towards an expanded understanding of workplace learning*. Singapore: Institute for Adult Learning.

Sadik, S. (2017). Non-permanent workers and their learning in a developmental state. In M. Milana, S. Webb, J. Holford, R. Waller, & P. Jarvis (Eds.), *International handbook on adult and lifelong education and learning*. London: Palgrave Macmillan.

Skule, S. (2004). Learning conditions at work: A framework to understand and assess informal learning in the workplace. *International Journal of Training & Development, 8*(1), 8–20.

Sung, J. (2006). *Explaining the economic success of Singapore: The developmental worker as the missing link*. Cheltenham: Edward Elgar Publishing.

Chapter 5

Integrated practice

Learning to be and become of and an occupation as a non-permanent worker is a constantly evolving process. The previous chapters have drawn attention to the integrated nature of occupational practices in which craft, learning-to-learn and entrepreneurial capabilities are developed and practiced variously according to the context, disposition and personal circumstances of the individual practitioner. These dimensions of our integrated practice model mediate the journey of the non-permanent worker. In this chapter, we pull these aspects together to present our conceptual frame which we call 'integrated practices'.

Chapters 1 and 2 signposted the value of the integrated practices model in making a significant contribution to conceptualising, designing and enacting the learning and development of non-permanent workers. The model is predicated on fundamental assumptions about learning and development that are illustrated through our working definition of learning. These assumptions are further spelt out later in the chapter. We consider learning to be a process contributing to an increased capability to act differently in the environment (Owen, 2017) leading to new sets of relations (Hager, 2002) in different contexts. Through the processes of developing capabilities, acting differently and creating new sets of relations in an environment non-permanent workers undertake journeys of being and becoming. Such a definition of learning is particularly pertinent to the non-permanent worker, as it is not a single workplace the freelancer needs to participate in, but multiple workplaces across a sector, or in some instances across industry sectors; the non-permanent worker constantly engages in multiple contexts. This means the environment in which capabilities to 'act differently' is not only the occupation, but the sector and its practices, thus the occupational capabilities required of non-permanent workers needs to be imbued with entrepreneurial and learning-to-learn capabilities in order to stay competitive. Engagement in practices contributes to our sense of who we are, our meaning-making and participation in different practices -our dispositions – in different contexts. The non-permanent worker is required to learn all this rapidly as they move from one organisation to another. Learning to act differently is not only about developing specific capabilities, but a constant process and journey of evolving identity and the enacted agency of those identities.

Our integrated practice model (see Figure 5.1), provides a way of thinking into both the growth and development of non-permanent workers and a framework for analysing the experience of the non-permanent worker, important in meeting the challenges of decent, good work, well-being and human flourishing. The integrated practices model provides a framework for addressing the challenge of how the development of non-permanent workers' capabilities can be supported over time and how the scaling up to the highly skilled workforces espoused by policies can realistically be achieved. In Chapter 2 we made reference to two theoretical lenses to interpret learning and development; one being the human capital lens and the other being social practice. Implicit within the integrated practice model is an assumption that humans are not a human capital resource, but people with innate abilities, and that all should have access to the resources, opportunities and affordances for development. For sectors that rely heavily on non-permanent labour market arrangements and the institutions within the sector that contribute in some way to workforce development of a labour market, it is necessary to understand the experience of the non-permanent worker in order to design and implement meaningful interventions for workforce development. Sector ecosystems, made up of educational institutions, professional bodies, government agencies, unions and employer bodies, skills councils and other bodies that have something to contribute or that impact on affordances, constraints, discourses of the sector, govern and have power to make changes. Thus the relations between these bodies is important in effecting change, as discussed in Chapter 4. Bodies in the ecosystem generate particular institutionalised orders and discourses creating and contributing to affordances or constraints for developing the non-permanent workers in their sector. Chapter 4 argued for occupational affordances that include opportunities for specialist work, linkages to enable ease of movement across work engagements and industry, occupational communities and for the choices of non-permanent workers to be heard collectively. Industry bodies that constitute the institutional governance of their industry sector ecosystems have the power to develop such affordances, provided they have a shared understanding of such intent (Bound, 2007; White, 2001).

Common in educational institutions is that craft capabilities, entrepreneurial and learning-to-learn capabilities are often considered as separate from each other and taught separately resulting in limited connection with the contexts in which future practitioners will truly begin their journey of being and becoming. Through the stories and examples discussed so far in this book, we make the point that craft, learning-to-learn and entrepreneurial capabilities, dispositions and context, are not separate but integrated. The whole, taken together, mediates the journey of the non-permanent worker, as shown in Figure 5.1.

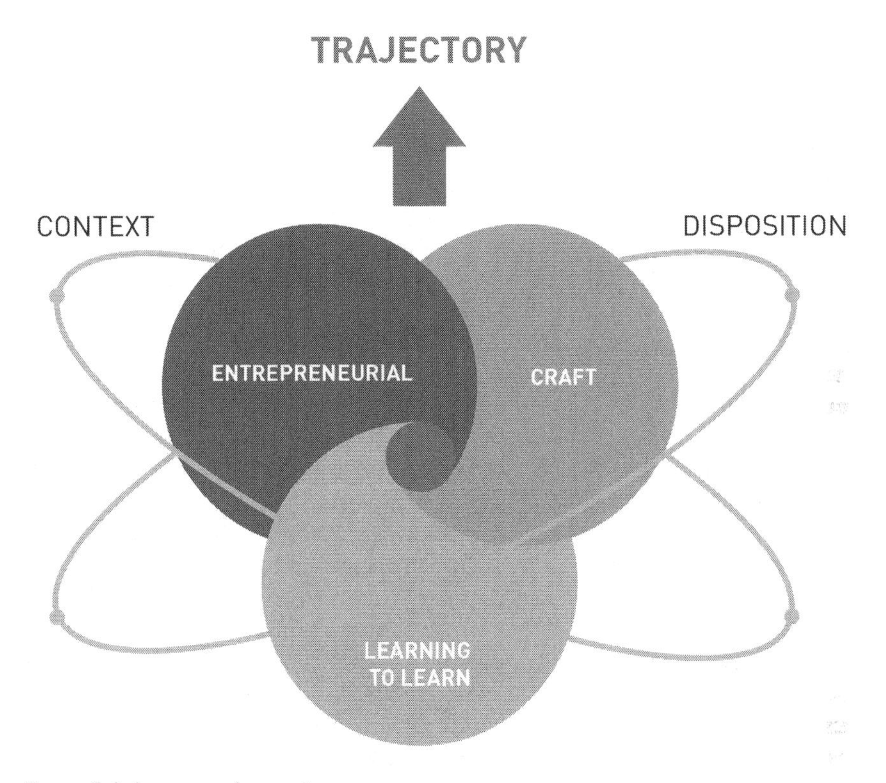

Figure 5.1 Integrated practice

The following sections expand on the dimensions of the integrated practice model: dispositions, context, capabilities and journey.

Dispositions

In Chapter 3, the major dispositions identified were, purposeful and broad, purposeful and contained, opportunistic and contained and opportunistic and broad. As discussed in Chapter 3, we used Bloomer and Hodkinson's (2000) explanation of dispositions, 'Linking meaning, participation and action is disposition. By disposition we mean orientation to practice' (p. 589). This social practice lens is used rather than the psychological perspective of character traits as Bloomer and Hodkinson's socio-cultural perspective links relations between how non-permanent workers we interviewed position themselves in relation to the occupational, sector- and site- specific practices they engage in, their self-narratives (Chappell et al., 2003) and their actions as they make meaning of their experiences.

For example, Zac's (rigger, technical theatre) orientation to his professional practice is 'getting the knowledge because tertiary wise I do not have anything. I want to learn new things, I want to explore what I can do, what is my capabilities'. Zac had no tertiary education; his curiosity and enjoyment of work in technical theatre contributed to him positioning himself as a constant learner, always seeking new possibilities to extend himself. As told in Chapters 3 and 4, Zac's story included five years of doing lighting, another five years of 'doing' sound; he then became 'hooked on rigging'. Zac's story, and that of others, resonates with Bakhtin's work that the self is constructed over time; it cannot be 'reduced to its here and now characteristics but can be reconstructed through its synchronous and diachronous projections' (1981, p. 153). There are constantly new possibilities for meaning-making that in Zac's case resulted in his actions of moving from lighting to sound to rigging. Zac's positioning of himself as a constant learner, as someone who strives (despite having 'no tertiary education', so he did not limit himself according to institutionalised educational discourses), and his decisions and actions in changing his area of expertise, his occupational practices, were mediated not only by his positioning and meaning-making but by the practices in the technical theatre sector. Teamwork across occupations such as sound, lighting, and rigging is how work is designed; these areas of occupational expertise do not work alone; together, they constitute a team. Zac was therefore able to 'see' and participate in the work of these different roles and practices and be exposed to the knowledge and capabilities involved. He saw possibilities in different specialisms through engaging in the industry practice of teamwork. Zac's story illustrates the intersection of the ellipse of context and his disposition (see Figure 5.1) of learning and curiosity. His self-narrative is inclusive of what Chappell et al. (2003) call relational identity and also reflexive identity. Relational identity in that through his work with other roles and their connections, he positioned himself variously over time as a lighting person, someone who works with sound and now as a rigger. His being and becoming is more than the technical capabilities required of these different occupational roles; he positions himself as *being* each of these occupational roles, so sees himself *in relation to others* who practice as a lighting person and so on. His self-narrative, what Chappell et al. (2003) refer to as reflexive identity, refers to his recounting of his history and his part in that story, evident in his account of himself as someone who wants to learn new things, to explore. So, disposition is entwined in context, context so far discussed as the situated practices in given sites, of occupational and practices and industry sector ways of working. Context is all these things and more. How, then, do the authors understand context, its entwinement with disposition and craft, entrepreneurial and learning-to-learn capabilities practiced by the non-permanent worker and their mediation of the non-permanent workers' journey?

Context

As discussed in Chapter 4, context is not simply the situated context or sets of practices, neither is it only that which is external to activity, to practices and individual meaning-making and action. Rather the authors argue that context is the socio-cultural, historical and economic norms, discourses, policies and practices of a nation, of an industry sector, an occupation and sites of work. Context is entwined variously in everyday practices (Bound & Rushbrook, 2015) and meaning-making. How so? Holland et al. (1998) argue that in the making of meaning, we author the world. 'But the "I" is by no means a freewheeling agent, authoring worlds from creative springs within' (p. 170). In making meaning we author the world; however, such authoring draws on, uses the words, the language of others to which they have been exposed. Such language carries within it ideology, social belief systems, particular perspectives of the world (Bakhtin, 1981). Language is a primary resource through which we make meaning and undertake everyday practices.

> Each word tastes of the context and contexts in which it has lived its socially charged life; all words and forms are populated by intentions. Contextual overtones (generic, tendentious, individualistic) are inevitable in the word. The word in language is half someone else's.
>
> (ibid., p. 293)

Context is embedded in everyday activity and actions (Bound, 2007; Bound & Rushbrook, 2015). Self-narratives and dispositions are mediated by context; the words become one's own when they are imbued with the speaker's intention (ibid), when the speaker appropriates (Wertsch, 1998) them. The 'speaker' or the 'I' uses language through which to make meaning, to participate and engage in practices. Practices – the doings, saying and relatings (Schatzki, 2012) of practices – are inclusive of tools that mediate practices through their embedded cultural norms and historical practices. That is, embedded in tools, are historical and cultural processes, ways of thinking and relating to others and to the environment (situated context). Language, however, is a primary tool. Practices are not fixed, stable entities but constantly evolve. Such complexity demands that through the continuous meaning-making non-permanent workers engage in, their own practice is constantly emerging.

Context creates affordances (Billett, 2001) for learning. Chapter 4 provides multiple examples. In the creative sector, access to challenging work, and therefore growth and development, is available through being engaged in the production of international shows and films, whereas local productions tend to be time and budget poor and task-based, severely limiting the exercise of aesthetic judgement, for example. Opportunities to engage with international productions is in large part due to a deliberate government policy for this sector. However, the context is of a highly competitive industry typified by alternating periods of frenetic activity and quiet. Malepart (2005) characterises the sector as being 'about the survival of the fittest' (p. 5). The result is that only some have access to international engagements. Without access to challenging work, opportunities for growth and development in the sector are limited. Another example is found amongst adult educators, who work in a sector as individuals, reproducing a discourse of lack of trust, where protection of trade secrets limits sharing and thus access to various forms of mentoring and support for non-permanent workers. The fragmented nature of the CET sector also limits ease of movement across sectors. The valuing of certain areas of expertise rewards individuals such as Xavier, who has expertise in re-engineering processes such as six sigma and lean manufacturing, but limits the income of adult educators such as Daisy, who teaches generic capabilities and literacy, despite this area of expertise requiring the greater pedagogical capabilities.

For the non-permanent worker, their dispositions, social circumstances and biography, enacted in particular contexts, enable them to 'see' possibilities (or not) within and across the different contexts in which they work. This is important for their journey. Working across sites, teams and practices exposes the non-permanent worker to multiple ways of being, exposure to and engagement in and with multiple practices. Zac's experience is a case in point. Specialists in the creative sector (e.g. lighting, sound, rigging) work in one form or another in teams, exposing Zac to these different specialisms. This affordance in the context of his work, in combination with his curious disposition, enabled his exploration of all of these specialisms before settling on rigging albeit that it required extensive learning on his part.

Because non-permanent workers work across sites and practices, considering affordances in one particular worksite has temporal importance, but constitutes only part of the experience of the non-permanent worker. The non-permanent worker needs to make sense of different practices in different organisations and settings. Francine, an adult educator, describes different practices within the sector, which can impact on getting a continuous flow of work:

> you get constantly of course, rated, every semester, and they emphasise very much on student surveys nowadays which I'm not sure exactly if that is totally accurate. Because this bunch of people [the students], you throw a few pizzas they adore you . . . So you get, you see some fellow staff members who try to like, so-called, bribe their way through their hearts. So I'm not sure about this whole system at all. I feel there has to be some caution to be exercised there. And there's a lot of ethical issues on the table as well.
>
> (Francine, adult educator, CET sector)

The 'student survey' is commonly referred to as the 'happy sheet', and it is the scores on these that play a major part in getting the next job both with a specific training provider and with other providers. This practice, across the sector, contributes to other practices, such as those in the pizza story, that subvert the intent of the 'happy sheet'. The pizza story is also reflective of sector practices that can quickly ascertain 'quality', important for for-profit organisations, as time is money, conveniently ignoring opportunities to develop quality provision. Different organisations and segments in the sector place differing values on such practices, meaning that the adult educator needs to be aware of the issues and position themselves accordingly. Another example is getting to understand the different rates of pay. Terrence comments:

> You are asked to do a lower rate. That's the reason why I decline some of the classes. I don't find it worthwhile for my time . . . But there are other trainers within that outfit who will go on and take. In Singapore there is a local term I think you might be familiar with. We call it 'spoil the market'.
>
> (Terrence: adult educator, CET sector)

Terence's comment highlights the lack of collective approach and the competitive nature of the sector. These two factors contribute to particular affordances common across the sector that the adult educator needs to constantly negotiate. Even in seemingly disarmingly simple matters such as planning the work, trainers can face the 'happy problem' of having clashes in their timetable. Negotiating this can impact a trainer's projected earnings and reputation. Keegan, for example, recently experienced moving his schedule around for an existing booking, only to find this booking rescheduled to another time. After this, he became very cautious of confirming dates before rearranging other clients. Keegan, like many, learnt this lesson the hard way; there were no mentors to prepare him for such exigencies, nor are such matters discussed in programs for adult educators in the sector. Such affordances are present across a sector, inherent in sector practices. For this reason, we extend the notion of affordances beyond its application to particular sites of work to include a consideration of affordances of an industry sector, as discussed in Chapter 4.

The dynamic embeddedness of context and disposition

Context and disposition are NOT separate from each other. Further, they do not just intersect, but are embedded each in the other. Understanding context as being embedded in disposition and disposition being embedded in context, brings a focus to the dynamic interplay between these dimensions of integrated practice and the capability development, and journey of the non-permanent worker. More specifically, lives are enacted within frames of meaning (Knorr Cetina, 2007), a key aspect of disposition. Frames of meaning are social constructs that help frame and interpret contexts, and all that constitutes a given context. These processes are sites of negotiation, constant disruption and evolution, requiring the non-permanent worker to be constantly engaged in a process of meaning-making and evolving an identity that contributes to their journey. Eteläpelto (2015) describes this identity making as a constant process of negotiation at the intersection of the individual and the social, as discussed in Chapter 2. Being mindful of the interplay between occupational practices, socio-cultural contexts and their own dispositions and personal circumstances is important in a freelancer's self-authoring and positioning, informing their self-narrative. As Dall'Alba and Sandberg note,

> practice is constituted neither by an objective structure constraining professionals' [occupational] action nor by the professionals' subjectivity, as sometimes claimed. Rather, practice is intersubjectively constituted through mutual understanding of a specific institutionalised order enacted by individuals.
>
> (2006, p. 385)

For example, Ron, a lighting designer in technical theatre, whose story was discussed in Chapters 2 and 4, could not readily access jobs until he undertook a diploma programme which afforded him access to and engagement with those who work in the sector. As told in Chapter 4, the sector works on networks, it is small and many of the key individuals know each other; it is therefore necessary to break into those networks to be able to access work. The recruitment practices of the technical theatre sector are not about looking at qualifications, rather those who engage others look to what the individual can do, how they react in problem situations. Ron's (lighting designer, technical theatre) story, told in Chapters 2 and 4, is a case in point. His advanced skills were not recognised until he met industry practitioners in a program he was undertaking. These industry practitioners recognised his capabilities and disposition, and only then did he gain access to work in the sector.

Importantly, it was not only the affordance of access to networks alone that opened up possibilities for him. It was his well-developed capabilities, his orientation to his practice, where he embraced the solving of complex, non-routine problems that was another part of the puzzle of getting into the sector. Affordances are more complex than a single explanation. In this example, what was also at play was the connection the educational institution had with industry. The educational institution's practices of engaging lecturers who continued to work in the sector, contributed to this affordance. For Ron, the affordances in the context in which he was studying and his disposition of embracing problem solving and seeking to constantly learn enabled him to be noticed and to take advantage of the opportunities the context afforded him.

Gavin's experience in the film and television sector provides another example. His experience was not so much about gaining access to work, as he had been part of the industry for a long time. Rather, it was about understanding the practices, the sayings, doings and relatings of the sector, the cultural norms and ways of being that enabled him to maintain a continuous flow of work. He states, you have to 'swallow a lot of pain. The more pain you swallow, the more popular you'll get'. Stamina and endurance are combined with a degree of performativity in the form of a willingness to stifle grievances that arise out of onerous working conditions. As Gavin further explains:

> And always remember . . . never put on a long face on the job. Even if you've been scolded or you've had a fourteen-hour day, you still have to put a smiling face because you're a non-salaried worker. . . . As a non-salaried worker, do not forget that your pay could be withheld.
>
> (Gavin, sound crew, film and television)

An aspect of Gavin's orientation to practice that framed his meaning-making (his disposition) involves him internalising these cultural practices of the sector. In this way, he and others reproduce those practices and norms. After all, meeting expectations set up by cultural norms and practices is a matter of knowing how to continue in the specific social practices; we act 'into' the social circumstances into which we must fit our action (Shotter, 1993). Individual non-permanent workers have little or no power to act otherwise. That non-permanent workers operate without any form of collective bargaining in a highly competitive, fast-moving sector, is a powerful reason why practices that sanction poor conditions, continue.

In addition to the dynamic interplay of dispositions, affordances and practices in an industry sector, there are the affordances and practices common across non-permanent work. These include late payment, poor rates of pay and non-payment. It is these experiences, which many of our interviewees spoke of, that engender the discourse of precariousness of the non-permanent worker who is always at risk. For those who are using non-permanent work as a form of transition to permanent work, the discourses of precariousness often play out. For example, Faris, aged 32 at the time of interview, was working in the security line before he left to take up a work-cum-study position to pursue a diploma in the construction industry. The job did not materialise when his new employer opted to retain him as a worker at a lower pay and did not send him for studies. As an interim measure, he took on a despatch job with a subcontractor that provided delivery services to a restaurant chain while applying for permanent positions. However, most jobs offered less than $1 500, which was unacceptable to him. The very restaurant chain that he supported offered him a full-time position at $1 100–1 200, which also came with wider responsibilities, as he had to cover island-wide delivery. Securing a job with a higher basic pay is important to him, as he is trying to apply for a Housing Development Board loan for his flat. It has been almost a year since he started his job search, and his current interim job adds little to his resume, as employers even ask if he might moonlight as a despatch rider if they were to take him. He is worried about his job prospects, as he is 'already 32', and no one employs him. Faris's disposition of seeking to improve both his income and his educational qualifications in taking the risk in leaving security and moving to the construction industry illustrates the relation between disposition, expectations and affordances in a context. That the construction company did not fulfil its promise of sending him for studies, opting instead to retain him at a lower paid rate is an example of an affordance that Faris has no control over. His decision to move to a despatch job to secure high income so he can buy a Housing Development Board flat is one that places priority on putting a secure roof over his head. He is caught in tension between what the job-market offers him, the requirements of getting a housing loan and securing meaningful well-paid work. Dispositions are enacted through the resources (such as meta-knowledge of systems and sectors, their norms and discourses, networks to contribute to learning and accessing work, a strong self-narrative) available to the individual. At the age of 32 in the Singaporean context, where benefits accrue to those who work (an aspect of his context), Faris has reason to be worried about his future, with no visible access to the resources he needs to turn around his situation. This seeming lack of access is a result of the affordances in the contexts he lives and works in.

The lived experience of low-wage workers such as Faris combine the discourses of choice (contingent workers) and being at risk (precious workers), as discussed in Chapter 1. For those who chose non-permanent work because of the larger take home pay, it was not necessarily a choice of 'free-will'. Rather, this group of non-permanent workers was constantly managing the boundaries between non-permanent work and permanent work as they grew tired of the perpetual struggle to maintain a flow of income and turned their attention to seeking permanent work. Contextual affordances such as policies governing permanent work and the lack of policy governing non-permanent work permeate the experience of non-permanent work for those engaged in peripheral work, as well as those in the more 'professional' occupations. Market forces that use labour as a flexible commodity are at work in creating and reproducing these conditions, that those with limited resources (e.g. language, knowing systems, meta-knowledge of sectors, extensive networks, etc.) struggle to become free of, whatever their disposition.

As shown in Chapter 3, the disposition of a non-permanent worker mediates his/her perception of learning affordances within their contexts, their ability to 'see' opportunities and their agency in utilising them. The capabilities of the non-permanent worker are another of the dimensions in the integrated practices model, which also contribute to the non-permanent worker's abilities to 'see' possibilities and negotiate affordances to their advantage where this is possible.

Capabilities

A range of capabilities that non-permanent workers require were introduced in Chapter 2, such as developing a strong self-narrative, being able to position oneself in the market, being a shapeshifter a constant learner and, of course, the need for strong craft capabilities, depending on the quality of the work being undertaken. Such examples point to the broader capabilities in Figure 5.1, namely, crafting, learning-to-learn and having entrepreneurial capabilities. These are not single sets of capabilities or skills, but are enacted and learnt on the job as integrated wholes. In this section, we delve deeper into what is meant by capabilities and the integrated whole of enacted capabilities.

Capabilities are far more than skills. Skills are often considered in relation to technical knowledge, skills and attitudes aligned to human capital requirements (Hinchliffe, 2013). Sen (1993) looks beyond the human capital perspective of skills, considering capability development as central to human well-being, which we can extrapolate to being central to occupational well-being (Hinchliffe, 2013). Capabilities, according to Sen (1993), are about values, social engagement, intellect and performance, which provide *opportunities* to function, act differently in our environment(s) (Owen, 2017) and create new sets of relations (Hager, 2002 in those environments. To consider capabilities in relation to occupations, Winch (2010, in Hinchliffe, 2013) argues that occupations are more than task-related skills and techniques;

> occupations includes broader-based abilities relating to the planning, communicating and coordination of work, the deployment of systematic knowledge (both technical and theoretical if needs be) and finally a series of normative dispositions including 'the ability to take responsibility for one's work, to develop personal characteristics of commitment to moral values, and to take responsibility for the consequences of the practice of one's occupation in a wider social and political context' (Winch, 2010, pp. 73–74).
>
> (Hinchliffe, 2013, p. 62)

Capability, then is about being and becoming a member of a particular occupation. It encompasses working with knowledge and experience to interpret/make meaning, justify and explain; it involves agency exercised through autonomy and responsibility, moral values and orientation to the practices of the occupation (Winch, 2010) or what we refer to as dispositions (orientation to practice through linking meaning, participation and action (Bloomer & Hodkinson, 2000). However, for the non-permanent worker, capability is more than the occupational capabilities; these capabilities are entwined in learning-to-learn and entrepreneurial capabilities, as discussed in Chapter 2. This is what we refer to as the integrated whole of enacted capabilities. It is what constitutes performance.

For example, Ashely, whose story was told in Chapters 2, 3 and 4, was involved in a programme that was excellent for developing technical capabilities at a specific theatre, but did not expose him to others in the industry. His entrepreneurial capabilities, so important in gaining a continuous flow of work, remained undeveloped, despite the fact that he was seen as a promising practitioner. His purposeful, contained disposition in the context of a single theatre left him with limited access to resources with which to make meaning of the recruitment practices of the sector he worked in and to make sense of how to learn about these processes and practices. Without these capabilities or exposure to their enactment by others, and access to resources to position himself as a freelancer, continuing as a freelancer was not possible for him, resulting in him finding a permanent job in the shipping industry.

Adult educators work in a highly competitive and segmented market. One segment is the consultants working directly with companies. These are the non-permanent workers who perhaps best fit the discourses of contingent work where choice and a good income are considered to be part of the package. Yet when we look at Xavier's story, there are elements of his being a 'contingent worker', just as there are elements of the precarity of non-permanent work in his story, albeit that the precarity is qualitatively different than that experienced by the low wage, casual worker. Xavier became a consultant when his company closed. However, his entry was not abrupt; he was already doing training for his department, the company and the company subsidiaries as part of his work in that company. He was well positioned within the sector and in his own narrative – 'I was already so-called, a pretty competent trainer' (Xiaver, adult educator-consultant). Xavier's disposition was purposeful and broad, mediating his meaning-making of experiences and the contexts he lived and worked in, contributing to his strong self-narrative and learning and development. He recounts that the first skills he picked up once he was consulting were costing and budgeting. In addition be reflected on additional skills he developed, such as managing multiple stakeholders.

> The other skill is I have to be always on the lookout, what's happened behind me. Because nobody is going to look out for you. So when that happened, beyond just training as a trainer now, facilitator, you also have to watch out what happened to the management and colleagues of the trainee. Because they may join in or when training, the trainee may spread the news to the management. So I became much, much more aware of the environment, not just on the trainee.
>
> (Xiaver, adult educator-consultant)

What is interesting about this account is that this ability to see the whole picture, the impact of his training activity up and down the line, and his awareness of the environment are not only part of his disposition (his orientation to his practice), where he is linking meaning, participation and action, but have become part of how Xavier positions himself as he works. Disposition, context and his evolving capabilities are evident in this statement, as is not only the craft of facilitation but of client management and positioning of self. These are entrepreneurial capabilities being exercised in everyday practices as a consultant trainer. How does Xavier learn all this? From his account, it is through trial and error, the making of mistakes and feedback from customers and associates. He also has a small group of people he shares with who he 'perceive[s] as someone who has more experience and someone who is willing to tell me what I went wrong, these are my mentors'. Sometimes, this group is widened to include friends of friends and contacts from other sectors. Having both close networks and extended networks is important for learning and gaining work and is evidence of the broadness of his disposition.

> Why do we invite these people? Three reasons. First reason: They are friends' friends; Second reason: We have potential projects in those areas; and the third reason is that we purposely want to enlarge our knowledge. It was intentional. The primary aim is to learn the trick of the trade. Content knowledge, and also maybe some cultural behaviour. The F&B people will never say no or bad things about what happened. And the medical people are always very direct to the point.
>
> (Xavier, adult educator-consultant)

Meta-knowledge is being used here as part of Xavier's meaning-making, as in the previous quote about awareness of his environment, in the awareness and knowledge of different cultural mores across occupational groups and sectors. The smooth flow of Xavier's integrated enactment of entrepreneurial, craft and learning-to-learn capabilities is perhaps why he gains some 90 per cent of his work through client referrals. Despite a seemingly good life as a consultant, Xavier's fears of potential precarity relate to no longer being relevant in his market, given the constant changes in processes and technology.

Xavier's experience contrasts with that of Daisy, a life skills adult educator who has been working freelance for some two years. Unlike Xavier, Daisy did not enter freelancing with well-established networks. After two years, Daisy was still trying to find out which 'particular market' she could do well in and reported needing to try out different sectors. Daisy's experience is not just a matter of her disposition (purposeful and contained), her linking of meaning, participation and action, which at the point of interview appeared to be nascent, but is also related to the context of her work. Xavier's work in quality control systems in manufacturing is a highly tangible product and comes with sets of pre-established, international standards. Life skills are much more amorphous, harder to market and comparatively valued far less than the products that Xavier offers. Daisy has much more work to do than Xavier at positioning herself. Her self-narrative is particularly important in these circumstances, yet it is one of uncertainty, 'but to pinpoint a particular market now is still quite early . . . I'm quite new and [need to] try out different sectors' (Daisy, adult educator, life skills). Her negotiation of the landscape she works within requires resources such as knowledge of the sector, its norms and discourses, networks to contribute to her own learning and accessing work and a strong self-narrative that enables her to be resilient and to position herself, yet if necessary to be flexible about the markets she works in and across. The contained element of her disposition, on the one hand, limited her access to resources that could assist her development of entrepreneurial capabilities, and, on the other hand, the context of her work provided no support and limited access to such resources.

The integrated enactment of craft, entrepreneurial and learning-to-learn capabilities is also evident in peripheral work (task-based with limited discretionary power). In Chapters 2 and 4, the stories of Borhan and Nazri provide illustrative examples. Borhan wanted to run his own kebab stall but struggled with numeracy; he did not perceive this to be an issue. Nazri, a furniture removalist who wanted to gain higher-quality assignments but did not have information about the range of opportunities in the sector, could indicate that it is not so much the lack of capabilities – which can be developed – that is an issue, but an orientation to their practice, perhaps arising from their socio-economic circumstances and life stories that contributes to limiting their opportunities. But this is only one aspect of the picture. It is easy to place responsibility for development solely on the individual (more akin to a human capital perspective). However, when analysed from the social practice perspective that is inclusive of the social relations of production, ready access to such resources is also required as part of affordances for individuals to be able to 'see' possibilities.

Chapter 2 discussed particular capabilities and their subsets. Figure 5.2 provides a general set of capabilities that are interconnected and embedded in each other, as indicated by the relationship connections between these dimensions. It should be noted that the capabilities named are not to be seen as definitive nor as a list. The mediating dimensions of disposition and context to the development and evolution of capabilities over time captures the integratedness of all the dimensions in the integrated practice model. All of these dimensions contribute to the journey of the non-permanent worker.

Journeys

In the integrated practice model, journey refers to future potential learning, career journeys and pathways of the non-permanent worker. Journey takes into account the interplay between all the dimensions of the integrated practice model. Elements of these dimensions include biographies, values (Fuller & Unwin, 2017), sense-making and the varying quality of the individual's engagement (Billett & Somerville, 2004) in different practices in different contexts. '[T]here is an interdependence between what is afforded individuals by social practice, and how they elect to engage with and construct what is afforded

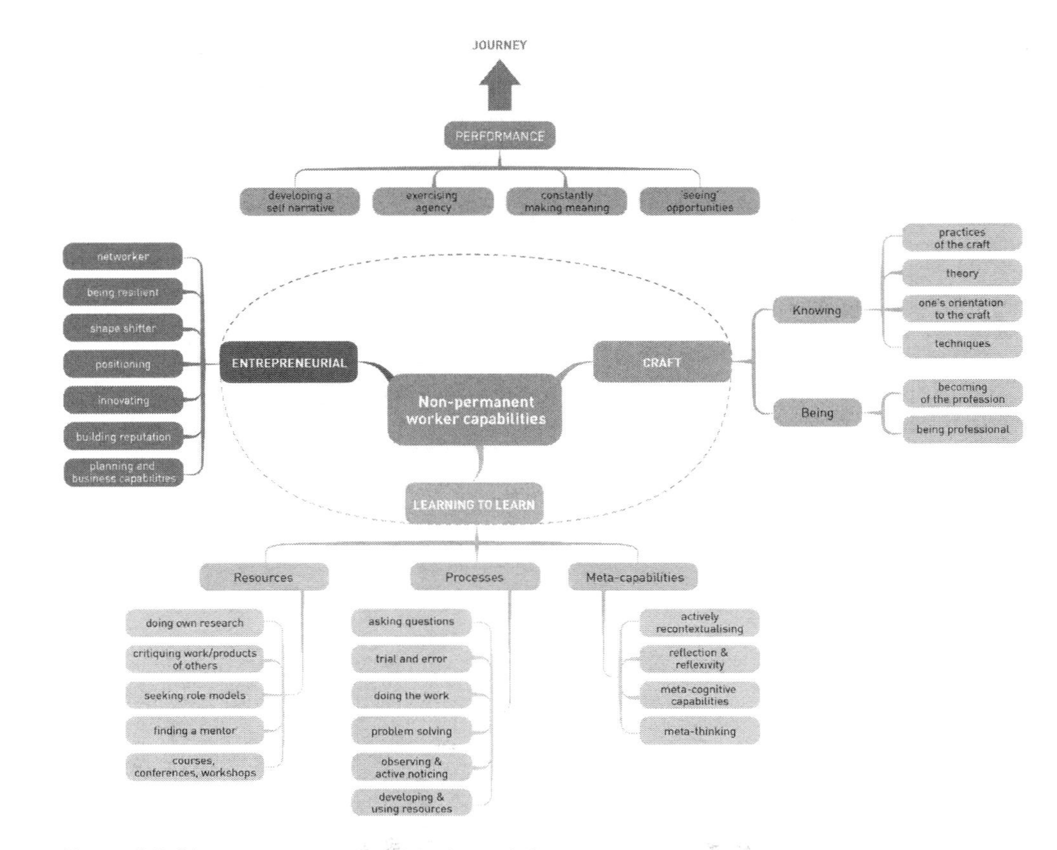

Figure 5.2 Non-permanent workers' capabilities

them by the social practice' (Billett, Barker, & Hernon-Tinning, 2004). The non-permanent worker is in many ways a job-crafter (Wrzesniewski & Dutton, 2001;), depending on the affordances in their work and their sector. Affordances and the disposition of the non-permanent worker interact dynamically with social narratives about occupational practices, societal discourses such as what is considered as success, gendered roles, team and work narratives. All of which are integral to learning; to how the non-permanent worker makes sense or figures their world (Holland et al., 1998), and constructs meaning that reinforces or challenges their orientation to practice (Bloomer & Hodkinson, 2000). Knowing, experience, and identity as a product of the social world is explained by Leontvev in Billett and Somerville (2004) as follows:

> The construction of concepts, procedures and objects is shaped by what individuals have experienced through their lives (Vygotsky, 1978; Scribner, 1985; Rogoff, 1990). Moreover, that experience is mediated by individuals' knowing, knowledge and sense of identity with its attendant dispositions and values that mediate that experience (Bloomer & Hodkinson, 2000; Hodkinson & Hodkinson, in press). These identities and subjectivities are therefore seen as being a product of the social world but appropriated by individuals in particular ways and for particular purposes.
>
> (Leontyev, 1981). (Billett & Somerville, 2004, p. 311)

Billett and Somerville note the dynamic interplay between what, in the integrated practice model, we call dispositions, and context (the social world). Leontyev's notion of appropriation of the product of individuals' social worlds is what, in this book, we call the embeddedness of context. Xiaver, for example, exhibited a strong sense of agency and identity, positioning himself seemingly unproblematically as a consultant whose work was highly valued. His sense making of the experiences of providing training where managers may drop in heightened his ability to manage multiple stakeholders, an important learning point and an indelible part of his expertise. His negotiation between self and social world dynamically contributed to expertise, positioning, agency and identity, and thus to his journey as a non-permanent worker. A contrasting example is Nazri (furniture removalist) and his limited exposure to industry knowledge, resources such as learning-to-learn through being reflexive, or what Billett and Somerville (2004) might refer to as the dynamic interplay between context, identity, agency and learning, contributing to limited pathways for him. The processes of thinking, acting and learning at and through work are not separate, but aspects of a process that contributes to learning identities directing intentional thought and action, monitoring knowing and how the individual engages with, makes meaning and appropriates social narratives (Billett & Somerville, 2004). As everyone's experiences and biography are different, so too is their meaning-making, their construction of concepts, procedures and ways of meeting needs. Occupational identities are a part of the social world, but are appropriated variously by different individuals. Likewise, being a 'free-lancer', a 'consultant' or a 'casual worker' involves a process of appropriating these identities from the social world according to the non-permanent worker's life history. Their construction of their self-narrative is a constant process of negotiation, depending on biography, experiences, disposition and context of the non-permanent worker. At a point in time, a non-permanent worker may hold a disposition that is, for example, purposeful and contained, such as Daisy. However, with access to resources and support, she could develop a disposition of being purposeful and broad. The context of her work as an adult educator – working in a fragmented market – and her speciality of teaching (lifes kills such as literacy, which is poorly remunerated) limit such possibilities. Working as an adult educator can be lonely work, unlike in the creative sector, where teamwork is common. Her negotiation between her disposition, life-history and her social world can become self-reinforcing of her nascent self-narrative or potentially develop into a broader and stronger self-narrative should she have access to support and resources she can use to make meaning of her experiences. Journeys are mediated by the lived realities of a non-permanent workers' context, disposition, life history and their capabilities.

These processes and the enactment of evolving identities involve social interactions which contribute to changing practices or to reproducing existing practices. For example, in the film and television sector, the discourse is that the less you complain about the long hours and the poor conditions ('the more pain you swallow'), the more jobs you will get ('the more popular you will be'). The reality of the role in different assignments and across them and the degree of agency enacted forge an identity with practice (Billett & Somerville, 2004), another example of the complex relations between the dimensions of integrated practice and their mediation of journeys.

Thus, to understand the varied journeys of non-permanent workers requires a close analysis of the contexts in which non-permanent workers work, their disposition, their biographies and their capabilities and the elements that constitute these dimensions of integrated practice. Journeys are mediated not only by the dynamic interplay between context, identity, agency and learning between self and social world but also by what resources the non-permanent worker has access to, their consumption of these resources, their exercise of agency and their self-narrative, which give 'permission' to be in and of an occupation as a non-permanent worker. It is very clear that those working in peripheral occupations have access to far fewer resources, including language, exposure to meta-thinking and meta-knowledge. These learning-to-learn capabilities inhibit access to possibilities. Exceptions such as Zac (rigger, technical theatre), who learnt complex mathematics through his own resources, exist and illustrate possibilities. What we learn from such exceptions is the importance of self-narrative and how this informs disposition in relation to context. Zac was exposed to possibilities through the type of work he was engaged in and the team processes that were part of the work design, whereas Borhan and Nazri were working in contexts that did not enable access to 'seeing' other possibilities; each largely worked alone, albeit within a loose community of similar workers, with similar life experiences.

Journeys are mediated by the complex relations between the dimensions and elements of the integrated practice model.

Conclusion

The power of the integrated practice model to explain the experience, the work and the learning of the non-permanent worker is considerable. It provides not singular explanations based on particular phenomena, but captures the complexity of the world of the non-permanent worker. For analytical purposes, we have discussed each dimension separately, but always linked each dimension to others. The model enables an explanation of non-permanent workers as a segment of the labour force and, importantly, enables examination of industry sectors and individuals. Policy-makers involved not only with workforce development, but with industry development, must see the dimensions holistically and in relation to each other when considering interventions. For example, the importance in the creative sector of having challenging assignments to develop expertise indicates a particular vision for the sector. Without such opportunities, the sector will not grow its local expertise. For educational institutions/private training providers, providing pre-service and continuous professional development, their educators and others involved with professional development, the integrated practice model provides a guide for curriculum design and consideration of delivery of learning. For other parties in a particular industry ecosystem that engages significant numbers of non-permanent workers, the model offers a framework for working collegially in developing the sector and the expertise in the sector. Although, not explicitly present in the model, the model assumes that everyone has potential and deserves opportunities to develop to that potential. Access to quality work is critically important for learning and development, just as the experiences afforded through educational institutions, be it for pre-service or continuing professional development, are also important. The next chapter considers the role of educational institutions, curriculum designers and facilitators of learning along with continuous professional development for non-permanent workers.

References

Bakhtin, M. M. (1981). *The dialogic imagination: Four essays by M.M. Bahktin* (M. E. Holquist, Ed.). Austin: University of Texas Press.

Billett, S. (2001). *Learning in the workplace*. Sydney: Allen and Unwin.

Billett, S., Barker, M., & Hernon-Tinning, B. (2004). Participatory practices at work. *Pedagogy, Culture and Society, 12*(2), 233–258. Retrieved from https://doi.org/10.1080/14681360400200198

Billett, S., & Somerville, M. (2004). Transformations at work: Identity and learning. *Studies in Continuing Education, 26*(2), 309–326. Retrieved from https://doi.org/10.1080/158037042000225272

Bloomer, M., & Hodkinson, P. (2000). Learning careers: Continuity and change in young people's dispositions to learning. *British Educational Research Journal, 26*(5), 583–597. Retrieved from https://doi.org/10.1080/01411920020007805

Bound, H. (2007). *Institutional collaboration, learning and context: A case study of Tasmanian information technology institutions*. Doctoral thesis, University of Tasmania, Tasmania, Australia.

Bound, H., & Rushbrook, P. (2015). Problematising workplace learning. In H. Bound & P. Rushbrook (Eds.), *Towards an expanded understanding of workplace learning*. Singapore: Institute for Adult Learning.

Cetina, K. K. (2007). Culture in global knowledge societies: Knowledge cultures and epistemic cultures. *Interdisciplinary Science Reviews, 32*(4), 361–375. Retrieved from https://doi.org/10.1002/9780470996744.ch5

Chappell, C., Rhodes, C., Solomon, N., Tennant, M., & Yates, L. (2003). *Reconstructing the lifelong learner: Pedagogy and identity in individual, organisational and social change* (Routledge Falmer, Ed.). London. Retrieved from https://doi.org/10.4324/9780203464410

Dall'Alba, G., & Sandberg, J. (2006). Unveiling professional development: A critical review of stage models. *Review of Educational Research, 76*(3), 383–412. Retrieved from https://doi.org/10.3102/00346543076003383

Eteläpleto, A. (2015). The role of work identity and agency in workplace learning. In *Towards a new understanding of workplace learning: The context of Singapore* (pp. 36–53). Singapore: Institute for Adult Learning.

Fuller, A., & Unwin, L. (2017). Job crafting and identity in low-grade work: How hospital porters redefine the value of their work and expertise. *Vocations and Learning, 10*, 307–324.

Hager, P. (2002). The conceptualisation and measurement of learning at work. In X. Beckett & P. Hager (Eds.), *Life, work and learning: practice in postmodernity*, Volume 14 of Routledge International Studies in the Philosophy of education, (Chapter 14). London: Routledge.

Hinchliffe, G. (2013). Workplace identity, transition and the role of learning. In P. Gibbs (Ed.), *Learning, work and practice: New understandings* (pp. 51–69). Dordrecht: Springer.

Holland, D., Lachicott, W., Skinner, D., & Cain, C. (1998). *Identity and agency in cultural worlds*. Cambridge, MA: Harvard University Press.

Malepart, A. (2005). *The feature film market in Singapore*. Canada: The Department of Canadian Heritage, Trade Routes Program.

Owen, C. (2017, March). *Enhancing learning in the workplace*. Institute for Adult Learning Roundtable paper, Singapore.

Schatzki, T. R. (2012). A primer on practices: Theory and research. In J. Higgs, R. Barnett, S. Billett, M. Hutchings, & F. Trede (Eds.), *Practice-based education: Perspectives and strategies* (pp. 13–26). Rotterdam: Sense Publishers. Retrieved from https://doi.org/10.1007/978-94-6209-128-3

Sen, A. (1993). Capability and well-being. In M. Nussbaum & A. Sen (Eds.), *Quality of life* (pp. 30–53). Oxford: Clarendon Press.

Shotter, J. (1993). *Conversational realities: Constructing life through language*. London: Sage Publications.

Wertsch, J. (1998). *Mind as action*. New York: Oxford University Press.

White, L. (2001). 'Effective governance' through complexity thinking and management science. *Systems Research and Behavioral Science, 18*(3), 241.

Wrzesniewski, A., & Dutton, J. E. (2001). Crafting a job: Revisioning employees as active crafters of their work. *Academy of Management Review, 26*(2), 179–201. Retrieved from https://doi.org/10.5465/AMR.2001.4378011.

Chapter 6

Using the spaces of NPW for learning, curriculum design and delivery type

What does integrated practice mean for educators in educational institutions and their practitioners (lecturers, trainers, facilitators, curriculum/instructional designers and so on)? In addressing this question, the authors challenge educational institutions and training providers to design and deliver learning and the enacted curriculum, not as separate pieces of a puzzle, but as an integrated whole, that is, to design, deliver and facilitate learning as integrated practice. There are whole sectors where the predominant form of work is non-permanent; this has been the case for many decades now, yet educational institutions cling to what has always been done. For an unknown future, learners need capabilities that enable them to:

- work across boundaries (disciplinary, professional, sites, forms of work etc.)
- to be curious, confident, capable learners
- to have strong craft capabilities (beyond technical skills) and, increasingly, various aspects of entrepreneurial capabilities.

Rather than individual sets of competencies (such as in competency-based training and human capital approaches) taught as separate from each other, there is a need to develop *understanding* of the work and industry landscape, a sense of being and becoming entrepreneurial and of being and belonging to a particular occupation. These understandings and senses are essential for non-permanent workers as they juggle operating a business, learning how to recognise and act on opportunities, being a valued professional who is masterful in their craft, a constant learner, and positioning themselves to gain a continuous flow of work and suitable income.

For those in educational institutions designing curricula, it is always useful to start at the end by asking the question, what is it we want our graduates to *be* and *become*? The authors will not be addressing this question in specific detail for various occupations in sectors where non-permanent work is the predominant form of engagement. What we will be doing in this chapter is illustrating how the integrated practice model can be used to address the important question: what is it we want our graduates to be and become? Before doing this, it is useful to understand current, commonly held beliefs and understandings of learning that get in the way of integrated practice.

Why the need to think differently about learning?

Occupational practices constitute an embodied understanding of practice which, when understood in certain ways, will be developed in that way (Dall'Alba & Sandberg, 1996; Sandberg, 2001; Sandberg & Pinnington, 2009). If educational institutions ignore non-permanent work or see it only as a series of stepping stones towards permanent work, then the development of the being and becoming of non-permanent workers will not be part of their repertoire, let alone a consideration in designing learning as integrated practice. Previous chapters have revealed the complexity of the entrepreneurial, occupational practices and learning of non-permanent workers; learning to be and become a non-permanent worker is far more than learning just sets of attributes, knowledge and skill. It entails a long-term process of development for survival as well as for personal and professional growth. Thus, addressing the question of what is it we want our graduates to be and become entails a deep understanding on the part of the educational institution and its practitioners of the work, the work arrangements in the sector and ways of being of an occupation that move well beyond technical competence. As indicated in Chapter 5, identity as a particular occupation involves processes of and what is it to be and become. The varied, changing spaces the non-permanent worker inhabits require strong entrepreneurialism intrinsic to a sense of being part of occupational ways of being. This sense of identity is likely to increase engagement, which in turn provides further opportunities to develop capabilities and grow. For example, Ashely felt he was not part of the social interaction associated with being a non-permanent worker in technical theatre, nor was he plugged into the social relations of production occurring through non-permanent networking in this sector. Consequently, he left for a permanent job in shipping. Xiaver (adult educator consultant in Lean and Six Sigma) had a strong sense of being engaged in and a part of the social practices related to his work in lean production and Six Sigma that he carried over from his permanent work. His core narrative demonstrates a strong sense of being a part of promulgating the expertise in his line of work. Daisy (adult educator), on the other hand, expressed an uncertain sense of being part of a field of expertise; she had not yet found her 'place', her niche, after two years of trying various markets. Her core narrative as a freelance adult educator reflects this; it is one of uncertainty and is not well developed. Being connected to a field of expertise is a dimension of the non-permanent core narrative that encompasses everyday contributions they make to their occupational practices; the recognition and support to others, in part, depend on the institutional and individual stakeholder perspectives on teaching and learning.

In the previous chapter, learning was defined as a process contributing to an increased capability to act differently in the environment (Owen, 2017) and in the process creating new sets of relations in those environments (Hager, 2004). What this means in practices where learners are involved with moving iteratively, across and between work and educational institutions is that as individuals develop capabilities, grow in confidence and have an increasing sense of being part of a particular occupation, they respond differently to and in the environments they are part of and engaged in. Over time, greater initiative, agency and responsibility are exercised. A growing sense of becoming contributes to responding to and interacting with the mental models active in a particular environment in more meaningful ways, including perhaps to question them, to critique in order to innovate. The sense of becoming is part of growing expertise, contributing to different, more purposeful engagement with and use of tools that are part of work, be they physical tools or mental (ways of thinking, ideas, mental models). Such change is often subtle, but if supported in meaningful ways is exciting to see, be it in a work, educational institution environment or both. Not all experiences are supported in ways that realise the potential for learning and development described here. Learning and development are mediated by a complex dynamic between learner disposition, biography, the situated context of the work and of the educational institution and of industry and national practices and cultural ways of being. Educators and those engaged in supporting learning in a range of environments cannot afford to remain ignorant of this complex dynamic.

Beliefs and assumptions about learning held and practiced by various stakeholders, both individual and institutional also contribute to learning experiences (positive and negative). Learning is inherently contextual. Acting differently, creating new sets of relations in an environment, implies that learning is not just that which takes place inside the head of an individual; nor is it a change in behaviour. Rather, learning is about change in the collective sense and is embedded in the social relations *between* people and artefacts, situated in places and spaces. Understanding learning as *only* cognitive – that which takes place inside an individual's head – is problematic, denying the social nature of learning through interaction with others, texts and other artefacts within which are embedded historical norms and practices that mediate our thinking, our mental models, our interactions, our practices. When learning is claimed to be a change in behaviour, this assumes we are interested only in demonstrated behaviour, not in the individual and collective sense-making, commitment, ethics and values, identity, connections and so on. Identity and agency are integral to acting differently in and relating to our environment. Instead, we can consider learning as an activity of being and becoming and incorporate what is useful from various theoretical perspectives. For example, Lemke uses an ecological perspective to explain the relation between context and mind:

> As people are participating in everyday practice they are functioning in microecologies, material environments endowed with cultural meanings; acting and being acted on directly or with the mediation of physical-cultural

> tools and cultural-material systems of words, signs, and other symbolic values. In these activities, 'things' contribute to solutions every bit as much as 'minds' do; information and meaning is coded into configurations of objects, material constraints, and possible environmental options, as well as in verbal routines and formulas or 'mental' operations.
>
> (1997, p. 38)

Lemke (1997) argues that biography, history and culture act *in* everyday activity and thus mediate learning. The dynamics of any 'ecosystem' depends on the networks that link, couple and connect this element with that and make this interdependent with that. Not only does Lemke highlight the interconnectness of context, people, their biographies in particular contexts and spaces within these contexts, as they interact with and engage artefacts. He also highlights that learning – 'contributing to solutions' – involves 'things' and minds, language and the affordances of a particular context. We would add that spaces also contribute to learning. For example, the community of practice literature implies that participation and engagement takes place within spaces that participants *belong* to. All of this tells us that it is critical to ensure opportunities for learning in the context, spaces and practices of an occupation. When that context is more often than not inclusive of non-permanent work, then how to *be*, how to relate and learning to act in the context, spaces and being a part of the practices of a community of practice are not just important, but critical.

Questioning current practices in educational institutions

Educational institutions have historical practices that are deeply associated with the particular institution. Universities, for example, typically use mass lectures and tutorials as forms of delivery. The focus is not on the learners and learning, but on delivering knowledge as a static product. Private education providers, so ubiquitous in the vocational and continuing education market, are motivated by profit and for this reason may choose to use similar traditional methods. It is common in educational institutions to see a divide between theory and practice, institutionalised into timetables (for example, theory on Tuesday morning and the practice/laboratory/simulator etc. on Wednesday afternoon). The theory-practice divide is also evident in documentation found in many competency-based training sets of standards under separate headings such as 'underpinning knowledge' and 'performance' or 'skills'. Such arrangements assume knowledge is static. The dualism of the theory-practice divide fails to capture the holistic nature of practice and the constant construction and co-construction of knowledge. Knowledge is culturally and socially shaped (Beckett & Hager, 2002) and is embodied holistically in practices (Lave & Wenger, 1991) and spaces. Knowledge is important in the making of workplace judgements that are socially and politically shaped and are about acting in the world and going through the consequences of those judgements (Beckett & Hager, 2002). Workplace practical judgement often starts with a judgement about what the problem is. Beckett and Hager (2002) note that a significant part of developing workplace practical judgement is learning to identify and respond to problems as a relatively autonomous practitioner. Practitioners look for patterns in workflow, peaks and troughs, standards, nature of interactions and so on (Beckett & Hager, 2002; Eteläpleto, 2008) that are particular to a space and its practices. Thus, the workplace is an important space for learning theory implicit in vocational [occupational] practices (Billett, 2001), seamlessly bringing together human reasoning, will and emotion, that is, 'cognitive, conative and emotive capacities of humans are all typically involved in workplace practical judgement' (Beckett & Hager, 2002, p. 177). In order to create spaces for holistically learning to be and become, teaching and learning practices require a critical reflexivity (Hinchliffe, 2013) on the part of educators, their institutions and their learners.

The provision by educational institutions of iterative movement between classroom learning experiences and being in work settings and spaces is important in developing the capability to make appropriate judgements and to act appropriately in the occupational practices of the non-permanent worker. Iterative movement between the spaces of practising an occupation as a permanent and as a non-permanent worker contribute to the pre-service student's sense of being and becoming.

Occupations have their own historically constituted roots and traditions, which have shaped their cultures and styles of working as well as the habits of those people working in the field (Eteläpelto, 2008). These historically constituted roots and traditions are embedded in the day to day practices of the non-permanent worker, which is why entrepreneurship and learning-to-learn and generic capabilities, for example, look a little different from one occupation to another. Within the film and television sector, differences in the specifics of learning-to-learn and deepening craft that also impact on entrepreneurial capabilities such as positioning of the non-permanent worker is described by Bound, Rushbrook and Sivalingham (2013):

> A script becomes an artefact for dialogue by working through it with the project team and/ or producer, for example, discussing how the lighting or grip work will be done. Problem solving how to achieve a certain effect with limited budget (such as a suicide jump from a high building) and sharing with another camera operator techniques for using a new camera are examples of work providing affordances for learning. More mundane examples include a new assistant director learning from experienced others how to complete paper work, thus learning about the process of production work. New equipment on a set is an opportunity for all roles to learn about it and its possibilities. Different genres develop specific skills. For example, live television events demand effective teamwork as pre- and post-production crews as well as distribution personnel work together in

> a high pressure environment. For a video editor, news training trains him to watch footage at a fast speed. Documentaries require a more deliberate and creative approach, generally developed by working with overseas production houses.
>
> (p. 35)

So the educator in educational institutions should seek to understand the social relations between the learner, their practical work activities and social and cultural relations in the workplace (Evans et al., 2006). To make the most of iterative movement between different sites or teams in real work settings requires an appreciation that workplace learning brings together multiple aspects of theory, practice and being and becoming. As learning in workplaces is embedded in social relations in the workplace, the content of what is learnt in different workplaces differs as does the ways in which learning and affordances for learning are embedded in the social relations in different work settings, occupations, and industry practices and ways of being. This is a consideration of the context of integrated practice, but implicitly it is also a consideration of the learners' orientation to practice and how they interpret and use the capabilities learnt, embodying learning from a range of experiences. Over time, such an approach enables evolvement into a more finessed, embodied understanding of the occupational capabilities as learners 'become' and constantly develop (Dall'Alba & Sandberg, 2006) as a non-permanent worker who belongs to a particular occupation.

Educational institutions frequently use the metaphor of transfer, assuming that what is learnt in the institution is seamlessly applied once the graduate is engaged in work. The transfer metaphor fails to recognise the contextualised, socially constructed nature of knowledge. In fact, a great deal of learning takes place in order to make sense of the different settings, requiring a reconsideration of what has been learnt previously in order to apply what has been learnt. Lobato notes that processes involved include attunement to affordances and constraints in the work environment; and that 'transfer' is distributed across mental, material, social and cultural planes. Skills and knowledge have to be developed and changed, as they are operationalised in the culture of new workplaces. Furthermore, it is not the skills and knowledge that develop, but the whole person, as s/he adjusts, with greater or lesser success, to working in different environments, as Hager and Hodkinson (2011) have argued. That adjustment depends as much upon the receptive or expansive nature of the new work setting, as upon the prior experiences, biographies and circumstances that workers bring to it.

Put differently, the processes entailed involve a series of knowledge recontextualisations (see Evans, Guile, & Harris, 2009; Evans et al., 2010; Evans & Guile, 2012) that can be significantly helped or hindered by the actions and dispositions of employers, co-workers, peers and practices in the spaces in which knowledge recontextualisation is required. Using the concept of recontextualisation concentrates on the ways in which different forms of knowledge are used and developed as people move between sites of learning and practice. All knowledge has a context in which it was originally generated. Contexts extend to the 'schools of thought', the traditions and norms of practice, the life experiences in which knowledge of different kinds is generated. For knowledge generated and practised in one context to be put to work in new contexts, it has to be recontextualised in ways that simultaneously engage with and change those practices, traditions and experiences.

This approach to recontextualisation has drawn on van Oers's (1998) idea that concepts integral to practice change as practice varies from one workplace to another. These notions have been substantially expanded to embrace the ways in which workers themselves change as they recontextualise concepts and practices. This is integral to how people think and feel their way into occupational and professional identities or think and feel their way beyond them and is highly significant for workers who move between workplaces as non-permanent workers. As non-permanent workers move between sites of practice, they think and feel their ways into occupational and social identities, necessitating different modes of knowledge re-contextualisation, as well as a capacity to develop and maintain 'mobility capital', or the ability to transition from one job to another (Forrier, Sels, & Stynen, 2009). Knowledge re-contextualisation, including attitudes, values and beliefs, leads to longer-term and ongoing 'whole person' development in professional life, part of the process of 'becoming', highlighted by Hager and Hodkinson (2011).

We can deduce from the discussion so far that learning-to-learn is important, particularly so for non-permanent workers who need to be constant learners (Bound, Sadik, & Karmel, 2015; Pittaway & Cope, 2007; Rae, 2006). Scardamalia (2002) makes the point that many students have explicit strategies for memorisation, but lack strategies for learning for understanding. Contributing to this problem is that students have little idea of the strategic activity involved in learning, largely because teachers do this work, and it is invisible to them. There is a need for teachers, lecturers and trainers to shift from 'being the sole engineer of the learning process' to sharing this responsibility and providing space and resources for learners to develop strategies for learning-to-learn, for making sense of their experiences and their orientation to practice. Scardamalia's interest is in the co-construction of knowledge in online communities is in school settings, yet her observations are pertinent here.

> Ideas are seldom treated in isolation. They are systematically interconnected – one idea subsumes, contradicts, constrains or otherwise relates to a number of others. To gain understanding is to explore these interconnections and to drill deeper while rising above, to gain broader perspective. Successful knowledge building we may say, exhibits deep embedding, both as regards the embedding of ideas in larger conceptual structures and the embedding of ideas in the practices of the knowledge building community.

> Participants share responsibility for community knowledge in addition to individual achievement.
>
> (Scardamalia, 2002, p. 75)

Knowledge, however, is more than relations between ideas. Nonaka and Toyama (2003) suggest that knowledge is created in a spiral 'that goes through seemingly antithetical concepts such as order and chaos, micro and macro, part and whole, mind and body, tacit and explicit, self and other, deduction and induction and creativity and efficiency' (p. 2). It is not surprising, then, that some use the term know*ing* as indicative of the active process of knowledge construction within given contexts. Blackler (1995) proposes that what is important is knowing the cultural historical systems or contexts in which knowledge is generated.

> Knowing is analysed as an active process that is *mediated, situated, provisional, pragmatic and contested.* Rather than documenting the types of knowledge that capitalism currently demands the approach suggests that attention should be focused on the (culturally located) systems through which people achieve their knowing, on the changes that are occurring within such systems, and on the processes through which new knowledge may be generated.
>
> (Blackler, 1995, p. 1021)

Attention to the contexts of practices is thus important for the educator, as is knowing the experience and background of learners. Gordon Wells's spiral of knowing (1999) provides a model of the processes involved which the educator can use in designing learning. The spiral of knowing starts with understanding based on past experiences that are brought to the present experience; to this is added new information that comes from feedback as a result of action and responses from others and artefacts involved in the action. However, for the information to lead to enhanced understanding, it must be individually appropriated and transformed through knowledge building (Scardamalia & Bereiter, 2006). Knowledge building involves collaborative action in relation to the object of the activity through dialogue in which participants make sense of and evaluate new information, relate it to what they currently believe, critically discuss alternative interpretations and implications and test their ideas through some form of further action. Each cycle leads to an increase in both group and individual understandings (Wells, 2008). Learning, then, is a process involving successive cycles. Inquiry-based approaches in which students select their own objects for inquiry and take responsibility with the teacher for determining how to proceed, foster such learning. Given the importance of dialogue, it is also important to build a community of inquiry. This is not dissimilar to the practices of many non-permanent workers.

Table 6.1 summarises much of the discussion so far, identifying traditional understandings and practices in the left-hand column, and those that are reflective of the integrative practices model in the right-hand column.

Table 6.1 Traditional and integrated practices assumptions about teaching, learning and knowledge

Traditional assumptions	*Integrated practice assumptions*
Learning is teaching knowledge, skills, attitudes	Learning is embodied: learners learn to use their senses, feel know*ing* in their bodies The practices of a vocation/profession encompass particular ways of being and knowing
Learning is acquisition Learning is assumed to be cognitive and behavioural	Learning moves beyond participation (practices of a vocation/profession are learnt through participating and engaging in the vocational/professional practices) to be about being, becoming and belonging Learning is assumed to be constructivist and socio-culturally situated
Learning is a product, measured in behavioural standards or outcomes Learning is 'transferred' unproblematically from one setting to another	Learning is a process incorporating social, cultural and political dimensions resulting in new sets of relations in a setting. Thus, learning is not 'transferred' from one environment or setting to another. Learning is not measured but assessment is a process of judging holistic performance
Learning happens within the confines of the educational institution	Learning happens through doing the work and (for new entrants for example) through participating in iterative movement between the spaces of the educational institution and work
Learning is a lock-step process	Practices in context are complex, multiple and varied requiring complex understandings, interpretations and judgements that need to be built into learning experiences
Knowledge is static Knowledge is held by the 'experts'	Knowledge is dynamic, distributed across tools, sites and people. It is co-constructed by those participating in the practices of the vocation/profession. Know*ing* better captures learning as an active, co-constructed process
Theory and practice are institutionally separated (e.g. through timetabling practices of classroom and laboratory/simulation/skills practice sessions; in curriculum documentation, etc.)	Learning in various work settings in the industry is integrated into the total learning experience, recognising that theory and practice are not separate but enacted together and that learning is embodied
The educator must do the work of ensuring learners learn	Future practitioners must be constant learners, so they must know how to learn. Learning must be designed such that learners learn and take responsibility for the strategic work of learning-to-learn.

Applying an integrated practice approach requires considerable rethinking of much that is taken for granted in educational institutions today. Despite much exciting work being done by many innovative, passionate educators, their work is often siloed and rarely has institution-wide application. Universities, polytechnics/technical education institutes, departments of education, and vocational education and training national quality assurance agencies are large beasts, difficult to turn to change direction, but change they must. Such change requires moving well beyond rhetoric and patchwork innovations. For example, where there is an emphasis on examinations designed to encourage memorisation or outputs of answers structured in particular ways that are not necessarily reflective of the practices of an occupation, then current practices will remain fundamentally unchanged, despite any claims to the contrary.

The following section provides some quite specific suggestions for developing pre-service non-permanent workers in educational institutional settings. There is an important assumption in the suggestions offered, and that is that there is in place strong strategies for engagement with non-permanent workers and strong engagement with the sector by the relevant department in an educational institution or by the private for profit training provider. Additionally, the approaches outlined below assume iterative movement between work settings and an educational institution, not just a single period of time in a work setting at the end of a programme. This is discussed further, later in the chapter.

Developing pre-service, non-permanent workers in educational institutional settings

When addressing the question of how to develop pre-service non-permanent workers, again, it is necessary to return to the question: what is it the institution/training provider wants their graduate to be and become? As the previous section has indicated, it is imperative that there are strong relations with the sector and its employers in order to provide students with multiple opportunities over the period of their course to be a non-permanent practitioner in the sector. Models of delivery that include iterative movement between educational institution and work-sector settings are required to make the most of affordances for learning in, through and for work. Examples of placing three- to six-month internships at the end of a three-year qualification such as those we found in our research minimise developmental opportunities for all stakeholders concerned: learner, educators and workplace supervisors. Additionally, the purpose and outcomes of each iterative cycle between educational institution and industry needs to be clear for all stakeholders; apart from the benefits for developing craft, entrepreneurial and learning-to-learn capabilities, this can also help manage potential for exploitation of students as indicated by Bound, Rushbrook and Sivalingham (2013) in their report on non-permanent workers in the film and television sector in Singapore:

> There is also a widespread sentiment in the [research project] reference group that internships need to be more effectively planned and tailored to the demands of the industry. The current state of many internships includes the use of interns (unpaid or paid at $500 per month) being given full responsibility for projects, with no access to support or mentoring. Not only is this highly stressful for the interns, but also exploitative and unethical.
>
> (p. 28)

It is necessary to design the building of capabilities to be and become a particular occupation, across a whole program. A cyclical, developmental approach enables building of confidence and degrees of expertise. Integrating the embodiment of craft, learning-to-learn and having entrepreneurial capabilities is a creative process with many different possibilities. Table 6.2 provides a few examples of learning activities that integrate the development of craft, learning-to-learn and having entrepreneurial capabilities. There is no universal panacea to learning design; rather, the key is to be aware of how to make the most of different spaces and possibilities and NOT to conceive of craft, learning-to-learn and having entrepreneurial capabilities as separate sets of skills. An emphasis on different aspects such as learning-to-learn will vary according to institutional practices in different countries. Finland, for example, develops students' learning-to-learn capabilities and responsibility for continual development very early in the education system. In Singapore, the education system emphasises learning for examinations, so these students need time and lots of opportunities to develop their learning-to-learn capabilities and to be aware of and take on for themselves the strategic thinking and doing involved in continuous learning and being responsibile for learning.

Table 6.2 lists some quite specific suggestions for making visible and developing craft, learning-to-learn and having entrepreneurial capabilities in integrated ways. Row one provides suggestions for learning (and continuous assessment if appropriate) activities for when pre-service learners are on placement. Collecting stories brings a focus to entrepreneurial capabilities and at the same time develops learning-to-learn and crafting capabilities. The stories become artefacts for reflection and being reflexive individually, with peers, back in the classroom, and outside the classroom and work spaces. Row two provides suggestions for recording craft and learning-to-learn experiences while on placement that, similar to row one, are artefacts for reflection in different spaces of learning, further building an integrated understanding of craft, learning-to-learn and entrepreneurial capabilities.

Table 6.2 Some pedagogical strategies for implementing the integrated practice model

Possible learning activities	*Aspects of integrated practice*		
	Craft	*Learning-to-learn*	*Entre-preneurial*
1. On-placement learners collect stories from work colleagues about: • market practices and labour market arrangements and how practitioners negotiate these • how their work colleagues gain work, how they manage CPD, tax, insurances etc. • about their mentors, how they approached their mentor, why the mentor agreed to be a mentor, what and how the work colleagues learnt from their mentors • who their role models are, why the work colleague(s) selected these individuals as role models, what they learnt • challenges work colleagues experienced (e.g. getting continuous work, solving particular problems, relating to other team members, etc.) and how they overcame these	Role of quality of work performance Deepening craft know*ing* 'Hidden' aspects of exercising your craft Belonging to the profession and being professional	Identifying resources Asking questions How to approach potential mentors Critical analysis Reflexivity	Meta-knowledge of the sector Gaining work Managing income stream Using networks Expected standards of performance Positioning Building resilience Shapeshifting Knowledge of industry practices
2. On placement learners record (photos, film – with consent – notes, lists, voice recording, drawings etc.) and reflect on through discussion and as part of an assessment, examples of: • what expertise they tapped into, when, why and how + *the value to the learner of this expertise* • what was new to them, how it links with what they already know. List the questions they asked, heard others ask. *What did they learn about who, when, where and how to ask to deepen their understanding?* What *in the environment enabled or constrained quality of performance etc.*) • their own and others use of trial and error. *How they critically appraised information and deepened their understanding and knowing*	Belonging to the profession and being professional Deepening craft know*ing*	Reflexivity Critical appraisal Active noticing Developing meta-cognitive capabilities Actively recontextualise Identifying resources	Tapping into expertise Establishing networks Industry norms and practices

The italicised suggestions are the value add and focus of discussions and part of possible assessment activities. 3. In undertaking project work • require learners to find examples of or develop innovative practices and explain why this is 'innovative' • projects can be assessed for entrepreneurial (e.g. project management), learning-to-learn and craft mastery • require learners to take risks • support learning by providing frameworks and theoretical principles (not only step by step processes) and expect learners to apply • involve learners in setting standards of performance (including assessment criteria) • build in peer and self-assessment	Push the boundaries of their craft Knowing standards of work performance Developing an orientation to practice Belonging to the profession and being professional	Finding and using resources Problem solving Critical appraisal Self- and peer evaluation capabilities	Developing a market edge Specific entrepreneurial capabilities such as project management, managing budget Resilience Knowing standards of work performance
4. As learners move iteratively between spaces of learning repeatedly pose questions such as[1]: • What surprised? • What challenged? • What patterns (in relation to a phenomena) did you notice? • Given the different context each learner was in, what was similar/different? (e.g. rules and culture, procedures, understandings of theoretical concepts?) Why? • How did the values, beliefs and ethics of different spaces and organisations differ? • Consider the reasons, the principles for x happening • What helped in building relationships in different spaces? • What entrepreneurial practices did you notice? What would you do differently? Why? • What does it mean for you to *be* a xxx?	Developing an orientation to practice Belonging to the profession and being professional	Reflexivity Critical appraisal	What it means to be entrepreneurial Knowing the necessity of being entrepreneurial

1 Refer to the dialogical inquiry map for a range of questions that encourage learners to think their way into being, becoming and belonging to a particular profession/vocation (Stack, 2007; Bound, 2010; Stack & Bound, 2012)

For example, networks are an important resource for learning, so finding out how experienced practitioner freelancers found mentors and why the mentor agreed to mentor that practitioner help make visible how to access resources for learning. Learning to be comfortable asking questions and, importantly, knowing when and how to ask questions that work around issues of power and face and help position the student positively for future work are learning-to-learn capabilities requiring practice, reflection and the seeking and giving of active feedback.

The learning-to-learn capability of being reflexive is critical for ongoing learning-to-learn and deepening of craft and entrepreneurial capabilities. Building on opportunities and strategies to be reflexive is important, as it too is a difficult capability to develop. Writing reflective journals is not the answer, as students often complete them just before they are due and tend to be descriptive rather than reflexive. Many of the strategies listed in Table 6.2 contribute to building reflexive capabilities, for example, considering what surprised, what challenged, what in the environment enabled or constrained quality of performance, what was new to the learner developing meta-knowledge of the sector and its labour market practices and so on. Meta-knowledge of a sector is important in preparing the pre-service student for work in the sector. Such knowledge, along with knowing the norms and practices, impacts on a learner's decision to continue with their studies or to try something else. It also indicates to the student what they need to pay attention to. For example, in the film and television sector in Singapore, only a minority of graduates from the polytechnics manage to stay in the sector. Meta-knowledge is important for decision making in navigating the territory and in making decisions about future journeys. Such knowledge might include the lack of regulation and union involvement contributing to realities such as late payments being an occupational hazard, or the 'lighted bulb' syndrome that describes 'hundreds of directors who came out and fade away' (Kevin, director, film and television); codes of conduct, such as certain clients belong to certain practitioners; and the requirements (e.g. standards of performance, rates of pay, ways of relating, language etc.) of different markets. Suggestions in rows three and four can be used in similar ways. Row four in particular can be used in any learning space and with other pedagogical strategies.

Specific implications include know*ing* the norms and practices in the film and television sector, for example, and include recognising and paying deference to chains of command on sets – important for building a reputation that will help maintain regular work, as is knowing that the quality of performance is important in gaining the next job. These social processes (which Coté (2006) describes as image projection) occur in contextually specific ways. For non-permanent workers moving between contexts and negotiating different expectations on a daily basis, this involves a high degree of what they sometimes describe, revealingly, as 'malleability', a term which refers to materials that have the property of being able to be hammered into shape without breaking or cracking.

The realities of the long hours and punishing work schedules that are norms, for example, in the film and television sector, lead to 'swallow[ing] a lot of pain. The more pain you swallow, the more popular you'll get' (Gavin, soundman, film and television). Identity as a practitioner in such sectors mediates decisions about continuing to be a non-permanent worker, and has implications for the journey of individual non-permanent workers. The self-narrative of the non-permanent worker impacts on their decisions to develop stamina and endurance, combined with a degree of performativity that appears as willingness to stifle grievances that arise out of onerous working conditions. Pre-service non-permanent workers need to be aware not only of these conditions, but to develop epistemic stances in relation to such norms and practices.

The need to pay attention to the development of entrepreneurial capabilities is highlighted by Nur et al. (2014) in their discussion of non-permanent workers in technical theatre in Singapore. These authors note that many freelancers appear unaware of the need to develop long-term plans for themselves that are appropriate to their future needs, both in terms of family life and state of health. Developing these capabilities while simultaneously building resilience and identity require careful deliberate curriculum design and close partnerships with the sector. There is much that can be developed in successfully designing learning that works across the spaces of work and educational institutions (Bound & Lee, 2014). Activities in Table 6.2 provide examples that integrate craft expertise, learning-to-learn and having entrepreneurial capabilities. Simultaneously, learners are asked and directed to actively notice specific aspects of the contexts they practice in and to develop their self-narrative. This might be done, for example, by asking learners to create a collage of themselves as a particular professional and to narrate (verbally or in prose) what the collage represents, at a point in time. Then, perhaps 12 months later, one could ask learners to revisit this narrative and express how they have changed. Tapping into self-narratives also can explicitly require tapping into meta-knowledge of the sector, of the craft and of reflexivity (an important part of learning-to-learn). Such activities also build an awareness of context and the ways in which it mediates activity in the sector and individual journeys. Capabilities, context and disposition are interwoven and interconnected with each other.

To consider being and becoming as core, rather than lists of knowledge and skills, is to break free of dichotomous understandings of knowledge and practice (Lum, 2013), instead focusing on development of expertise. Such an approach focuses instead on being capable in an occupation: 'one must in effect be able to "see" and make sense of an entire world of meanings, purposes and involvements, and this is something that clearly has to be learnt' (Lum, 2013, p. 29). Lum expounds this idea in his earlier work, saying that our becoming capable would seem to be first and foremost

> about our gaining certain fundamental understandings and abilities relating to how that particular world works, how to cope in it and find our way

> around it – rather than necessarily being able to exhibit the secondary and derivative behavioural or propositional manifestations of those understandings. In becoming capable we learn to adopt a particular stance, a certain interested and purposeful viewpoint which in turn structures our consciousness and our experience. We thus come to be equipped with a certain kind of 'readiness'; we are able to see things *as* certain things, we are able to interpret what we experience and extrapolate from it in a way which is appropriate to the world in which we wish to operate.
>
> (Lum, 2009, p. 113)

Conceptualising learning as dichotomies such as separating theory and practice, positions educational institutions and educational practitioners to overlook what it is the practitioner needs to *understand* and to under-estimate what is required (Lum, 2013). The integrated practice model offers a powerful alternative to such traditional approaches.

Continuous development of non-permanent workers

Supporting continuous development of non-permanent workers can be looked at from both the perspectives of minimising risks and expanding potential. These are two sides of the same coin that also apply to permanent workers who have to take account of the possibilities of job loss at any stage of their career and protect against these possibilities as well as expanding their capabilities within their present role and future journey. For non-permanent workers, the risks are intensified, and there is no clear line of sight to development opportunities, which can rarely be accessed through contracting organisations. These are the ever-present realities that an integrated practice approach has to confront.

Ways of minimising risk for non-permanent workers can be viewed in individual and institutional terms. The UK study 'Boosting the living standards of the self-employed' (RSA, 2015), for example, searches for ways of minimising risk by promoting the earning potential of non-permanent workers by boosting their 'personal capital, human capital and social capital'. Conceptualising the issues in terms of capital can imply a zero-sum approach that concentrates disproportionately on gaining individual advantages through acquisition. A wider resources-based analysis better indicates the dimensions of non-permanent workers' development that integrated practice approaches have to embrace if risks are to be minimised and development potential realised. For example, it is an accepted tenet of 'human resources development' that people develop when they are able to access support for their well-being at work as well as suitable opportunities for personal and professional development. An example is that the efficacy of continuing professional development depends fundamentally on mental and physical well-being. Many non-permanent workers operate in poorer conditions with fewer protections than those typically experienced by employees in companies that have the support of human resource and safety systems. A challenge for non-permanent workers is identifying anchor institutions that can provide advice and support relating to occupational health, for example, and developing their awareness and agency to avail themselves of support where needed for their well-being.

A further challenge for education and training providers is how to provide continuing personal and professional development opportunities that align with what their intended participants, the non-permanent workers, want, need and feel disposed to participate in. Here, the technocratic solution of enabling non-permanent workers to draw down elements of transferable skills and competences from an elaborated competence framework offers a 'solution' the logic of which might appear to address the 'problem'. But, views of non-permanent workers and their actual participation patterns among our respondents suggest the approach is wide of the mark. Across all the sectors in which we interviewed non-permanent workers, attending structured training was described as an opportunity-cost involving both the cost of the course and loss of income while attending training. Additionally, for those unaware of how to access available systems and support, the complexity of the systems is a barrier, as indicated in Luqman's story described in Chapter 3. Luqman wanted to undertake a course to be a tower crane driver, but cost considerations and the complexity of the application processes posed seemingly impassable barriers to gaining access.

Solutions have to respond to the contextualised preferences of non-permanent workers according to the functionings they seek. This approach, drawing on Sen (1993), explains why technically rational solutions offered by competence and skills packages, generic or otherwise, are inadequate to meet the challenges and expressed preferences of non-permanent workers. Furthermore, continuing professional development also depends crucially on forging social relationships through work and the development of work contacts, both proximal and distal. Additionally, the extent of challenge or not in the work offers potential, or not, for forging social relations and thus professional development. The social relationships embedded in the contracting organisations are much less available to non-permanent workers and have less significance than their personal and occupational networks forged through connections.

The differences between the continuous professional development experiences of non-permanent workers and permanent workers can be seen more clearly when we consider the specific ways in which the workplace supports, directs and gives meaning to learning opportunities at work. Building on Evans, Guile and Harris (2011), the continuing professional development of workers that takes place in and through the workplace entails:

- **Enculturation –** 'learning how we do things here'. For permanent workers, whether in a leading blue-chip company, a local small-medium enterprise (SME) or non-government organisation (NGO) or a public-sector institution continuing professional development entails learning and keeping up to date with organisational procedures and protocols as well as the brand 'values' to which all workers are meant to subscribe. For non-permanent workers joining organisational teams as agency staff, casuals, contract staff, freelancers, adjuncts and so on, moving between assignments within an organisation or, more usually, between organisations, entails continuous learning, as these workers have to learn to 'read' norms and expectations quickly and put their capabilities to work according to the situation.

- **Developing performance to standards –** learning to achieve and perform to occupational and organisational standards and meeting the demands of increasing regulations and health and safety standards and introducting new systems. For permanent workers, competence development is often a supervised process of learning and performing the job and defined work roles. In larger companies, this will be supported by appraisal systems and access provided in or through the workplace to continuing training where that is deemed necessary or desirable. For the non-permanent worker, this process is non-linear, can involve meeting a multiplicity of performance expectations and requirements and depends on capabilities to use judgement to assess new situations to bring those new situations under control.
- **Improving practice, innovation and renewal –** Practice improvement is a purpose that is often driven from the 'bottom up' in organisations; innovation is more often 'top down'. For permanent workers, employee-driven innovation is starting to receive more attention with implications for knowledge flows and power relations between levels of the permanent workforce. Learning to do what has not been done before involves significant work-based and workplace learning and occurs every time a new set of demands is introduced. For non-permanent workers, as for permanent workers who have had several job moves, their different configurations of prior experience and know-how can be brought to bear on work problems to the organisations' benefit, but non-permanent workers who are regarded as marginal are rarely seen by organisations as a resource in this situation. This is ironic, as our data contains many stories of non-permanent workers learning innovative practices, processes and producing novel solutions as they move across different projects, sites and work with international practitioners. For example, in the film and television sector, problem solving is used in finding out how to achieve a certain effect with limited budget such as a suicide jump from a high building.
- **Equity, ethics and social justice –** refers to the process of systematically reflecting on practice within a set of professional concerns about ethics, values, priorities and procedures. The organisation of learning through Trades Union structures and workplace representatives foregrounds social justice and corporate social responsibility and also embodies some of these purposes. These structures are at best only patchily available to non-permanent workers, often through mutual or co-operative enterprises.

- **Development of capabilities –** encompasses the development of professional and occupational capabilities; learning the capabilities necessary to 'do the next job' at the same time as performing the present job; learning to work in different cultures and environments. The impetus may come from the organisation or the occupation as well as the individual's need for career development. For permanent workers, development of wider capabilities while working on the current job can come from 'acting up' in the present work context to anticipatory training and development in succession planning programmes in larger organisations or from seeking development opportunities beyond the workplace, with a view to a planned occupational move. For non-permanent workers, development of capabilities depends most heavily on the quality of serial assignments and on networks to access personal sponsorship and opening of doors. Lack of quality assignments, in which the worker has to move from one exploitative, routinised or corner -cutting assignment to the next to sustain their income, potentially undermines and restricts capabilities' development and thereby a longer-term direction to their working lives: 'no trajectory, no career, no security'.
- **Occupational/ professional identity development –** refers to new entrants 'thinking and feeling' their way into an occupation and coming to identify with it and with others who are participate in it. Experienced workers develop and reconstruct identities in and through work as positions, roles and contexts change (see Hodkinson & Hodkinson, 2004). For permanent workers, much of this development takes place within relatively stable work groups and overlapping social networks. For non-permanent workers, identity development takes place through serial engagements in practice and is dependent to a greater degree on forging enduring relationships-in-action beyond assignments and practice engagements. Identity development for non-permanent workers involves complex relations with space and place as well as relationships. An identity may be seen in terms of expectations regarding a role, expectations which are normative, technical and epistemological. A precondition of this is the person's ability to enact a particular practice in terms of learning the language and vocabulary and the goals and purposes and the broader environment in which a practice takes place. However, an identity is not fashioned merely through enactment of a practice. A strong degree of reflexivity is required as the worker starts to inhabit a role with identity at best only partly formed. Some degree of self-reflection is required to make the transition into the new identity based both on reflection in action and on reflection after the event (Hinchliffe, 2013, p. 52).

This reflexivity can also be understood as intrinsic to the processes by which different forms of knowledge are continuously and iteratively put to work, as continuous professional development potentially enables non-permanent workers to become knowledgeable practitioners with a sense of who they are, a working knowledge of the occupational practice communities to which they belong to and confidence in the capabilities they can offer to the organisations that use their services.

All these processes build, for both permanent workers and non-permanent workers, on pre-service education, training and experience. They are integral to becoming a knowledgeable practitioner. Whether a non-permanent worker or permanent worker in an organisation or in an established trajectory of development, these forms of continuous professional development are very relevant to all levels of the workforce, although this is often insufficiently recognised at the lower levels of the earnings distribution. For non-permanent workers, many of these development processes are not embedded in day-to-day organisational life but have to be actively constructed – development takes place but presents additional challenges of how to sustain development and counter potentially de-skilling and dis-integrating experiences. For example, channels of support for mental and physical well-being are not obvious; accessing training and development through employers does not exist for non-permanent workers – they are on the periphery of organisations, and access is limited to the social and commercial networks that are integral to specific workplaces. In working life, integrated practice is intrinsic to the continuing professional development of non-permanent workers, with learning-to-learn and entrepreneurial capabilities being crucial ingredients in actively constructing the pathways to knowledgeable practice.

Knowledgeable practice is practice that is characterised by the exercise of attuned and responsive judgement when individuals or teams are confronted with complex tasks or unpredictable situations at work. The concept of knowledgeable practice enables us to focus on the practice while attending to the knowledge frameworks that underpin the directing of work and the exercise of judgement that is involved in working with others to vary or change practices or products at work (Evans, 2009, 2015). The knowledge that underpins knowledgeable practice is developed by forging connections between theory and practice. In the workplace, chains of recontextualisation are forged day by day as, for example, people are stretched and challenged at work and have to exercise judgement in making decisions and taking action. Reflection on and in practice, much rehearsed in the literature, is insufficient unless it is connected to deliberation and action-taking. Seen in terms of putting different forms of knowledge to work, the challenges for non-permanent workers are how to cope with the continuous change and how to progressively develop their capabilities and work identity.

Knowledge is recontextualised, it is not static; it is context specific and the practitioner develops know*ing* in practice while moving between successive assignments of variable quality and navigating unpredictable organisational environments. For non-permanent workers, integrated practice at work entails and embodies learning in and through the work assignments, through observation of others; through mentorship, coaching and peer learning and by drawing on new ideas and experiences accessed both through work and often beyond work. This invisible learning (Allan et al., 2016) is triggered by the activity and the context. Knowledge recontextualisation takes place when the non-permanent worker recognises a new situation as requiring a response and uses knowledge – theoretical, procedural and tacit – in acts of interpretation in an attempt to bring the activity and its setting under conscious control (van Oers, 1998). When the interpretation involves the enactment of a well-known activity in a new setting, an adaptive form of recontextualisation takes place as existing knowledge is used to reproduce a response in parallel situations (Evans, 2017). Where the interpretation leads the learner to change the activity or its context in an attempt to make a response, a productive form of recontextualisation takes place as new knowledge is produced. Forms of knowledge are embedded in routines, protocols, artefacts and networks as well as in organisational hierarchies and power structures (Allan et al., 2016; Evans et al., 2010). Continuing professional development for non-permanent workers depends in part on the extent in which they can use work problems as a 'test–bed', learning through observing, inquiring, acting and moving on. Progressive development of capabilities is dependent in part on what they can 'make of' different environments, finding tactical ways in which they can leverage greater control of their situation (including decisions on which assignments they turn down and why), using tacit skills, seeking mentoring and recognising the value and benefits of mutual peer support. Non-permanent workers, through developmental knowledge recontextualisations, come to self-embody knowledge cognitively and practically. This is a process that is invisible, as it is difficult to detect and appreciate.

These processes tend to be better understood for non-permanent workers whose work is recognised as using professional, managerial or specialist knowledge and skills associated with extended initial education and training. They are less well understood for those non-permanent workers undertaking task-based forms of work that is held to be easily learnt. Further light is shed on these workers, and some of the wrong assumptions that are made about them through textured accounts of what adult life at work means in practice for people whose life journeys lead them to enter it at the low-wage, low-graded end of the labour market.

Fuller and Unwin (2017) have identified the 'crafting' involved in low-graded work in a study focused on hospital porters. This research has shown how porters became knowledgeable practitioners able to mobilise diverse forms of expertise in 'crafting' their job as patient care, with many forms of care work activity, despite the absence of this activity from their job description. The findings showed how employers 'misrecognised' the actual skills and knowledge workers possess and use day by day, while the porters themselves who identified as job crafters recognised that providing care and seeing themselves as part of the healthcare workforce deviated from the occupational identity ascribed to them. In this case, the public-sector workers were part of a stable organisational team characterised by a strong sense of being part of the organisation, of belonging, but the observations seem to hold for other low-graded employees and non-permanent workers who are often also mis-recognised as somehow 'locked-in' to routine work roles from which they have neither motivation nor the capabilities to escape.

Evans and Waite (2013) inquiry into the retrospective views of adults in low-graded work highlighted the significance of earlier experiences that led workers to restricted work options. For those whose limited educational attainments or engagement with schooling restricted their work options, shifts towards more positive orientations to learning often emerged in adulthood and changed with contingencies and new roles in adult life. This exploration of employees' personal accounts of adult learning shows how specific workplace experiences and activities can act as 'activating events' in so far as they have the potential to not only trigger new 'learning orientations' (values, attitudes towards learning) but may also forge new working life orientations. The range of orientations found among adults holding low-graded positions at work might surprise many who hold a deficit perspective. The complex sets of adult motivations and beliefs that were shown to constitute the 'work orientations' of low-graded workers were captured, in Evans and Waite (2013), by the following categories: 'content with current role' 'reconciled to current role'; 'struggling to overcome barriers'; 'stand-by opportunism'; and 'aspirational'. The category 'content with current role' signified a satisfaction with current employment status as well as preference not to be promoted or experience change in the workplace. 'Reconciled to current role' denoted an acceptance of current employment status which may also be shaped by a lack of employment and training opportunities within the organisation (thereby making promotion prospects unlikely) as well as by a lack of opportunity to undertake training outside of work (e.g. as a result of family commitments). 'Stand-by opportunism' denoted not only an attitude of satisfaction with current employment status but also a willingness to take advantage of any learning or career advancement opportunities that may become available. Such an attitude is therefore based on the reasonably optimistic premise that the work environment is sufficiently favourable for such opportunities to materialise. 'Aspirational' career orientations signify a wish for advancement through work. 'Active aspirational' as opposed to 'passive aspirational' attitudes entail actively seeking out learning or work opportunities that align with the aspiration. If such opportunities are not available through present work such a disposition often entails active steps to move onto more challenging work or find support for further learning outside work: for example, the cleaner who moved onto care work, developing her literacy and language skills to a level that eventually enabled her to enter nurse training. Moving between non-permanent work assignments in the search for more stretching, challenging or rewarding kinds of activity is modus operandi for at least some low-wage workers. At least some of the ingredients of integrated practice are present in such purposeful activity. The evidence from our sample of non-permanent workers shows that the potential among low-wage workers for continuing professional development supported by integrated practice should not be overlooked or under-estimated.

This section began with a discussion supporting the continuous development of non-permanent workers from two perspectives: minimising risks and expanding potential. The challenges non-permanent workers face in addressing these perspectives suggest that we need innovative approaches to address these challenges. The authors reject the human capital, technically rational approaches as inadequate. Rather, we argue that in considering continuous professional development for non-permanent workers, it is necessary to tap into their learning processes and to address structural issues. The integrated practice model along with the dispositions framework expanded on in Chapter 3 and the concept of occupational affordances discussed in Chapter 4 offer frameworks for doing this. Typical learning processes include being mentored, having role models, observing practices and the work of others, engaging in dialogue, asking questions, accessing expertise through networks, self-initiated accessing of information, repeated practise and doing the work. For example, the richness of learning opportunities in working with others whose work is well respected can involve partial mentoring, dialogue and doing the work as shared by Ron, as he works with a lighting designer.

> I would sit down with [him] . . . , not like he is teaching me but because he will tell me, I want this channel at this per cent, you start to see his working process . . . When you are working with someone of that calibre and experience, you would pay attention to everything he is doing, how he communicates and what he is trying to do. A lot of times you don't understand what he is trying to do. Just going through the entire process of 2–3 weeks of working with him building up the show step-by-step, you learn that this is [his] way of doing things, what works, what doesn't, why it works and how do you get that – it is a tremendous privilege.
>
> (Ron, lighting designer, technical theatre)

Ron shares the richness of learning opportunities when working alongside knowledgeable practitioners with deep expertise. Structural issues such as access to continuous professional development and expertise are illustrated in Adi's explanation of how he and his team of technical crew friends picked the brains of international practitioners whom they worked with on shows:

> We read, we learn from the foreigners – the English, the Australians, the Americans. We learn from them. We copy everything that they do. We ask them questions because experience is everything to us . . . we know there are something that they need to do like let's say the chandelier is going to fall down, how are they going to achieve that? We don't know but know

> that it's automation but then we do it with them then we learn . . . , then they will explain.
>
> (Adi, rigger, technical theatre)

On the surface, Adi's explanation appears to suggest expansive learning opportunities in the industry. Consistent with the warning raised in the literature on the limitations of workplace learning, a closer examination suggests that the low barriers to entry tend to lead to haphazard development of core capabilities, as there is a lack of opportunities for the structured development of expertise (Sadik et al., 2014). The comments from Adi, who first joined the industry in the 1990s, are telling:

> How did I progress? . . . There are no professional people because the professional people are us, which is not professional. We're not trained, we're untrained, so we're very raw but we're willing to learn.

This haphazard development of core capabilities is linked to how freelancers fit into the production process, and the general industry expectations that they learn on the job. Ben, of British nationality, is a director at a theatre venue and feels that there is a lack of appreciation of the depth of expertise required of a technical theatre practitioner:

> [In lighting for instance] we don't just turn up for a few lights up there and turn them off. There are various theories of physics or psychology involved in lighting design in other parts of the world. I do not see that in Singapore . . . They watched visiting companies and picked up all the bad habits . . . There's no underpinning knowledge and the quality ain't there.
>
> (Ben, director, technical theatre)

These examples illustrate structural issues of access to knowledgeable practice. Systematic, not haphazard, access to theoretical knowing, the bringing together of practice, theory, embodiment and meta-knowing, for example, are critically important in enabling the non-permanent worker to grow and develop (see Wheelahan, 2010) and to make the most of opportunities. Other important structural issues relate to the quality of work opportunities, or, rather, the lack of such opportunities. Job quality is a key ingredient for continuous development. The availability of specialist roles and the quality of assignments are important structural aspects for the development of non-permanent workers. 'In the absence of career progression structures typically available for permanent work, specialist roles that the market demands and rewards provide a signpost for the non-permanent worker to seek out work and evolve . . . in deeper way[s]' (Bound, Sadik, & Karmel, 2015, p. 36). For example, in film, television and technical theatre, the low quality of assignments available locally was seen as a major barrier. This is tied to the high number of imported productions and low budget set aside for local productions. A freelance producer explains, 'The projects are not exciting enough for us to move forward. It's always the same . . . The freelancers doesn't upgrade, but the projects don't require them to upgrade as well' (producer, technical theatre). In some sectors such as technical theatre, those wishing to move, for example, from being a technician to a lighting designer had to make a deliberate disrupter in their career, resulting in a lower income and, once again, more than the usual precariousness until they became established.

Continuous professional development conceived as delivery, such as providing courses, attending seminars, conferences and so on, is clearly not appropriate as a major strategy for continuous professional development for non-permanent workers. Rather, continuous professional *learning* and development are contingent on addressing structural issues such as quality of assignments and access to credible expertise. It is the lack of opportunity to develop knowledgeable practice, not a lack of willingness to learn, that is the issue. As indicated in Chapter 3, non-permanent workers who have a broad disposition that values growth continuously seek opportunities through the learning strategies listed above.

The spectra of dispositions framework presented in Chapter 3 is helpful for understanding non-permanent worker's orientation to practice, important as a contribution to understanding the potential journey of the non-permanent worker. The occupational affordances framework (see Chapter 4) helps in analysing and framing up what it is that non-permanent workers in different sectors and those supporting them need to understand about the contexts in which they work and their affordances for development and growth. Not the least of the issues surfaced in this framework is the need for occupational affordances related to the quality of assignments that provide challenges and satisfying work. Integrated practice as a model is valuable for the same reasons discussed in the section on pre-service non-permanent workers. Work is enacted not as separate sets of skills and knowledge, but as complex wholes of integrated capabilities that are deeply embodied. For example, in the case of Adi, theoretical knowing of physics and psychology of lighting is linked to his ability to position himself in the labour market (an aspect of entrepreneurialism) and having a frame for understanding what he knows and does not know in order to frame up his questions and dialogue – aspects of learning-to-learn. Reflexive, knowledgeable practitioners, aware of their self-narrative and their evolving identity is the intent of using the integrated practice model.

Collaboration between educational institution/ provider and the sector

> For freelancers in Singapore's creative sector, reflection has become a 'general pedagogic stance' (Edwards, 1998, p. 386) that is vital to the effective navigation of shifting work patterns and a fast-changing technological environment. But

> not only do individuals need to be reflexive, so too does the governance of the infrastructure that supports the industry. De-standardised and flexible working patterns call for greater reflexivity on the part of institutions and individuals as well as a greater emphasis on learning (Edwards, 1998, p. 382). The recursive examination of social institutions, practices and ideas that characterises reflexivity in the contemporary era (Beck, 1992; Giddens, 1990, 1991) has important implications for learning in educational, work and personal contexts (Edwards, 1998; Edwards et al., 2002).
>
> —(Bound, Rushbrook, & Sivalingham, 2013, p. 36)

Interactions and relationships between educational institutions, the industry sector (including employers, professional bodies, employer organisations and so on) and learners are important because they determine performance standards and requirements that could shape and/or provide affordances for good assessment, learning design (Bound, Chia, & Karmel, 2016) and recognition of prior learning. Interactions and relationships between educational institutions and the relevant industry sector provide spaces for developing evolving and innovative understandings of current practices and potential future needs. Such relationships are critical aspects of governance of a sector that recursively flow back to participating institutions and organisations. Such relations are *not* to say that educational institutions are behoven to industry, but do say that educational institutions can be cumbersome beasts that often lag far behind current practices and tend to operate from the supply perspective, rather than a demand perspective. This is startlingly evident when examining programs that prepare students for being and becoming a particular occupation that is predominantly engaged as non-permanent work in particular sectors.

Collaborative partnerships between educational institution(s) and employers change the spaces for and of learning. Such collaborations of one kind or another have been in place for many decades in many countries (Germany, Australia, Britain etc.), and there is a considerable literature about such arrangements that consider practice approaches. The complexity and richness of learning through and at work have long been recognised and are now an entrenched aspect of the higher education landscape in many countries, impacting upon learning, teaching and research, providing a new dimension to the role of the modern university (Garnett, 2013). Vocational institutions have long been in these spaces. Given that 'work is an inescapable component of our being' (Gibbs, 2013, p. 1) and that work is organised for production or service provision, not learning, it is behoven on educational institutions in particular to move away from impoverished understandings of 'theory and practice', of competence with its separation of 'skills', (the practical aspects of 'doing') and of underpinning knowledge to a holistic appreciation of being and becoming in and to a particular occupation in the activity of work. Such approaches place new demands on all in collaborative partnerships, but especially upon educational institutions, to understand what the activity of work entails. Focusing on the activity of work means that dominant work arrangements, such as non-permanent work, cannot be conveniently ignored, but instead must become an integral part of the epistemological approaches of educational institutions and a permanent aspect of their reflexivity. It also means that educational institutions can claim a space in the ecosystem to contribute to the design of 'good' jobs.

Typically, in developing capabilities that involve workplace practicums for pre-service students, the educational provider develops close working relationships with individual employers. These relationships involve discussions about the whole program, the desired outcomes for the learner of the practicum, the types of opportunities the workplace provides, the pedagogical and assessment tools used for making the most of learning opportunities and, of course, discussions between learner and their supervisor and learner, supervisor and lecturer. These sets of relations assume the work in the sector is 'permanent' work. In their research report on non-permanent workers in Singapore, Bound, Sadik and Karmel (2015) note that '[f]rom the data, it appears that there is inadequate support from social institutions [including educational institutions] in Singapore that tend to design programmes and policies based on a "permanent work paradigm"' (p. 39). However, where the work is predominantly non-permanent, provision of opportunities is needed for the pre-service student to experience permanent work settings *and* to come to 'know' the necessity for and to value the set of capabilities required for being and becoming *a non-permanent worker*. This needs to be woven into developing core narratives and evolving dispositions so that pre-service learners develop holistic understandings of what it is to be and become a particular occupation to which non-permanent work is integral.

Bound, Sadik and Karmel (2015) suggest that a useful approach to support holistic development, to provide the experience of non-permanent work for the pre-service student and for continuous professional learning and development, is to identify, recognise and accredit industry masters who are rewarded financially for mentoring practicum students. Students would be attached, not to an organisation, but to a 'master' who is a non-permanent worker. Student might initially shadow their assigned 'master', undertaking purposeful, active noticing. Such experience is built on by gradually increasing the level of responsibility the student has over the multiple times they undertake their practicum. Students would gradually develop not only awareness of and an appreciation of the importance of capabilities such as those identified in Table 6.2, but, importantly, begin to build their sense of being and becoming of and part of the profession and the sector. Such an approach also emphasises the need to develop understanding, to capture the whole of what is required to be and become. It takes creative expertise and different epistemological stances on the part of the educator and institution(s) to design learning and assessment that move away from the measurement of specific competencies and skills, that focus on behavioural outcomes and to move instead to assessing holistically and focusing on developing being and becoming. Non-permanent work arrangements in particular need attention to know*ing* that entrepreneurial and learning-to-learn capabilities are not exercised separately, that capabilities are not exercised in a vacuum. Rather, the disposition and the importance of having an evolving core narrative are critical aspects of learning to be and become a non-permanent worker providing a particular occupational (craft) expertise. Context provides various affordances and constraints for exercising agency and developing a core narrative and disposition and, thus, developing various capabilities.

Different places and spaces of learning take on different thought patterns and ways of being; educators need to find ways of making these explicit and cross-fertilising concepts and experiences. Their role, therefore, is not to impart information but to initiate critical and reflective discourse where students learn to imagine and think of other possibilities, including learning how and why we fail – a critical aspect of self-directed learning that develops a capability for constantly improving and builds resilience. Such experiences weave into core narratives and dispositions. For the message to be consistent, not only educators from the educational institution, but also workplace supervisors and trainers need to have a shared understanding of how trainees are progressing through their learning journeys (Bound & Lee, 2014). A curriculum that calls for learners to relate different forms of learning in context and to conceptualise their experiences in different ways requires the educator to pose problems to encourage learners to 'analyse their experiences and arrive at a critical understanding of their reality' (Guile & Griffiths, 2001, p. 125). Developing the ability to self-assess and assess the work of others that is relevant to the context, purpose and required standards is what Boud (2000) calls sustainable assessment; it is an integral aspect of being a non-permanent worker and simultaneously contributes to learning-to-learn capabilities. Collaborative partnerships offer rich possibilities only if what is brought to the table are deep understandings of the work, the sector, its affordances and the dispositions of learners.

Conclusion

The notion of multiple parties introduces new dimensions that suggest new models of thinking and working between educational providers, employers, professional bodies and other relevant, fit-for-purpose bodies/agencies in an ecosystem. Collaborative partnerships and learning ecosystems involve complicated interactions and relationships, differences and negotiation, which, in turn, create new spaces for learning of those involved. Collaborative partnerships in and of themselves do not meet the needs of non-permanent workers. A reflexive stance is required not just by educational institutions and employers, but by the governance structure of a sector.

The integrated practice model offers those involved in supporting the growth and development of non-permanent workers (including the workers themselves) a framework, a way of thinking about designing learning that develops being and becoming in and of a particular occupation situated in a labour market that predominantly engages these occupations as non-permanent workers. To develop graduates and continuous professional learning and development opportunities that build on their agency, and thus participation and engagement that increase their sense of connectedness, is to contribute to opportunities to guide their own journey and to be less of a pawn of labour market fluctuations.

References

Allan, H. T., Magnusson, C., Evans, K., Ball, E., Westwood, S., Curtis, K., & Johnson, M. (2016). Delegation and supervision of healthcare assistants' work in the daily management of uncertainty and the unexpected in clinical practice: Invisible learning among newly qualified nurses. *Nursing Inquiry, 23*(4), 377–385. Retrieved from https://doi.org/10.1111/nin.12155

Beckett, D., & Hager, P. (2002). *Life, work and learning: Practice in postmodernity*. Routledge. Retrieved from www.amazon.com/Learning-Routledge-International-Philosophy-Education/dp/0415161894/ref=sr_1_1?s=books&ie=UTF8&qid=1326741846&sr=1-1

Billett, S. (2001). *Learning in the workplace*. Sydney: Allen and Unwin.

Blackler, F. (1995). Knowledge, knowledge work and organizations: An overview and interpretation. *Organization Studies*. Retrieved from https://doi.org/10.1177/017084069501600605

Boud, D. (2000). Sustainable assessment: Rethinking assessment for the learning society. *Studies in Continuing Education, 22*(2), 151–167. Retrieved from https://doi.org/10.1080/713695728

Bound, H. (2010). Developing quality online dialogue: Dialogical inquiry. *International Journal of Teaching and Learning in Higher Education, 22*(2), 107–119. Retrieved from www.eric.ed.gov/ERICWebPortal/detail?accno=EJ930136%5Cnwww.eric.ed.gov/ERICWebPortal/contentdelivery/servlet/ERICServlet?accno=EJ930136

Bound, H., Chia, A., & Karmel, A. (2016). *Assessment for the changing nature of work*. Singapore: Institute for Adult Learning.

Bound, H., & Lee, W. (2014). *Teaching and learning across boundaries: Work, classroom and in between*. Retrieved from http://tlc.unisim.edu.sg/research/AdvSOTL/helen.html

Bound, H., Rushbrook, P., & Sivalingham, M. (2013). *The entrepreneurial self: Becoming a freelancer in Singapore's film and television industry*. Singapore: Institute for Adult Learning. Bound, H., Sadik, S., & Karmel, A. (2015). *Developing non-permanent workers in Singapore*. Singapore: Institute for Adult Learning.Coté, J. (2006). Identity studies: How close are we to developing a social science of identity? – An appraisal of the field identity. *An International Journal of Theory and Research*. Retrieved from https://doi.org/10.1207/s1532706xid0601_2

Dall'Alba, G., & Sandberg, J. (1996). Educating for competence in professional practice. *Instructional Science, 24*, 411–437. Retrieved from https://doi.org/10.1007/BF00125578

Dall'Alba, G., & Sandberg, J. (2006). Unveiling professional development: A critical review of stage models. *Review of Educational Research, 76*(3), 383–412. Retrieved from https://doi.org/10.3102/00346543076003383

Eteläpelto, A. (2008). Perspectives, prospects and progress in work-related learning. In S. Billett, C. Harteis, & A. Eteläpelto (Eds.), *Emerging perspectives of workplace learning* (pp. 133–247). Rotterdam: Sense Publishers.

Evans, K. (2009). *Learning, work and social responsibility: Challenges for lifelong learning in a global age*. Dordrecht: Springer.

Evans, K. (2015). Developing the creative potential of the workforce: Rethinking the part that work-based learning can play. In *Towards a new understanding of workplace learning: The context of Singapore* (pp. 17–35). Singapore: Institute for Adult Learning.

Evans, K. (2017). Bounded agency in professional lives. In M. Goller & S. Paloniemi (Eds.), *Agency at work: Professional and practice-based learning*. Cham: Springer.

Evans, K., & Guile, D. (2012). Putting different forms of knowledge to work in practice. In J. Higgs, R. Barnett, S. Billett, M. Hutchings, & F. Trede (Eds.), *Practice-based education*. Rotterdam: Sense Publishers. Retrieved from https://doi.org/10.1007/978-94-6209-128-3

Evans, K., Guile, D., & Harris, J. (2009). *Putting knowledge to work: The exemplars*. London: WLE Centre for Excellence, Institute of Education, University of London.

Evans, K., Guile, D., & Harris, J. (2011). Rethinking work-based learning, for education professionals and professionals who educate. In M. Malloch, L. Cairns, K. Evans, & B. O'Connor (Eds.), *The Sage handbook of workplace learning* (pp. 149–162). London: Sage Publications.

Evans, K., Guile, D., Harris, J., & Allan, H. (2010). Putting knowledge to work: A new approach. *Nurse Education Today, 30*(3), 245–251. Retrieved from https://doi.org/10.1016/j.nedt.2009.10.014

Evans, K., Hodkinson, P., Rainbird, H., & Unwin, L. (2006). *Improving workplace learning*. London: Routledge. Retrieved from https://doi.org/10.4324/9780203946947

Evans, K., & Waite, E. (2013). "Activating events" in adult learners' lives: Understanding learning and life chances through a retrospective lens. In H. Helve & K. Evans (Eds.), *Youth and work transitions in changing social landscapes*. London: Tufnell Press.

Forrier, A., Sels, L., & Stynen, D. (2009). Career mobility at the intersection between agent and structure: A conceptual model. *Journal of Occupational and Organizational Psychology, 82*(4), 739–759. Retrieved from https://doi.org/10.1348/096317909X470933

Fuller, A., & Unwin, L. (2017). Job crafting and identity in low-grade work: How hospital porters redefine the value of their work and expertise. *Vocations and Learning, 10*, 307–324.

Garnett, J. (2013). Forward. In P. Gibbs (Ed.), *Learning, work and practice: New understandings*. Dordrecht: Springer.

Gibbs, P. (2013). *Learning, work and practice: New understandings* (P. Gibbs, Ed.). Dordrecht: Springer.

Guile, D., & Griffiths, T. (2001). Learning through work experience. *Journal of Education and Work, 14*(1), 113–131. Retrieved from https://doi.org/10.1080/13639080020028738

Hager, P. (2004). Lifelong learning in the workplace? Challenges and issues. *Journal of Workplace Learning, 16*(1/2):22–32

Hager, P., & Hodkinson, P. (2011). Becoming as an appropriate metaphor for understanding professional learning. In L. Scanlon (Ed.), *"Becoming" a professional: An interdisciplinary analysis of professional learning* (pp. 33–56). Springer. Retrieved from https://doi.org/10.1007/978-94-007-1378-9_2

Hinchliffe, G. (2013). Workplace identity, transition and the role of learning. In P. Gibbs (Ed.), *Learning, work and practice: New understandings* (pp. 51–69). Dordrecht: Springer.

Hodkinson, P., & Hodkinson, H. (2004). The significance of individuals' dispositions in workplace learning: A case study of two teachers. *Journal of Education and Work, 17*(2), 167–182. Retrieved from https://doi.org/10.1080/13639080410001677383

Lave, J., & Wenger, E. (1991). *Situated learning: Legitimate peripheral participation*. Cambridge: Cambridge University Press.

Lemke, J. (1997). Cognition, context, and learning: A social semiotic perspective. In *Situated cognition: Social, semiotic, and psychological perspectives*. London: Lawrence Erlbaum Associates.
Lum, D. (2009). *Vocational and professional capability: An epistemological and ontological study of occupational expertise*. London: Continuum Studies in Education.
Lum, G. (2013). The role of on-the-job and off-the-job provision in vocational education and training. In P. Gibbs (Ed.), *Learning, work and practice: New understandings* (pp. 21–32). Dordrecht: Springer.
Nonaka, I., & Toyama, R. (2003). The knowledge-creating theory revisited: Knowledge creation as a synthesizing process. *Knowledge Management Research & Practice*, *1*(1), 2–10. Retrieved from https://doi.org/10.1057/palgrave.kmrp.8500001
Nur, S., Bound, H., Karmel, A., & Sivalingham, M. (2014). *Masters of their destiny? Identities, learning and development of freelance workers in Singapore's technical theatre industry*. Singapore: Institute for Adult Learning.
Owen, C. (2017). *Enhancing learning in the workplace*. Singapore: Institute for Adult Learning Roundtable paper.
Pittaway, L., & Cope, J. (2007). Entrepreneurship education. A systematic review of the evidence. *Internal Small business Journal: Researching Entrepreneurship, 25*(5), 479–510.
Rae, D. (2006). Entrepreneurial learning: A conceptual framework for technology-based enterprise. *Technology Analysis & Strategic Management*, 18(1), 39–56.
Royal Society of Arts. (2015). *Boosting the living standards of the self-employed*. London: RSA.
Sandberg, J. (2001). Understanding the basis for competence development. In *International perspectives on competence in the workplace* (pp. 9–26). Dordrecht: Kluwer.
Sandberg, J., & Pinnington, A. H. (2009). Professional competence as ways of being: An existential ontological perspective. *Journal of Management Studies*, *46*(7), 1138–1170. Retrieved from https://doi.org/10.1111/j.1467-6486.2009.00845.x
Scardamalia, M. (2002). Collective cognitive responsibility for the advancement of knowledge. In B. Smith (Ed.), *Liberal education in a knowledge society* (pp. 67–98). Chicago: Open Court Publishing Company.
Scardamalia, M., & Bereiter, C. (2006). Knowledge building: Theory, pedagogy, and technology. In R. K. Sawyer (Ed.), *Cambridge handbook of the learning sciences*. New York: Cambridge University Press. Retrieved from https://doi.org/10.1598/RT.61.2.5
Sen, A. (1993). Capability and well-being. In M. Nussbaum & A. Sen (Eds.), *Quality of life* (pp. 30–53). Oxford: Clarendon Press.
Stack, S. (2007). *Integrating science and soul in education: The lived experience of a science educator bringing holistic and integral perspectives to the transformation of science teaching*. Curtin: University of Technology.
Stack, S., & Bound, H. (2012). *Exploring new approaches to professional learning: Deepening pedagogical understanding of Singapore CET trainers through meta-cognition and practitioner-based research*. Singapore: Institute for Adult Learning.
Van Oers, B. (1998). The fallacy of decontextualization. *Mind, Culture & Activity*, *5*(2), 135–142. Retrieved from https://doi.org/10.1207/s15327884mca0502
Wells, G. (1999). *Dialogic inquiry: Towards a sociocultural practice and theory of education*. New York: Cambridge University Press.
Wells, G. (2008). Dialogue, inquiry and the construction of learning communities. In B. Lingard, J. Nixon, & S. Ranson (Eds.), *Transforming learning in schools and communities: The remaking of education for a cosmopolitan society*. London: Continuum Studies in Education.
Wheelahan, L. (2010). *Why knowledge matters in curriculum: A social realist argument*. Abingdon: Routledge.

Chapter 7

Implications for workforce development

A comparative perspective

The preceding chapters have put forth integrated practice as a model to support the capability development of non-permanent workers. In this chapter, we outline how the model can offer new ways of organising workforce development in the context of disruption to the standard employment model.

Non-permanent workers in most industrial societies now make up between one-fifth and one-third of the total labour force, although figures vary depending on how workers are categorised as identified in Chapter 1. From a broader labour market perspective, non-permanent work is not simply a unique category of labour but epitomises a wider employment shift whereby workers are expected to undergo more frequent job and career changes across their working lives (Ross, 2008). Globalised finance and the introduction of new ways of organising production, enabled by the spread of new technologies, have increased the interdependence of national economies with profound consequences for the organisation of national labour markets. To a degree, this meant that national governments lost some of their influence over the operation of capital and labour markets. There is now a high level of experimentation in the labour market, with a proliferation of new contractual arrangements such as zero-contact hours and app-enabled on-demand work that blur the distinction between who is a worker or an employer and the traditional set of relationships that undergird them.

In this dynamic context, workforce development needs to be imagined in new ways, requiring a fundamental rethink of the relationship among work, education and employability. By workforce development, we do not refer to simply employment training as though workers have particular deficits in need of rectification. Jacobs and Hawley (2009) put forth a broader definition of workforce development as referring to 'the coordination of public and private sector policies and programmes that provides individuals with the opportunity for a sustainable livelihood and helps organizations achieve exemplary goals, consistent with the societal context' (p. 2561). In this regard, the focus is on societal goals of self-actualisation and the dignity of work that include how individuals continuously develop themselves through work and how organisations enable those learning opportunities for workplace performance. As

Leadbeater and Mulgan (1997) argue, work is a means for 'people to find connection to the wider society, that they find a sense of purpose and self-respect' (p. 198). Consistent with the experience of non-permanent work detailed in the preceding chapters where workers traverse across diverse work settings, we do not limit organisations to just firms but also include professional associations, industry bodies, unions and other national entities that contribute to supporting workplace performance. We also do not limit workforce development to existing labour market participants; the pre-employment school system is central in any workforce development effort. Learning to be and to become, which sits at the core of the integrated practice model, requires fundamentally new ways of preparation for work.

The chapter is organised in the following way. We preface our discussion on the integrated practice model with two observations. First, we argue that there can be no universal workforce development policy nor provision for non-permanent workers. There is no evidence of a single 'precariat class' (Standing, 2011) or a class of 'boundaryless workers' (Arthur & Rousseau, 1996). Different national institutional structures are generating different conditions of non-permanent work that are always relative to other employment options in those markets. Any provision for workforce development for non-permanent workers must necessarily be context dependent.

Second, we argue for workforce development efforts for non-permanent workers to begin from a broader understanding of capability development, beyond the discourse of rights, protection and benefits. As highlighted in Chapter 1, characterisations of decent and good work permeating the non-permanent work discourse pay scant regard to the human development aspect. Precariat understandings of non-permanent work have led to protracted efforts to establish particular categories of such workers that enable regulation to tie them to the traditional model of industrial relations based on an employee-employer relationship. The pigeon-holing of workers into specific categories does not sit well with the empirical data outlined in preceding chapters that shows many workers deploying their capabilities in a range of settings with different contractual arrangements, depending on the job they take up. Attempts to categorise non-permanent workers may in fact rob them of their agency prematurely. A more constructive discourse is to encourage the compatibility of some of these non-permanent forms of work with larger societal investments in education.

We go on to discuss how the integrated practice model can transform our understanding of national capability-building, challenging the front-loading model of education systems in most industrial societies and giving depth to lifelong learning policies. The focus on embodied practice and the space for a higher level of agency in non-permanent work for workers to chart out their own work journeys highlight fundamental new ways in how we should think about education, learning and development. While there is no one universal policy intervention that can be used to tackle the issues raised by non-permanent work, we will outline how the use of the integrated practice model in each country can highlight the areas where policy issues for country-specific provision could be developed.

Significance of national institutional structures in generating different conditions of non-permanent work

The growth of non-permanent work is a global phenomenon, but it is national institutional structures that are generating locally specific conditions of non-permanent work. The forms of non-permanent work in each country need to be understood in the institutional context of national labour markets, relative to other forms of employment arrangements in those labour markets. National institutional conditions shape non-permanent work in each country, including the level of wages, form of income and employment rights. When viewed comparatively, there is little sense to make categories such as 'precarious work' or 'boundaryless work' into uniform concepts applicable across labour markets because the characteristics of that work and the experience of it vary so much. It challenges us to develop new ways through which to understand the experience of these workers. A comparison of 'low-wage' non-permanent work in the UK, Singapore, India and South Korea highlights the nationally specific conditions of non-permanent work that escape any easy universal conceptualisation.

In the liberal market economy of the UK, the spread of globalised finance, new ways of organising production and declining trade union power have led to a hollowing out of jobs as managerial roles and skilled jobs were lost and job content transformed. The high levels of unemployment of the 1980s prompted significant market deregulation and the curtailment of trade union power in a crude process of job creation with limited attention to the quality of employment. At the lower levels, labour markets became more flexible and workers more insecure as income levels fell or remained relatively static. Low-wage non-permanent workers in the UK face the prospects of long spells of unemployment between jobs with the threat that exposes them to reducing their employability. Many UK low-wage non-permanent workers would prefer permanent jobs and are additionally constrained by the lack of opportunities to continue in non-permanent work. Whitton (2003) highlights that the precarious position of low-wage non-permanent work in UK is inextricably linked to the benefits accrued from permanent work as a result of atypical workers being kept at the fringes of the labour market and being denied the advantages that core workers enjoy. Daune-Richard (1998) likewise argues that the trade unions' focus on improving the protection of part-time workers had the effect of strengthening the labour market segmentation of such workers, instead of a more empowering agenda of how the specific skills and productivity in part-time work can be enhanced. More recent research on the self-employed in the UK has revealed that the use of non-permanent work is pervasive throughout the economy and takes diverse forms (CRSE & IES, 2017). Indeed, 30.7 per cent of the self-employed are in technical, managerial and professional occupations where the employment is relatively secure and where they have mid-to-high levels of pay and report relatively high levels of job satisfaction. This contrasts with a total of 17.1 per cent who are in low-paid, insecure jobs such as cleaners and carers.

The shape of non-permanent work in low-wage occupations takes a remarkably different form in Singapore than in the UK. Singapore has had strong job creation since its independence in 1965. The developmental state set up the institution of permanent work as an integral component of its state-led macroeconomic planning that cherry picks desired economic growth sectors, with a high focus on labour discipline (Sung, 2006). This model of economic growth continues to be sustained through the influx of migrant workers at depressed wage levels and with rigid work conditions, creating a mismatch between the jobs available and the aspirations of some segments of the local population. Low-wage non-permanent work emerges as a site of resistance for those who reject permanent work opportunities when such work cannot deliver the kind of socially acceptable levels of income or opportunity. As we outlined in preceding chapters, non-permanent workers in low-wage occupations in Singapore have little difficulty securing permanent work but opt for non-permanent work arrangements to enjoy higher pay and greater flexibility than they would have in permanent work. As one food and beverage casual worker explained in this research study, 'this is permanent . . . every day work, every day money . . . either I want or don't want [sic]'. In the context of full employment in Singapore, they do not face the kind of employment uncertainty encountered by their counterparts in UK and other Western economies. These non-permanent workers often point out that employers have offered them permanent employment. However, it is in non-permanent work that the workers would have the potential to scale their income to double or triple what they would have earned in permanent work by putting in longer hours if they so wish, which would not be possible if they were to accept fixed wages as a permanent worker in the very same occupation. This in no way suggests the desirability of their situation. On the contrary, fatigue from routinely physically demanding work, a sense of lack of progression and exclusion from medical benefits and the national savings scheme, namely the CPF, prompt many to continuously seek out alternative permanent work at their desired wage levels.

Like gig workers in Singapore, India's gig workers do not display the level of precarity associated with such work as described in Western advanced economies. Surie and Koduganti (2016) surveyed perceptions of security and risks of platform economy drivers in Bengaluru and found that platform economy companies in fact have given its drivers a 'stable, mid-term period of time to accumulate wealth' and 'bear the risks of flexible working conditions in the short-term with more confidence' (p. 2). The favourability of gig work in Bengaluru is linked to the pervasive informal economy in India that is dominated by unpaid, subsistence and daily wage work where work and income uncertainty is the norm. Many of these platform drivers had already been driving for a living in work where traditional middlemen presided over the distribution of jobs. The standardisation of work in platform economy removes the role of the traditional middlemen to enable these drivers to predict with more confidence their income levels over a longer period in the context of clearer job certainty.

This is not to say that the precarious character of non-permanent low-wage work is unique to Western, advanced economies. The South Korean non-permanent labour market exhibits a similar characteristic. It underwent extensive casualisation due to the reforms mandated by the International Monetary Fund, following the Asian financial crisis in 1997 (Cooke & Jiang, 2017). One in two South Korean workers may be in some form of non-standard work, much of which is linked to in-house sub-contracting (Shin, 2013). In contrast to Singapore, where trade unions are managed at the national level through tripartite dialogue spearheaded by the government, the developmental state of South Korea relies on enterprise-led trade unions as a mechanism for instituting labour discipline. Regular work carries with it significant employee protection. The passage of the Non-Regular Employment Law in South Korea in November 2006 stipulates that only full-time, regular workers could be members of unions in companies where they work. Non-regular workers thus have to express their discontent and demands on their own, leading them to find support for their struggle outside workplaces, specifically in social movement organisations, with varying levels of success (Lee & Lee, 2017).

We have used low-wage non-permanent work across these four countries to highlight the importance of institutional contexts in generating particular conditions of non-permanent work. The precarity experienced by low-wage non-permanent workers in the UK has parallels with their counterparts in South Korea, but stands in sharp contrast to the experience of such work in Singapore and India. What the comparative analysis suggests is that non-permanent work in and of itself is neither necessarily problematic nor desirable, but always dependent on its status and position relative to other employment arrangements in the national labour market. Any provision for workforce development for non-permanent workers must necessarily be context dependent. It also means that a policy focus on non-permanent work should not be at the expense of tackling other labour market issues. For instance, in the UK, quality job creation remains an important conversation. In Singapore, the design of permanent work in low-wage occupations has to continue to be a top policy concern.

Categorising non-permanent workers and the challenges they create for workforce development policy

It is perhaps inevitable that to provide better support for non-permanent workers, unions and other interested members of society have mounted various efforts to categorise different types of non-permanent work in a bid to select some categories that could be tied to some form of employee or worker relationship with businesses to co-share some risks, particularly related to income uncertainty and health benefits. Shin (2013) outlines how the term 'non-regular worker' in South Korea came under significant political contestation following the IMF's institution of neo-liberal reforms, prompting the government to take the lead to forge a new consensus of who counts as a non-standard worker. Despite a widening of the term to include limited-term workers, part-time workers and atypical workers, consensus-building is far from complete, as the existing definition excludes permanent temporary workers and what is said to be 'bogus self-employed persons'. In the UK, a recommendation was made to the UK government in 2017 that people who work for platform-based companies, such as Deliveroo and Uber, be classified as dependent contractors (Taylor, 2017).

Universal meaningful categories remain elusive and will continue to be so given the pace at which new technologies are being deployed in a neo-liberal economic order that is enabling a high level of experimentation in the labour market. Zero-hour contracts and app-enabled on-demand work are some recent innovations in the labour market. What is of concern is that the pigeon-holing of workers into specific labour categories does not sit well with the empirical data we outlined in preceding chapters that shows many workers deploying their capabilities in a range of settings with different contractual arrangements, depending on the job they take up. In Singapore's technical theatre, workers can take up jobs as hourly rated crew, as well as project-based assignments. In other words, they are both on zero-hour contract as well as operating as an independent contractor. The opportunity to deploy their capabilities in diverse settings allows them to take advantage of expansive jobs and minimise the risks associated with restrictive jobs. Attempts to categorise them and keep them beholden to particular contractual arrangements may in fact rob them of their agency prematurely.

The focus on categorisation of workers also means that advocacy and interventions are always ex-post, as a reaction to the effects of a contractual arrangement. A single-minded focus on rights, protection and benefits obscures the need for deeper debates on creating work that enables self-actualisation and affords dignity to workers. It fails to consider that permanent work can be just as stifling and self-limiting, whereas workers may benefit more in terms of craft development when they can deploy their capabilities in wider settings. It also ignores the reality that the security of permanent work is far from certain in the current context.

A more constructive discourse is the extent to which flexible contractual arrangements can be deployed in ways that are capability-enhancing and compatible with larger societal investments in education. As demonstrated in this volume, non-permanent work arrangements challenge conventional understanding of the division of labour based on wage, skills or formal qualifications. Where specialist work is available in the industry on a non-permanent basis, entry-level low-wage work may in fact be a stepping stone to developing deeper expertise if adequate support is provided, as the case of Singapore's technical theatre demonstrates. On the other hand, non-permanent work, even in occupations requiring higher educational qualifications and greater work complexity, limits capability-building if there is no opportunity for specialisation on a non-permanent basis.

There is the threat that new technologies deployed by firms in a neo-liberal economic environment may create more task-based gig work in the likes of Uber and TaskRabbit. This is not limited to just low-wage work but also professional work that is undergoing Digital Taylorism in terms of being broken into discrete tasks that can then be parcelled out as on-demand work. However, technological innovation does not take place in a vacuum. There are far wider gains when workforce development efforts are equally focused on encouraging and incentivising industries and businesses to deploy non-permanent work arrangements in ways that enhance the capabilities of the workforce. The agenda of innovation cannot be seen as incompatible with workforce development. More importantly, this volume has shown that non-permanent work arrangements are not necessarily detrimental to workers. Such arrangements have the potential to be capability-enhancing because practitioners can deploy themselves in diverse settings and not be limited to just one employer, unlike in permanent work. In information technology, for instance, software engineers are increasingly engaged in non-standard work arrangements where they can build their portfolio through diverse projects with multiple clients. Gigster and Toptal are two niche developer platforms for freelance work in the information technology and finance industries with a series of screening processes before one is accepted as a platform member and where challenging and lucrative work is posted.

We do not in any way suggest the futility of rights-based or protection-based advocacy for non-permanent workers. Some forms of universal provision are necessary, such as medical coverage for the broad spectrum of non-permanent workers, not just particular types. However, we argue that rights-based advocacy tends to be ex-post and is thus limiting. Such advocacy has to be coupled with capability-development advocacy to push an agenda where technology can be deployed in new ways that is capability-enhancing. In the absence of such discourse, the costs of individual 'skills' curtailment or atrophy, aggregated at the national level, have considerable implications for capability levels in the workforce and carry societal risks.

Integrated practice & lifelong learning provisions

At its core, the integrated practice model is about learning to be and to become. As we noted in Chapter 6, to consider being and becoming, rather than referencing from a list of knowledge and skills, is to break free of dichotomous understandings of knowledge and practice. Learning to be and become focuses on the long-term process of capability development for personal and professional growth that is well beyond technical mastery. It is a journey of self-discovery that is not limited to the minds of individuals, but anchored in the social process of building capabilities and relations and creating new ones. The journey is never linear, but rather marked by elements of navigation, uncertainties and serendipity with unclear and yet-to-be discovered pathways. Tried-and-tested ways are but mere signposts for the non-permanent worker who needs to constantly differentiate himself or herself in the marketplace of work and develop his or her own pathways.

While the starting point of the integrated practice model is the development of non-permanent workers, we argue that the model is not without relevance to the wider workforce that can expect to experience more frequent job and career changes across their working lives. In fact, the model potentially builds higher resilience in the context of greater employment uncertainty by orienting an individual not to a particular job or a career that is highly limiting, but to the wider occupation or a practice. The model does not in any way presuppose that occupational contexts are static. Quite the contrary, occupational contexts are dynamic spaces for interpreting new or different ways in which practice can be enacted – be it technological advancements, new ways of working or new career paths. Our dataset supports the dynamism of occupational contexts for example, how practitioners in the creative industry are also lecturers and entrepreneurs and how they need to constantly keep up with the latest technology, by understanding what it can and cannot do. In other words, occupational contexts are expansive and string together a range of occupational practices. The model does not presuppose that an individual always remains in the same occupation. Rather, participation in any occupation, new or otherwise, entails a longer-term process of learning to be and become, rather than a simple process of picking up technical skills. However, the expansive nature of occupational contexts enables more dynamic ways to reconstitute occupational practice, thus challenging the paradigm that the new practitioner always has to begin as a novice.

Below, we outline four ways in which workforce development needs to evolve in the context of the integrated practice model.

From front-loading to lifelong learning

Learning in the context of being and becoming fundamentally challenges the front-loading model of national education in most industrialised societies, where young adults spend a significant amount of their youth picking up knowledge and skills in isolated educational institutions with the occasional exposure to industry through career talks, industry projects, internships and other related activities. We recall the critique of the modern education system as a 'great sorting machine' (Kirp, 1974), with the hidden goal of stratifying society and placing workers in a socially-constructed hierarchy of professions.

High-stakes examinations decide who qualifies for entry to this or that profession. The limits of this front-loading model may have been accommodated under traditional forms of organising production where there is stability not only in the professions and occupational competences, but also in employment, providing significant space for the individual to learn to be and to become through the actual work. Unfortunately, in a period of change where jobs and careers are disrupted rapidly, the deficiencies of this front-loading model are laid bare as workers now find that they need to pick up new ways of doing things or switch to a new job.

Continuing education systems attempt to plug the gaping hole created by the modern education system by giving opportunities for adults to develop themselves, be it to get better at their current jobs or occupations or to enter new ones. Unfortunately, the dominant model of such systems mimics the front-loading model of education through the wide-spread provision of adult classroom training designed to equip learners with technical skills, with scant regard to the social processes of learning. Singapore's continuing education system is especially culpable, with the government's investment in adult education spawning an entire industry focused on competence-based training provision. The response of Singapore's non-permanent workers to such learning provisions is understandably lukewarm. Their typical learning processes include observing practices and the work of others, engaging in dialogue, accessing expertise through networks and doing the work. Indeed, there is a strong desire to learn particularly from more experienced workers, but such opportunities are hard to come by and rarely delivered through the continuing education system.

The evidence points to the importance of lifelong learning to anchor the learning and development of not just non-permanent workers, but the broader workforce, across their working lives. Lifelong learning is not a value left to the agency of individuals, but deliberately facilitated through educational provisions rooted in situated practice that needs to be imagined in new ways due to disruption of stable, site-specific understanding of work and work communities.

The place of pre-service education has to be re-examined in the context of wider lifelong learning provisions. Rather than broadly viewing lifelong learning as a compensation for initial education, pre-service education becomes the front-end of an integrated educational system that caters for further learning, career switches and reorientation. A core aspect of pre-service education must be to create safe spaces that enable a journey of exploration of craft identity or identities, anchored in an individual's interests and facilitated through exposure to a range of work opportunities and communities. What this entails is a relook at high-stakes examinations that currently sort out students' access to various courses, based on test scores instead of passion or interests. Pre-service education also needs to develop entrepreneurial capabilities in a broad manner in terms of the diverse ways of seeking out work and strategies to build a niche in the marketplace, given the privatisation of risk, performance and responsibility to individuals. Lecturers, teachers, career counsellors and parents play an important role in facilitating these journeys of self-discovery, as highlighted in Chapter 6. A generous view of the capabilities of each individual sits at the heart of the transformation of the education system based on the integrated practice model.

From human capital to embodied practice

The focus on embodied practice allows one to break free of dichotomous understandings of knowledge and practice and didactic instruction. Work is enacted not as separate sets of skills and knowledge but as complex wholes of integrated capabilities that are deeply embodied.

The space for workforce development opens up dramatically with this focus on embodied practice. It puts the learner at the core in a journey of learning and developing across various settings. In earlier chapters, we observe the opportunity for linking up experienced freelancers with beginning practitioners in a mentoring arrangement that is embedded in the production process. These may be industry masters who are recognised and rewarded financially for mentoring the practitioners. When twinned with iterative movement from educational institutions, it enables systematic, not haphazard, access to theoretical knowing and the development of meta-knowing that enables the non-permanent worker to grow and develop. Entrepreneurial and learning-to-learn capabilities can be developed by providing a space for learners to seek their own work and reflect on the experience.

There could be other new ways to develop capabilities beyond educational institutions. Platform applications are excellent in linking up producers and consumers without an intermediary and offer the possibility of matching experienced practitioners with beginning practitioners in a loose apprenticeship model. Workplaces could also emerge as sites for professional development. In technical theatre, a manager in a theatre venue was exploring the possibility of engaging an experienced freelancer on an adjunct basis to mentor younger freelancers.

In all, the focus on embodied practice necessarily creates a decentred approach to learning. In Singapore, the government recently issued training credits to individuals to spur their engagement in lifelong learning activities. The problem is that such credits can be used only for classroom-based training approved by the government agency overseeing continuous education and training. There is practically no recognition of the importance of embodied practice.

Lifelong learning provisions, if they are to truly work well, will have to break free from their human capital origins that see competence development as focused wholly on the 'supply side', without addressing the contexts, spaces and their practices in which capabilities are used and developed. Favouring training programmes that draw down elements of 'transferable skills' and competences from an elaborated competence framework denies the embodiment of practice. The recognition by funding bodies of the need to facilitate broad-based, embodied practice will open up a range of innovations in lifelong learning provisions to support the broader-based learning and development of workers.

From stratification to differentiated development

Lifelong learning also has to create space to understand dispositions and prior biographies of workers and facilitate the recontextualisation of knowledge in new ways. Learning and development are mediated by a complex dynamic between learner disposition, biography and the situated context of the work. Particular dispositions may come in the way of how learners see the affordances that are available to them, as noted in Chapter 3.

Indeed, our dataset has a sizeable number of individuals who 'fall into' non-permanent work, in that they seek out non-permanent work simply to be gainfully employed, rather than with a deliberate view to practice in the occupation. These workers may opt for non-permanent work because of prior retrenchment and their subsequent struggle to secure suitable employment. The adult education industry is replete with such examples. Other workers may join an industry by tagging along with their peers without an appreciation of the industry, as in the case of some of our respondents in the creative industries. Due to their disposition, these individuals lack the dexterity to identify the opportunities for development. For example, in technical theatre, many technical crew are unable to see the need to build an appreciation of the creative arts, which limits their ability to make more meaningful contributions to a production. This also stunts their development prospects.

The need to consider dispositions and prior biographies in lifelong learning provisions cannot be emphasised enough in the context of wider employment changes that workers are expected to undergo. Too often, work transitions do not take place well because of the alleged deficient mindset of the individual worker, causing frustrations to all involved, including the worker, peers, human resource personnel and line managers, the educational provider and other stakeholders. The integrated practice model posits that such transitions should not be conceptualised as abrupt, as though the past is of little value or even incompatible with the current transition. Rather, there are more dynamic ways to reconstitute occupational practice, and the 'new' practitioner does not always have to begin as a novice. Learning to be and to become requires a process of meaning-making through recontextualisation of past knowledge and experiences in new ways. It is a social process that can be supported by educators, workplace managers and peers, once there is a better appreciation of the learner's disposition and biography.

From just supply-side to including demand-side

The integrated practice model demands the availability of challenging work. Without such work, there is little space for workers to develop themselves meaningfully. Adaptability cannot be institutionally separated from the structure of opportunity. Advocacy to push for capability-enhancing non-permanent work must accompany the deployment of the integrated practice model. As Brown, Lauder, and Ashton (2011) highlight, there is a sharp disjunction between how national governments understand competitiveness and productivity and how firms develop their business strategy. Whereas national governments focus on knowledge and skills rather than profits, companies are focused on getting smart things done at a lower price. Leaving it to the market to experiment with new employment arrangements unfettered leads to high risks of incongruence with large societal investments in education.

Chapter 4 outlines two separate types of non-permanent jobs, namely jobs where specialist positions are available on a non-permanent basis in the industry and jobs that keep workers strictly at the periphery. For the former, strengthening labour market linkages across jobs is vital, as otherwise, it leads to situations of only a few succeeding in the industry, while the rest are stagnating. This problem of inequitable distribution of job opportunities for independent contractors has received limited attention, given the overwhelming policy and public focus on what is seen as more 'precarious' work such as gig drivers and those on zero-hour contracts.

For peripheral jobs where there are no prospects for specialisation on a non-permanent basis, the integrated practice model emphasises the need to develop policy measures that can enhance the capability level of such jobs by improving the demands of the tasks, such as rotating workers between jobs with different tasks, using teamwork, creating a demand for team-working skills and encouraging the use of devolved management, thereby requiring workers to develop communication and problem-solving capabilities.

In summary, the integrated practice model offers fundamentally new ways to organise workforce development in support of the learning and development of non-permanent workers, alongside the wider workforce, which is likely to experience more frequent job and career changes. The model demands a central place for lifelong learning, overturning the front-loading character of modern education systems. It eschews didactic practices to focus on embodied practice, creating more socially-situated and decentred spaces for learning. It puts learners and their biographies centrestage to allow for differentiated development in their journey of learning to be and to become that builds upon their past experiences. It also highlights the need to give attention to demand-side configuration of jobs by employers and the industry.

Implications for national education and lifelong learning systems

The most striking policy issues for country-specific provision of the integrated practice model is the absence of lifelong learning provisions in many established industrial societies, including the UK, the United States of America (USA) and

Germany. Government investments in education in these countries continue to concentrate on the preparation of youths for work in the context of high youth unemployment and temporary employment. The UK government invested in a large-scale modern apprenticeship scheme targeted at youths aged 16–24 that provides off- and on-the-job training leading to an industry-approved qualification. A target of three million new apprenticeships by 2020 has been set. UK employers are required to contribute to the scheme by paying a levy. Bynner (2017) highlights the failure of the UK to develop a system of lifelong learning. While there are still odd programmes in the UK that encourage learning at work, such as a scheme to subsidise 'training' in SMEs and a trade union initiative to support learning at work, there is a lack of systematic provision. The focus on one-off skills means that the system is not preparing workers for the demands of the modern labour market. Germany's vocational training system demonstrates the value of embodied practice, but offers mainly high levels of initial training, with limited provision thereafter (Institut Arbeit und Technik, 2012). In a study by Hanushek et al. (2015) that uses data from OECD's International Adult Literacy Survey (IALS), it was found that the initial labour-market advantage of vocational education to general education decreases with age. Among the three apprenticeship countries in their dataset, they found that lifetime earnings in vocational education were larger in Switzerland, as compared to Germany and Denmark, which had higher economic growth. The findings led the authors to conclude that general education was more adaptable to a volatile economy. There is some support for this finding from our integrated practice model that requires the development of broad-based entrepreneurial and learning-to-learn capabilities that modern apprenticeship programmes tend not to develop (Guile & Lahiff, 2012). The focus on apprenticeships as a solution to tackle high youth unemployment and temporary employment is necessary in the context of the non-standard work arrangements in these countries. However, the evidence suggests that such models of intervention are short-term solutions which will not build a foundation for lifelong development for work and learning and may even be limiting in how workers are exposed to work and networks in only one firm.

In South Korea, community-based adult education has made way for more formalised and individualised approaches to adult learning that is increasingly taking on segmented forms in what has been called 'learning capitalism' (Han, 2008, p. 517). Companies deliver the bulk of vocational training to workers through a large private market, while the government focuses its investment on providing open learning as a credible pathway for university accreditation (Kwon, Schied, & Kim, 2011). In other words, the government's investment in lifelong learning is about improving life chances based on qualifications. There are significant limits to this model. The privatisation of lifelong vocational education and training means that corporate objectives are prioritised over the broader needs of workers such as entrepreneurial capabilities. The government's open learning provisions also do not deliver on their intent, as the credentials do not offer the same degree of professional opportunities for adult learners (Han, 2008; Kwon, Schied, & Kim, 2011). In other words, South Korea's lifelong learning model is not bold enough in making lifelong learning complementary to its pre-service school system and preparing workers for dynamic change.

Like South Korea, Singapore has stepped up its investments in lifelong learning provisions. Unlike South Korea's largely compensation-based model, the provisions in Singapore have been conceptualised as complementary to the national education system in a bold experiment towards 'gradually erasing the lines between pre-employment training and continuing education and training' to support a lifelong pursuit of mastery and excellence (Ministry of Education, 2016). In this regard, the approach finds support from the integrated practice model. The city-state is moving towards more public provisions, carving out a significant role for adult learning in its traditional institutes of higher learning, including universities and polytechnics. Some of the training programmes being delivered are in cutting-edge areas such as data analytics and cybersecurity in a bid to prepare its citizens for the looming digital disruption. Subsidised training is widely available, alongside a training credit scheme that every Singaporean aged 25 and above can utilise for courses. The limits of the Singapore model against the integrated practice model are immediately apparent. Contrary to the decentred approach envisaged in the integrated practice model, the shape of Singapore's lifelong learning model is highly centralised with minimal efforts to involve workplaces and industry practitioners in lifelong learning provisions. There is limited space for facilitating embodied practice, as didactic instruction dominates. Here again is the focus on training that separates theory from practice, doing from knowing. A training discourse often focuses on specific skills and works from a deficit model within a supply-driven model as opposed to learning, where the learner is the centre, taking responsibility for their learning and being situated in a demand-driven model. In all, the complementary model of Singapore's lifelong learning provision is a step in the right direction, but represents a missed opportunity in its failure to anchor the provisions on a stronger pedagogical foundation based on both the getting of work and the doing of work.

In India, the global discourse on lifelong learning has prompted the Indian government to shift towards competitive skills-oriented policies on lifelong learning in a bid to propel knowledge-based economic growth, thus overturning the traditional notion of lifelong learning in India that typically seeks to cater to the high number of illiterate and poorly literate citizens. Mandal (2013) highlights how this shift raises deep issues of what is 'nationally realistic and globally viable' in policy-making for an economy with a large proportion of the population still living below the poverty line. Regardless of the shifts, lifelong learning provisions remain underfunded by the government and are largely left to a private market that relies on corporate and individual investments that tend to benefit those who are already socially advantaged.

What is clearly apparent is that there is no single model of lifelong learning provision. Each country's unique socio-economic structures are generating different forms of provisions. This is certainly desirable, but the analysis of the lifelong learning provisions against the integrated practice model demonstrates the limits of some of these provisions. In the UK, the modern apprenticeship system does not build the kind of entrepreneurial capabilities required by the workforce to navigate the labour market over the long-term. In South Korea, the privatisation of lifelong vocational education and training prioritises corporate interests, with limited attention to the capabilities required to build broader-based skills. Singapore is ahead of most countries in its systematic provisions that seek to empower workers to navigate labour market changes more confidently, but the provisions rest on weak pedagogical foundations given the heavy reliance on didactic approaches. India faces the challenge of dealing with high levels of illiteracy and a large informal sector, which limits how lifelong learning and embodied practice can be meaningfully enacted in the context of high power asymmetry. Still, the integrated model suggests the potential for entrepreneurial and learning-to-learn capabilities to guide craft development more decisively to overcome contextual challenges.

Conclusion

In this chapter, we have argued that the context of dynamic change demands for workforce development to be imagined in new ways, involving a fundamental rethink of the relationship among work, education and employability. We have outlined how the integrated practice model can offer new ways of organising workforce development in the context of disruption to the standard employment model. We note that any provision for workforce development must necessarily be context dependent, given the significance of national institutional arrangements in generating different conditions of work in each country. We have emphasised that non-permanent work does not necessarily lead to precarity, but may even be capability-enhancing in particular forms of work and contexts. There is also no evidence that non-permanent work in low-skilled occupations, in and of themselves, pay poorly and lead to precarity. In Singapore, non-permanent work in low-skill occupations may in fact pay better, and in some sectors provide greater scope for capability-development than higher-skilled non-permanent work.

We have argued that learning to be and to become, which sits at the core of the integrated practice model, requires fundamentally new ways of preparation for work. We challenge the front-loading model of education systems in most industrial societies, arguing instead for lifelong learning systems to sit at the centre of educational provisions. We highlight the importance of embodied practice and the space for a higher level of agency for workers to chart out their own work journeys. We also note that adaptability cannot be institutionally separated from the structure of opportunity. Advocacy and regulation for capability-enhancing work must accompany the deployment of the integrated practice model.

The successful take-up of the integrated practice model hinges on the partnership of a range of stakeholders. There must be a commitment by government agencies of the need to invest more in workers throughout their working lives, rather than just in the early stages of their youth. There must also be support for a decentered and differentiated approach to lifelong learning provisions, anchored in embodied practice, which necessarily entails messier ways of delivering those provisions. Workplaces must also step up to provide the social spaces for learning, as do industry practitioners. Educational institutions and educators also play a central role in this transformation.

There are four points that are immediately apparent in our examination of lifelong learning provisions in selected countries. First, the government must necessarily play a significant role to provide such provisions, as the cases of Singapore and South Korea show. Second, models of lifelong learning have greater depth when they are conceptualised to play a complementary, not compensatory, role in national education systems in the context of dynamic change. Third, a shift from a focus on training to learning creates the spaces for potentially innovative, decentred approaches to learning. It also recognises that much of this learning already currently takes place, as illustrated in our data. The difficulties for policy makers are that training is easily 'seen' and accounted for when spending public monies. Learning is more amorphous, happening anywhere, anyhow and at any time. It is difficult to pin down. This is an issue that policy makers must grapple with given the rapid changes in work, labour markets and technology that give us access to huge quantities of information. Policy makers have been slow to grasp the limits of a training model, but leading firms have not been so slow and have invested significantly to support intensive workplace learning (Sung & Ashton, 2015). Finally, much of learning provisions have always been provided to support the achievement of company objectives. What this research has shown is the urgent need to provide additional support for the worker's development needs whose requirements for entrepreneurial capabilities is a separate need that employers are not going to meet. The dynamic context of more frequent job and career changes implies that the getting of work and the doing of work will increasingly diverge. Provisions have to be put in place urgently to enable workers to navigate the increasingly more complex terrain of work and learning with more confidence.

References

Arthur, M. B., & Rousseau, D. M. (1996). *The boundaryless career: A new employment principle for a new organizational era*. New York: Oxford University Press.

Brown, P., Lauder, H., & Ashton, D. (2011). *The global auction: The broken promises of education, jobs and incomes*. New York: Oxford University Press.

Bynner, J. (2017). Whatever happened to lifelong learning? And does it matter? *Journal of the British Academy*, *5*, 61–89.

Cooke, F. L., & Jiang, Y. (2017). The growth of non-standard employment in Japan and South Korea: The role of institutional actors and impact on workers and the labour market. *Asia Pacific Journal of Human Resources, 55*, 155–176.

CRSE & IES. (2017). *The true diversity of self-employment*. London: Centre for Research on Self-Employment & Institute of Employment Studies.

Daune-Richard, A. M. (1998). How does the "Societal Effect" shape the use of part-time work in France, the UK and Sweden? In J. O'Reilly & C. Fagan (Eds.), *Part-time prospects: An international comparison of part-time work in Europe, North America and the Pacific Rim*. London: Routledge.

Guile, D., & Lahiff, A. (2012). *Apprenticeship and freelance work: A de-centred and distributed model of learning to develop media production apprentices' vocational practice and social capital*. London: Centre for Learning and Life Chances in Knowledge Economies and Societies. Retrieved from www.llakes.org

Han, S. H. (2008). The lifelong learning ecosystem in Korea: Evolution of learning capitalis? *International Journal of Lifelong Education, 27*(5), 517–524.

Hanushek, E. A., Schwerdt, G., Woessmann, L., & Zhang, L. (2015). General education, vocational education, and labor-market outcomes over the lifecycle. *The Journal of Human Resources, 52*(1), 48–87.

Institut Arbeit und Technik. (2012). *Mapping the German landscape of tertiary lifelong learning*. Discussion paper, 4:3. Accessed 21 February 2018.

Jacobs, R. L., & Hawley, J. (2009). Emergence of workforce development: Definition, conceptual boundaries, and implications. In R. Maclean & D. Wilson (Eds.), *International handbook of education for the changing world of work*. Bonn: UNEVOC International Centre for Technical and Vocational Education and Training, & Springer.

Kirp, D. L. (1974). The great sorting machine. *The Phi Delta Kappan, 55*(8), 521–525.

Kwon, T., Schied, F. M., & Kim, J. (2011). Towards a learning society: Lifelong learning policies and practises of South Korea since the 1997 IMF crisis. *Widening Participation and Lifelong Learning, 13*, 2.

Leadbeater, C., & Mulgan, G. (1997). The end of unemployment. In G. Mulgan (Ed.), *Life after politics*. London: Fontana.

Lee, B. H., & Lee, S. S. Y. (2017). Winning conditions of precarious workers' struggles: A reflection based on case studies from South Korea. *Industrial Relations, 72*(3), 524–550.

Mandal, S. (2013). From policy to guidelines: Metamorphosis of lifelong learning in India. *International Journal of Lifelong Education, 32*(2).

Ministry of Education. (2016). *Opening address by Mr Ong Ye Kung, acting minister for education (Higher education and skills), at the MOU signing ceremony for the power engineering sector*. Accessed 21 February 2018. https://www.moe.gov.sg/news/speeches/opening-address-by-mr-ong-ye-kung--acting-minister-for-education-higher-education-and-skills-at-the-mou-signing-ceremony-for-the-power-engineering-sector

Ross, A. (2008). The new geography of work. *Theory Culture & Society, 25*(7), 31–49.

Shin, K. Y. (2013). Economic crisis, neoliberal reforms, and the rise of precarious work in South Korea. *American Behavioural Scientist, 57*(3), 335–353.

Standing, G. (2011). *The precariat: The new dangerous class*. London: Bloomsbury Publishing.

Sung, J. (2006). *Explaining the economic success of Singapore: The developmental worker as the missing link*. Cheltenham: Edward Elgar Publishing.

Sung, J., & Ashton, D. N. (2015). *Skills in business: The role of business strategy, sectoral skills development and skills policy*. London: Sage Publications.

Surie, A., & Koduganti, J. (2016). The emerging nature of work in platform economy companies in Bengaluru, India: The case of Uber and Ola cab drivers. *E-Journal of International and Comparative Labour Studies*, *5*(3), 2–30.

Taylor, M. (2017). *Good work: The Taylor review of modern working practices*. Report submitted to the UK government. Accessed 21 February 2018. https://assets.publishing.service.gov.uk/government/uploads/system/uploads/attachment_data/file/627671/good-work-taylor-review-modern-working-practices-rg.pdf

Whitton, T. (2003). The growth of precarious employment in Great Britain. In *Revue Française de civilisation Britannique*. Paris: Centre de Recherche et d'Études en Civilisation Britannique.

Appendix A

The research project

Genesis and methodology

The genesis of our research project on non-permanent workers and their learning and identity came from a Roundtable discussion of international scholars on the topic of workplace learning and the mediation of context held in Singapore in 2011. The Roundtable was funded by the Institute for Adult Learning, Singapore (IAL) and organised and conducted by IAL's research Centre for Work and Learning (CWL). The Roundtable included international and local academics with expertise in workplace learning. In our breakout discussions related to specific potential projects, Professor Karen Evans, who facilitated the group that developed the research proposal for the non-permanent workers project, was particularly interested in how workers think and feel their way into particular occupations. The group then identified that non-permanent workers were a growing segment of the labour market that were little understood in Singapore. After much discussion, we settled on the addressing the following research questions:

1. How does the experience of non-permanent work **contribute** to or **constrain** the **learning** of workers?
2. How do non-permanent workers **identify** with their work, and how does this **influence learning opportunities**?
3. How can the **learning** of non-permanent workers be **supported and enhanced**?

We conducted the project iteratively, beginning with film and television, then adult educators, followed by technical theatre and, finally, what we, at that stage, called the 'low-wage' occupations. Five reports were generated, one for each of these groups of occupations, and in our final report, we undertook an analysis across the sectors. It was at this stage that we developed the integrated practice model. All five reports are available on the IAL website, under research publications.

They are:

- Bound, H., Rushbrook, P., & Sivalingham, M. (2013). *The entrepreneurial self: Becoming a freelancer in Singapore's film and television industry*. Singapore: Institute for Adult Learning.

- Karmel, A., Bound, H., & Rushbrook, P. (2013). *Identity and learning for freelance adult educators in Singapore*. Singapore: Institute for Adult Learning.
- Nur, S., Bound, H., Karmel, A., & Sivalingham, M. (n.d.). *Masters of their destiny? Identities, learning and development of freelance workers in Singapore's technical theatre industry*. Singapore: Institute for Adult Learning.
- Sadik, S., Bound, H., Karmel, A., & Tan, J. (2015). *Haphazard occupational narratives: The work and developmental experiences of non-permanent workers in low-wage occupations in Singapore*. Singapore: Institute for Adult Learning.
- Bound, H., Sadik, S., & Karmel, A. (2015). *Developing non-permanent workers in Singapore*. Singapore: Institute for Adult Learning.

The following section on our sample provides an overview of the total sample, followed by an outline of our analysis across the case studies. These sections are followed by a description of the background, sample and analysis for each of the separate studies.

Our sample

The interviewees were selected based on purposive and convenience sampling (Lankshear & Knobel, 2004) to obtain a range of job roles, gender and years of experience. As is typical of qualitative research, the sampling is not representative of the population. As the population is not currently defined or captured statistically, a representative sample would not have been possible, had we desired to draw the sample in this way. Conducting some 30 interviews per sector (see Figure 1), however, resulted in 'saturation' of the data where common stories and themes were being expressed by the participants. Participants were

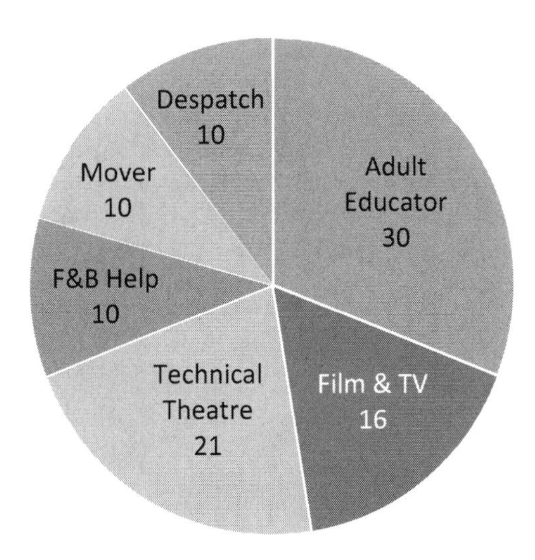

Figure 1 Total sample of non-permanent workers (n=97)

Table 1 Sample selection criteria

Included	*Excluded*
• Singapore citizens or permanent residents • Workers who are engaged on fixed-term contracts of less than 12 months or who engage in work without formal contracts • Workers who have been working on short, fixed term contracts/no contract/as casual workers for *at least* six months	• Non-Singapore citizens or non-permanent residents • Permanent employees and workers whose work contract terms extend for 12 months or more; students, pre-national service men • Workers who have been working on short, fixed-term contracts/no contract/as casual workers for *less than* six months

identified through industry contacts, personal contacts of the research team, advertisements and snowballing with an eye on our selection criteria listed in Table 1. Figures 2–5 show the demographic data of our participants.

The profile of the non-permanent workers we interviewed is varied, as indicated by Figures 2–5. The breakdown of respondents by sector or occupations is in Figure 1. Our respondents were undertaking non-permanent work across the age groups (Figure 2). Notably, adult educators are predominantly between 40–64 years of age, reflecting the need to have existing work experience before becoming an adult educator. There were fewer creative workers beyond the age of 49, perhaps indicative of the heavy work and often gruelling hours. Low-wage respondents are spread across the age groups. The ethnicity of our respondents is somewhat of the population at large (Figure 3). Notable, however, is the large number of adult educators who are Chinese, compared to proportions in our sample who are Malay or Indian. In the creative and low-wage sectors, our respondents are more evenly spread across the different ethnicities that are dominant in Singapore. In terms of gender, the larger number of males in our sample is reflective of the gender distribution in the creative and low-wage industry sectors (Figure 4). Adult educators are more evenly distributed. In terms of educational qualifications, adult educators in our sample are the group that holds post-graduate qualifications, as would be expected. Creative workers in our sample predominantly hold a degree, or a diploma or O/N Levels, with two holding only secondary qualifications. As would be expected, the low-wage workers in our sample hold lower levels of educational qualification from O/N Levels to primary, although one respondent held a degree and another a diploma (Figure 5).

Analysing the data

On completion of the specific studies in each of the sectors, we undertook a systematic analysis across the cases, drawing on the reports and also returning to

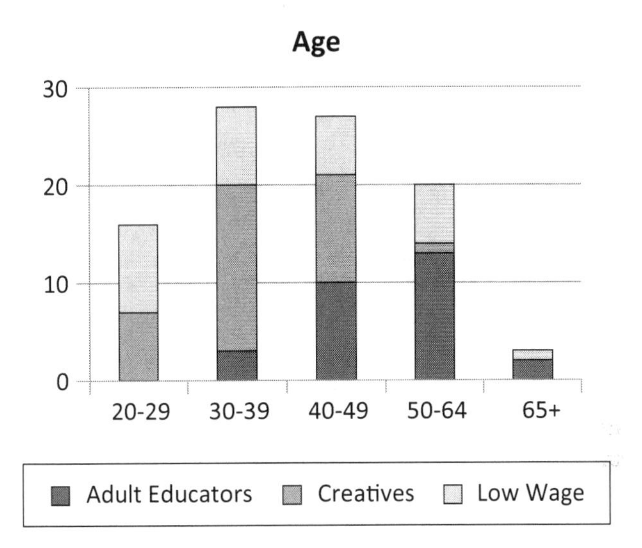

Figure 2 Age of respondents

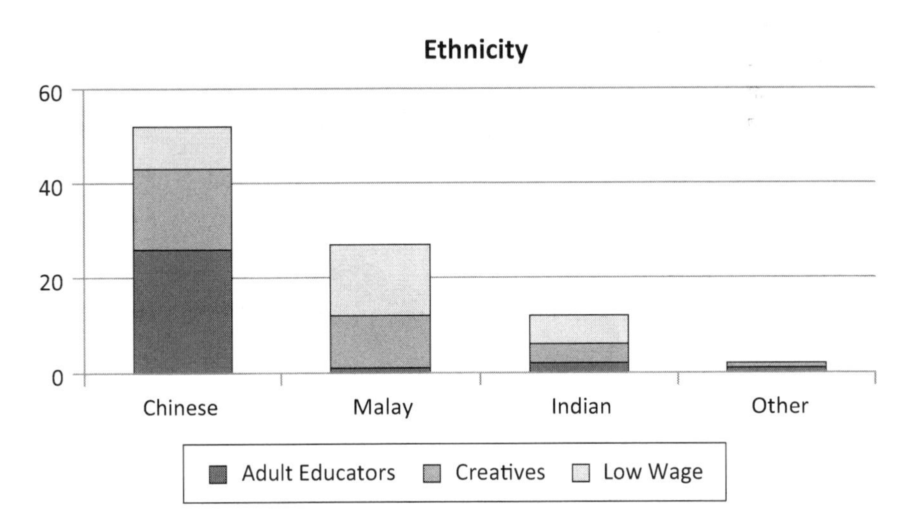

Figure 3 Ethnicity of respondents

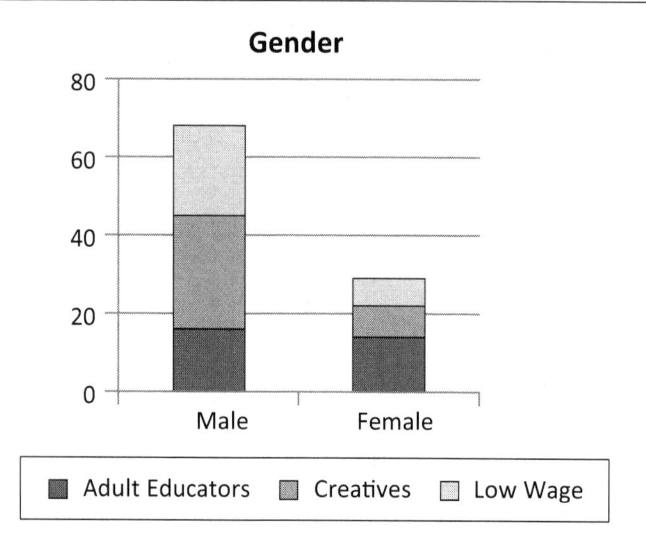

Figure 4 Gender of respondents

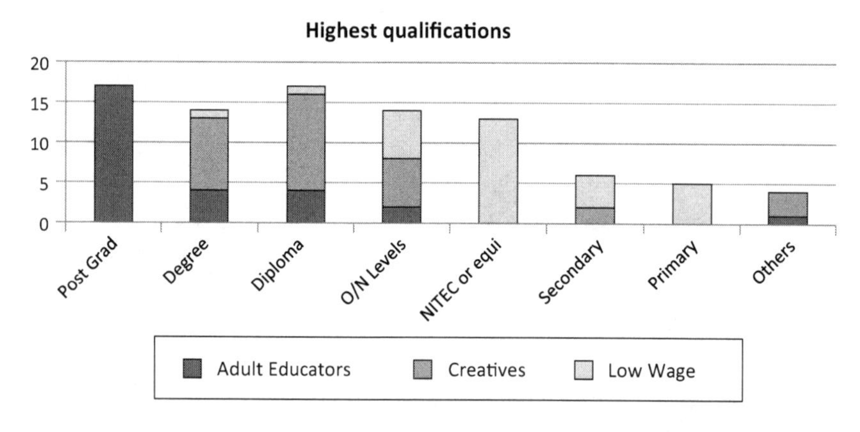

Figure 5 Educational qualifications of respondents

the data. Firstly, we undertook a systematic analysis across the sectors and then focused on key dimensions we identified to inform our conceptual frame: namely integrated practice (entrepreneurialism, craft identity and learning-to-learn skills), dispositions, context and journey.

Once we focused on the dimensions listed above, we quantified aspects of our qualitative data. We used this method to confirm our interpretation and as a means to further access deeper insights and identify dominant and divergent patterns in the data. The process of undertaking this kind of analysis requires a tighter categorisation and naming its characteristics to identify the 'identity variables', journeys, and other characteristics of these workers. This analysis confirmed the criticality of having well-developed entrepreneurial, craft and learning-to-learn capabilities. We then went back to the data again to establish why different workers with different forms of integrated practice were experiencing different journeys. This process confirmed and deepened our conceptualisation of dispositions and occupational affordances and their importance for growth.

Given the large number of qualitative interviews and the multi-faceted nature of the analysis, it is reasonable to assume our findings are generalisable with two important caveats. The first caveat relates to the nation of Singapore and its developmental and policy environment, which may make the experience of non-permanent work in Singapore distinct compared to the experience in developed nations, particularly for those experiencing lower incomes (across all the sectors). The second caveat relates to our sample selection, as we have selected only workers with contract or employment periods of one year or less or with no contracts. Clearly, the closer the group is to our sample, the more generalisable our findings are to that group. This particularly applies to findings that relate to dispositions and journeys. However, given findings from international studies, we consider that our contribution of well-developed entrepreneurial, craft and learning-to-learn capabilities, mediated by motivations and context and resulting in different journeys at different points in time, are widely generalisable. New concepts we have introduced to the field, such as 'integrated practice' and 'occupational affordances', offer rich potential for further development.

Film and television

With a relatively small population of around five million people, Singapore's creative arts sector is commensurately small. However, given the country's central location in Southeast Asia, its economic prosperity, cultural diversity and status as a market and transport hub, it is well placed as a site for artistic production for domestic and regional consumption. Working in this sector largely revolves around tender or contract-based projects typified by alternating periods of frenetic activity and quiet. This 'boom and bust' business cycle (Kong, 2011, p. 56) has produced a highly competitive industry which, as characterised by one market analyst, is 'about the survival of the fittest' (Malepart, 2005, p. 5). Within the Singaporean Film and Television industry, anecdotal evidence suggests that some 70 per cent of the workforce are freelancers.

Historically, the small Singaporean film and television sector was dominated by the Singapore Broadcasting Authority (SBA), a state-based institution. Employment was more permanent, and workers learned their skills on the job under the guidance of experienced personnel. As a result of restructuring in 2001, the Media Corporation of Singapore (MediaCorp) was brought together from previously semi-separate SBA entities in television, broadcasting and radio. It was from this time, under the umbrella of MediaCorp's monopoly, that production houses proliferated, and caused the shift to what in the industry is called freelance work. To address this trend, there has been considerable funding directed to filling the gap in educational institutional infrastructure for the industry. Funding, though, for local productions through the Media Development Authority (MDA) tends to be modest compared to that for international production houses. To meet budgets, smaller production crews are used so those hired need to occupy more work roles. Combined with the growing availability of small jobs (e.g. weddings and corporate work) and a simultaneous lack of bigger projects, freelancers often juggle multiple jobs to cover the 'feast or famine' nature of available work (Kong, 2011).

In addition to on-the-job training and work experience, educational institutions provide pre-employment film and television training. Polytechnics such as LaSalle-SIA College of Arts, Nanyang Academy of Fine Arts (NAFA) and the Nanyang Technological University (NTU) provide a range of programmes. The Singapore Media Academy (SMA) also offers a similar combination of programmes, nearly all of which develop television, film and theatre skills. In 2010, the Workforce Development Agency (WDA) and the national manager of competency-based CET Workforce Skills Qualifications (WSQs), in partnership with SMA, introduced the Creative Industries Apprenticeship Scheme (CIAS). According to Kong (2011), in a comment on a possible disconnect between pre-employment education and the industry and the need for more CET provision, 'these initiatives [e.g., CIAS] recognise the fact that the normal routes of academic success are insufficient to develop the full potential of future participants of the creative industries economy, and need to be substantiated with practical experience'.

This study adopted qualitative methods to collect data from workers operating in the film and television sector in Singapore. One-hour semi-structured interviews (n=16) with cameramen, video editors, sound recordists, gaffers, key grips, makeup artist, producers, directors and owner-operators of two production houses were conducted and transcribed. In addition, individuals from production houses, training providers and relevant government agencies were interviewed to provide further industry context and insights (see Table 2). Online sources such as *Mandy.com* and *LinkedIn* were consulted. The selection of interview participants was a mix of purposive and convenience sampling, that is, initial interviewees were selected through snowballing, and once we had entered the industry enough to gather our own interviewees, we selected to ensure we had a representative sample of roles undertaken within the industry. We also deliberately sought interviews with women to balance the gender bias in the industry that was reflected in our interviewees. All informants were guaranteed anonymity, and pseudonyms are used.

Interview transcripts were then analysed by the team of researchers who looked for common themes. NVivo software was used to organise the data

Table 2 Film and television interviewees

Interviewees occupation	*No. interviewed*
Freelancers (non-permanent workers)	
Producer	3
Director	1
Editor	2
Camera crew	3
Gaffer	1
Key Grip	2
Sound crew	3
Make-up artist	1
Sub-total	16
Production Houses	
Executive producers	3
Editor	1
Film & TV Training Providers	
Singapore Media Academy	1
Singapore Polytechnic	1
Media Development Authority	1
Government Agency	2
TOTAL	25

into these themes. In addition to interviews with freelancers in the film and television industry, a reference group was held to illuminate the findings from the perspectives of multiple industry stakeholders. These stakeholders were from the Ministry of Manpower (MOM), MDA, WDA, Ngee Ann Polytechnic, Temasek Polytechnic, ITE, SAE Institute, NAFA, NTU, National Trades Union Congress (NTUC) Legal Services, NTUC Learning Hub and IAL. This was significant, as bringing industry stakeholders together enabled them to hear first-hand the voices, experiences and issues of those they may not have direct contact with. It also helped to deepen or extend networks, which is important in developing influence and reach. With deep, extensive knowledge and industry experience, reference group members collectively added depth and also credibility to our findings.

Technical theatre

Singapore's technical theatre industry has undergone a profound transformation in the last 15 years, as arts and cultural production assumes a more prominent role in the city-state's economic and nation-building strategies (Bound et al., 2013; Kong, 2011; Ministry of Culture, Community & Youth, 2012). Where previously, the local theatre scene comprised a handful of arts houses and modest performance venues, it is now anchored by three large non-profit and commercial venues namely, the Esplanade, Resorts World and Marina Bay Sands, as part of a strategic plan to position the country to seize a greater portion of the cultural tourism pie, while concurrently growing its local arts industry. The government's expenditure on arts and culture grew steadily at 11 per cent each year, increasing from S$230.2m in 2005 to S$478.9m in 2012. Correspondingly, the total nominal value-add of the arts and cultural sector scaled to S$1.3b in 2011, from S$0.8b in 2003. The number of music, dance and theatre productions has been on an upswing, growing by an average of 10 per cent annually to hit 3 343 productions in 2012 (Ministry of Culture, Community & Youth, 2013). A fourth venue, the Singapore Sports Hub, adds international sports to the heady mix of live entertainment options in the city-state. A regional wing is developing, as local arts production houses begin touring their shows in the region, while superiorly equipped local companies make inroads to supply equipment, technology and staff to international concerts and conferences in the fast-growing emerging economies of China and ASEAN.

Like other creative industries, the technical theatre industry in Singapore relies on freelance work arrangements that appear to be the vanguard of a post-Fordist globalised economy characterised by shorter business cycles, knowledge jobs, flatter structures and outsourcing (Brown et al., 2011; Evans & Gibbs, 2009, Felstead & Ashton, 2001; Kalleberg, 2009). The core freelance jobs in the industry relate to technical, design and production jobs in the areas of lighting, sound, and stage/production. Freelance craftspeople form the backbone of the industry, and are engaged for work periods ranging from hours, days to months. The total full-time employment in the arts and cultural sub-sector stood at 24 400 workers in 2011, up from 20 900 workers in 2003. The performing arts segment specifically grew by 6 per cent annually, from a total of 4 500 workers in 2003 to 7 100 workers in 2011 (Ministry of Culture, Community & Youth, 2013). Statistics on the freelance pool, however, are not available. It has been estimated that freelancers made up 30 per cent of all those working in the creative industries (cited in Institute of Policy Studies, 2010). Indicative figures from the range of organisations that employ them suggest that the proportion of freelancers in technical theatre may be even higher. A flagship performing arts venue in Singapore, for instance, employs 250 permanent staff and engages 700–750 freelancers annually, of which 250 are technical crew. A leading arts production house in Singapore has seven permanent staff and engages up to 50 technical and non-technical freelancers for a production and up to 80 for a festival.

Something to note is that the description of the sector as 'technical theatre' is contested in Singapore and elsewhere (see, for example, the discussion in Farthing, 2012). Although the sector has origins in theatre, it has since grown to include the wider music and entertainment industry (e.g. concerts, festivals, mass display events) as well as the Meetings, Incentives, Conferences and Exhibition (MICE) industry, which comprises a wide range of activities, from major exhibitions to wedding banquets. 'Live Events' has been proposed as a more apt description of the sector. In addition, the term 'technical' itself is seen as a clumsy catch-all term covering technology, design, craft and management without sufficient specificity (Farthing, 2012). This study retained the term 'technical theatre' for expedient reasons to be consistent with the terminology used by local government agencies that oversee industry and workforce development.

Using data collected from interviews with 23 freelance technical theatre professionals and six organisations that engage them, the research investigated the triple challenge of a shortage of skilled labour, concurrent stagnation and the lack of professionalism in the technical theatre sector. Interviewees were selected based on convenience and purposive sampling (Lankshear & Knobel, 2004) to obtain a range of job roles, genders and years of experience. All informants were guaranteed anonymity, and the report uses pseudonyms. We deliberately sought out former and returning freelancers to capture comparative perspectives. We looked for common themes across the interviews, as well as developed a vertical analysis of each narrative (Coffey & Atkinson, 1996; Strauss & Corbin, 1990). We also augment the data with interviews with six organisations that engage freelance practitioners to provide a wider contextual understanding. In addition, a reference group session was organised involving 23 key employers, policy-makers, educators and freelancers to discuss the preliminary set of findings and jointly identify potential recommendations.

Adult educators

Singapore's adult educators face a large responsibility; adult educators (and the rest of the TAE community) need to 'help deliver high productivity and increased competitiveness, and to secure Singapore's sustainable growth in a global marketplace' (IAL, unpublished). This important role for adult educators stemmed from the transformation of Singapore's Continuing Education and Training (CET) sector to support industry growth, bridge skills gaps, raise industry standards and enhance the employability of workers. The demand for flexibility has seen short-term project work become the norm for the majority of adult educators who conduct face-to-face or other types of workforce learning and development activities. Such work arrangements are often used to cover peak training periods, for teaching whole units over a period of time or for guest lecturing. There are seven main categories that adult educators can work in, as represented in Figure 6.

A freelance adult educator may offer services to learners by working as non-permanent staff with private education institutes (with 72 per cent of private education institute teachers in non-permanent employment (CPE annual report 2012/2013)1); WSQ-approved training organisations (institutions such as IAL2 have over 70 per cent adjunct staff); public-sector training institutions (Civil Service College reported the amplification of adjunct or associate training staff at the Capability Development Forum 20133); and post-secondary education institutions and private training consultancy organisations (PTCOs).

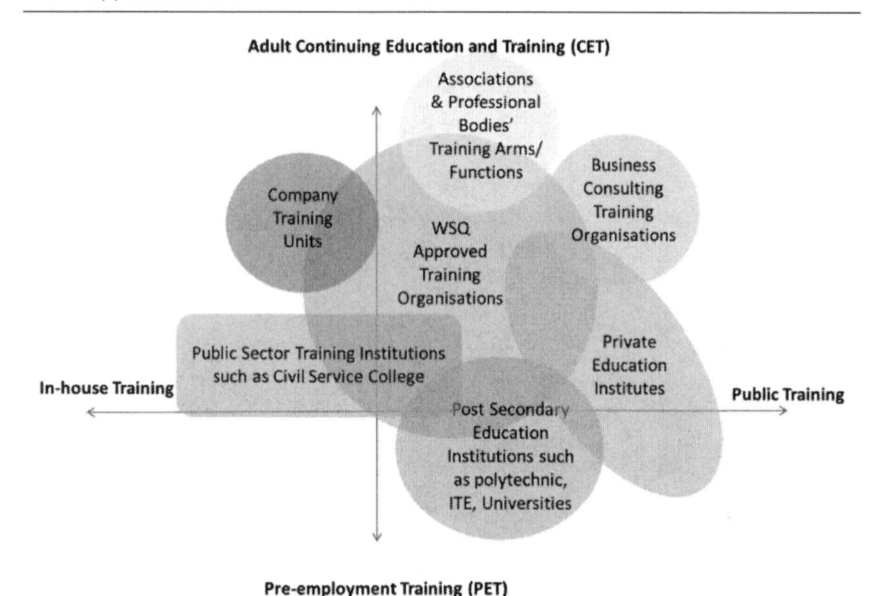

Figure 6 Segmented market

Source: IAL. Unpublished. Part 1: Strategic Intelligence TAE Landscape & The Changing Demand

They may also be a PTCO themselves and provide services directly to businesses seeking their expertise (thus cutting out the services of a middleman). A freelance adult educator may have work with one or many of these types of learning institutions and may have learning and development expertise in one or more area. The type of organisation with which freelance adult educators work and the relationship they foster can determine whether new skills/ approaches and innovative delivery methods can be effectively applied as well as the willingness of freelancers to provide feedback for improving courseware design. Sole proprietors who seek work with businesses, for example, are likely to have more scope for creativity and innovation than freelance adult educators who work for WSQ-approved training organisations (ATOs) concerned with their guidelines.

Like other countries, the profile of Singapore's adult educators is characterised by diversity. These adult educators come from diverse occupational backgrounds and interact with learners from a multitude of industries. The different types of freelance adult educators include: industry experts who hold a main job in their industry and occasionally conduct training (such experts often have weaker pedagogic practices); people with caring responsibilities; retirees with previous careers; people with study responsibilities; and people, often sole proprietors, who offer customised training solutions for corporate clients (Shorne, 2008 in Jacques, 2012).

This study involved semi-structured, in-depth, qualitative interviews with 30 adult educators and one marketing agent in Singapore. Through purposive sampling, adult educators with varying years of experience and from a range of industries, operating in both the WSQ and private markets, were invited. Participants were identified through industry contacts, the Adult Education Network database, IAL's ACTA graduate database, the Centre for Workplace Literacy's Trainer Database, and personal contacts of the research team.

All interviews were recorded and transcribed before being imported into NVIVO. Themes were developed through reading the data, referring back to the literature and multiple coding by various members of the research team. Each transcript was then coded by the established themes before being further analysed into sub-themes.

After the initial analysis, a reference group met to validate and provide feedback on the report. Many members of the reference group felt that the report captured what it is like as a freelance adult educator. Their suggestions included providing more differentiation between the different types of freelance adult educators so that a more nuanced understanding of the different systems could be gained and recommendations could become more targeted. Their other comments and recommendations also influenced the shape of the final report.

Low wage report

The growing interest in the plight of the low-wage workers in Singapore stems from a growing wage gap in Singapore. In 2013, the city-state registered the highest Gini coefficient globally at .4784, indicating a correspondingly high level of inequality in income distribution that has significant economic and political implications (Loh, 2011; Ng, 2013). A slew of measures has been introduced progressively to improve the plight of this group of workers, beginning with Workfare in 2007 as a key income supplement that included cash payouts and top-ups to the workers' Central Provident Fund. Currently, workers are eligible for Workfare if the average gross monthly income during the period worked is S$1 900 or lower. The island-state's tightly regulated union additionally champions the Progressive Wage Model or PWM, which was formalised in 2012. Under this model, business licensing is tied to the adoption of a tiered wage ladder that also supports workers' skills upgrading and enhanced productivity. The most extensive application of the PWM is in the cleaning industry, where a basic wage of $1 000 is mandatory for any cleaning business to secure an operating license.

In a tight labour market where employers are screaming for permanent workers, odd-job workers form a critical pool to supplement or bridge the gap while recruitment is on-going. In industries such as food and beverage and retail, manpower initiatives have been introduced to tap into part-time/casual labour pool to provide enterprise flexibility, but such programmes face significant challenges in attracting and retaining such workers.

The research team relied on a range of sources to secure interviewees. Significant difficulty existed in locating these workers, as well as in gaining their trust and interest to participate in the study. To secure interviewees, we first relied on GumTree, an online free classified listing. We indicated that a $30 shopping voucher would be given as a token of appreciation for their time. At the same time, we cast the net wide among our personal contacts. Interviews secured through personal contacts proved to be the most valuable in helping the research team gain an initial understanding of the workers. These personal contacts pointed us to 'ports' where casual workers tend to congregate. For instance, despatch riders have meeting points at two coffee shops in Tanjong Pagar, among others. Removalists congregate in several ports, such as a coffee shop in Holland Drive and an alley in Sixth Avenue. These are not mere meeting points, but entire support communities where workers not only report for work or seek work, but also hang out with one another after work, accompanied by their family members at times. The research team devoted time at the different ports to introduce themselves and the research project to the workers in order to build rapport and gain their goodwill to participate in the research. Many were apathetic, and some were hostile and suspicious of our intentions. Over time, some of the workers agreed to participate, driven mainly by the recognition of the effort put in by the research team. Our interviewees also informed us that they rely on Facebook pages that advertise part-time and temporary jobs, so we advertised the call for interviewees in those pages as well. Those who responded to our online advertisements were mainly motivated by the $30 shopping voucher. Given the time taken to build relationships and to ensure that the interviewees were sourced from a range of sources, data collection inevitably stretched from July to November 2014. A good mix mainly in terms of age and ethnicity was ensured.

We also sought inputs from five employers, one work supervisor, two representatives from self-help groups, and two career coaches. This data was collected through face-to-face meetings, email or phone interviews.

All data collected was subsequently analysed using the principles of analytic induction (Charmaz, 1983). Interview transcripts were coded iteratively as and when new categories emerged. This process entailed repeatedly returning to earlier coded transcripts for recoding. When the categories that emerge failed to support findings in existing academic literature, another round of transcript examination was undertaken. Interpretations stemmed from our understanding of theory and research, which was developed in a process that always called for a return to the data for support.

The preliminary findings were then put up for discussion through a reference group session that was organised in January 2015, which comprised 31 representatives from the government, companies, unions, self-help groups and academia. The reference group session also discussed the implications arising from the findings, and suggested areas for intervention.

References

Brown, P., Lauder, H., & Ashton, D. (2011). *The global auction: The broken promises of education, jobs and incomes*. New York: Oxford University Press.

Charmaz, K. (1983). The grounded theory method: An explication and interpretation. In R. Emerson (Ed). *Contemporary field research: Perspectives and formulations*. Boston: Little Brown.

Coffey, A., & Atkinson, P. (1996). *Making sense of qualitative data: Complementary strategies*. Thousand Oaks, CA: Sage.

Evans, K., & Gibb, E. (2009). *Moving from precarious employment to decent work*. GURN Discussion Paper No. 13. International Labour Office, Global Union Research Network (GURN).

Farthing, A. (2012). *Mapping technical theatre arts training*. A report for the Higher Education Authority, Arts and Humanities, UK. Retrieved from https://www.heacademy.ac.uk/system/files/headdm- farthing2012mappingtechtheatretraining.pdf.

Felstead A., & Ashton, D. (2001). Paying the price for flexibility? Training, skills and non-standard jobs in Britain. *International Journal of Employment Studies*, 9(1), 25–60.

Jacques, N. (2012). *Improving workforce planning and development: perspectives of sessional VET practitioners*. Adelaide: NCVER.

Kalleberg, A. L. (2009). Precarious work, insecure workers: Employment relations in transition. *American Sociological Review*, 74, 1–22.

Kong, L. (2011). From precarious labor to precarious economy? Planning precarity in Singapore's creative economy. *City, Culture and Society*, 2, 55–64.

Lankshear, C., & Knobel, M. (2004). *Teacher research: From design to implementation*. England: Open University Press.

Loh, J. (2011). *Bottom fifth in Singapore. Social Space, 88-90*. Singapore: Lien Centre for Social Innovation.

Malepart, A. (2005). *The feature film market in Singapore*. Canada: The Department of Canadian Heritage, Trade Routes Program.

Ministry of Culture, Community and Youth. (2012). *The report of the arts and culture strategic review*. Singapore: Ministry of Culture, Community and Youth.

Ministry of Culture, Community and Youth. (2013). *Singapore cultural statistics 2013*. Singapore: Ministry of Culture, Community and Youth.

Ng, I. (2013). Multistressed low-earning families in contemporary policy context: Lessons from work support recipients in Singapore. *Journal of Poverty*, 17(1), 86–109.

Strauss, A. L., & Corbin, J. (1990). Basics of qualitative research: Grounded theory procedures and techniques. London: Sage.

Index

Note: Page numbers in *italic* indicate figures. Page numbers in **bold** indicate tables.

action 51
advancement-oriented individuals 14
agency 16–17
Airbnb 4
authority, distrust of 61–62

becoming 123–124
borderlessness 33

capability(ies): defined 99; development of 127; integrated practice and 99–102; skills vs. 99
career changers 15
career journeys 36–39
churn 6
collaboration: between educational institution/provider and sector 133–136
community, occupational 80–84
conditions, institutional structures and 142–144
context: dynamic embeddedness in 95–98; global 71; integrated practice and 92–93, 93–98; learning and 80–84, 116; linkages and 77–80, 86–87; meaning-making and 70; mind and, in ecological perspective 111–112; occupational affordances and 71–74, *74*, 93–94; pathways and 72–73; practitioners and 73–74; sites of work and 69–70; technology and 70; voices and 84–86, 87
contingency 5–8
continuous development 124–133
crafting 129–130
culture, organisational 16–17

decent work 7
development 11–12; of capabilities 127; continuous 124–133; defined 140; differentiated 150; in educational settings 118–124, **120–121**; embodied practice and 149–150; of entrepreneurship 123; holistic 135–136; human capital 29–31, *30*, 149–150; of identity 127; institutional structures and 142–144; of performance to standards 126; policy, and categorisation of workers 144–146; in practice 21–23, *23*; pre-service education and 148–149; as social practice 32; technology and 146
digital platforms 4–5
dispositions: defined 49; dynamic embeddedness of 95–98; focus and 53; integrated practice and 91–93; opportunistic *52*, 52–53, 60–65, 66–67; purposeful 51–52, *52*, 54–60, 66; reflexivity and 50, 55; spectra of 51–52, *52*; towards learning 49–50
distrust of authority 61–62
dynamic embeddedness 95–98

East-West interfaces 9–10
ecological perspective 111–112
embodied practice 149–150
enculturation 125–126
entrepreneurship: capabilities and 99–102, 119; career journeys and 38–39; development of 123; educational institutions and 90–91; learning and 111, 113; pedagogical strategies for **120–121**; purposefulness and 54, 56–57; work-centred individuals and 14
environment, workplace 16–17

equity 126
ethics 126

false self-employment 4
family 14, 19, 50
figured worlds 69
flexibility 14–16, 60, 62
frames of meaning 95–96
Freelancers Union 5
front-loading 147–149

gig economy 4
good work 7–8

higher income, fear of 61–62
holistic development 135–136
hospitality 4
human capital 149–150
human capital development 29–31, *30*

identity 16–17, 34–36, 38–39, 105, 127
identity formation 35–36
income, higher, fear of 61–62
India 5, 143–144, 153–154
innovation 126
institutional structures 142–144
integrated practice 150–151; capabilities and 99–102; context and 92–93, 93–98; development and 146–147; dispositions and 91–93; journeys and 102–106, *103*; learning and **117**, 146–147; model 90, *91*; pedagogical strategies for **120–121**

job changers 15
journeys: career 36–39; integrated practice and 102–106, *103*
justice, social 126

knowledge, meta- 101
knowledgeable practice 128, 132–133
knowledge recontextualisation 20–21, 114–115, 128–129

language 93
learning: agency and 16–17; collaborative partnerships in 133–136; context and 116; in context of organisational work practices and cultures 16–17; disconnects 12–13; dispositions towards 49–50, 66 (*see also* dispositions); enculturation and 125–126; front-loading model in 147–149; as human capital development 29–31, *30*; identity and 16–17; integrated practice and **117**, 146–147; issues with 11–12; and knowledge recontextualisation 114–115; to learn 43–44, 115–116; in 'liquid lives' 17–19; and organisation of work 13–14; as part of occupational community 80–84; passion and 59–60; in practice 21–23, *23*; pre-service education and 148–149; questioning current practices in 112–118, **117**; reflexivity and 17–19, 122; situated 33; social organisation 31; social organisation of 32; as social practice 31–32; strategies 12–13; thinking differently about 110–112; and transfer metaphor 114; workplace 72
linkages 77–80, 86–87
liquid lives 17–19, 50
lived experiences 32–34, 98

malleability 40–41
meaning, frames of 95–96
meaning-making 51, 69, 70, 93, 112–113
meta-knowledge 101
moving across 77–80

neo-Taylorism 12–13
non-permanent work: as contingent 5–8; defined 3; as precarious 5–8; prevalence of 2; reasons for use of 3–5
non-permanent workers: agency of 16–17; development of 11–12; flexibility of 14–16; identity and 34–36; identity of 16–17; learning of 11–12; lived experiences of 32–34; recontextualisation of knowledge by 20–21
Non-Standard Employment 2

occupational affordances 71–74, *74*, 93–94
occupational community 80–84
occupational identity 127; *see also* identity
opportunistic disposition *52*, 52–53, 60–65, 66–67
organisational culture 16–17
organisational work practices 16–17

participation 51, 62–63
passion 59–60
pathways 72–73
performance to standards 126
personal interests 50
policy, workforce development 144–146

positionality 39
practitioners 73–74
precariousness 5–8
precarious occupational biography 14
pre-service education 148–149
production process, specialist integration into 74–77
professional identity 127; *see also* identity
purpose 50–51
purposeful disposition 51–52, *52*, 66

recontextualisation, of knowledge 20–21, 114–115, 128–129
reflection 43–44
reflexivity 17–19, 43–44, 50, 55, 122, 127–128
renewal 126
responsibility 57–58, 62
retail 4
return to labour market 14
risk minimisation 124–125

self, senses of 50–51
self-authoring 39
Self-Employed Women's Association 5
self-employment: aiming for 15; false 4
shapeshifting 40, 43
sites of work 69–70
situated learning 33
social dialogue approach 9, 10–11
social justice 126
social organisation learning 31
social practice: learning as 31–32
South Korea 142, 144, 152–153, 154, 155
spaces, of non-permanent workers:
  and questioning current practices in educational institutions 112–118, **117**;
  and thinking differently about learning 110–112
specialist integration, into production process 74–77, 86
stagnation 59–60
Standing, Guy 6
stratification 150

Taylorism 12–13
technology: context and 70; development and 146; faceless 5; gig economy and 4; work communities and 70
term contract workers 10, 12, 15, 16, 17, 19, 24n2
trade unions 2, 5, 24n4, 45, 90, 141, 144
transfer metaphor 114

unemployment 6, 11, 142, 152
unions, trade 2, 5, 24n4, 45, 90, 141, 144

voices 84–86, 87

work-centered individuals 14
workforce development *see* development
workplace learning 72
work practices, organisational 16–17